C-3810   CAREER EXAMINATION SERIES

This is your
PASSBOOK for...

Staff Services Analyst

Test Preparation Study Guide
Questions & Answers

NATIONAL LEARNING CORPORATION®

COPYRIGHT NOTICE

This book is SOLELY intended for, is sold ONLY to, and its use is RESTRICTED to individual, bona fide applicants or candidates who qualify by virtue of having seriously filed applications for appropriate license, certificate, professional and/or promotional advancement, higher school matriculation, scholarship, or other legitimate requirements of education and/or governmental authorities.

This book is NOT intended for use, class instruction, tutoring, training, duplication, copying, reprinting, excerption, or adaptation, etc., by:

1) Other publishers
2) Proprietors and/or Instructors of "Coaching" and/or Preparatory Courses
3) Personnel and/or Training Divisions of commercial, industrial, and governmental organizations
4) Schools, colleges, or universities and/or their departments and staffs, including teachers and other personnel
5) Testing Agencies or Bureaus
6) Study groups which seek by the purchase of a single volume to copy and/or duplicate and/or adapt this material for use by the group as a whole without having purchased individual volumes for each of the members of the group
7) Et al.

Such persons would be in violation of appropriate Federal and State statutes.

PROVISION OF LICENSING AGREEMENTS – Recognized educational, commercial, industrial, and governmental institutions and organizations, and others legitimately engaged in educational pursuits, including training, testing, and measurement activities, may address request for a licensing agreement to the copyright owners, who will determine whether, and under what conditions, including fees and charges, the materials in this book may be used them. In other words, a licensing facility exists for the legitimate use of the material in this book on other than an individual basis. However, it is asseverated and affirmed here that the material in this book CANNOT be used without the receipt of the express permission of such a licensing agreement from the Publishers. Inquiries re licensing should be addressed to the company, attention rights and permissions department.

All rights reserved, including the right of reproduction in whole or in part, in any form or by any means, electronic or mechanical, including photocopying, recording, or by any information storage and retrieval system, without permission in writing from the Publisher.

Copyright © 2024 by
National Learning Corporation

212 Michael Drive, Syosset, NY 11791
(516) 921-8888 • www.passbooks.com
E-mail: info@passbooks.com

PUBLISHED IN THE UNITED STATES OF AMERICA

PASSBOOK® SERIES

THE *PASSBOOK® SERIES* has been created to prepare applicants and candidates for the ultimate academic battlefield – the examination room.

At some time in our lives, each and every one of us may be required to take an examination – for validation, matriculation, admission, qualification, registration, certification, or licensure.

Based on the assumption that every applicant or candidate has met the basic formal educational standards, has taken the required number of courses, and read the necessary texts, the *PASSBOOK® SERIES* furnishes the one special preparation which may assure passing with confidence, instead of failing with insecurity. Examination questions – together with answers – are furnished as the basic vehicle for study so that the mysteries of the examination and its compounding difficulties may be eliminated or diminished by a sure method.

This book is meant to help you pass your examination provided that you qualify and are serious in your objective.

The entire field is reviewed through the huge store of content information which is succinctly presented through a provocative and challenging approach – the question-and-answer method.

A climate of success is established by furnishing the correct answers at the end of each test.

You soon learn to recognize types of questions, forms of questions, and patterns of questioning. You may even begin to anticipate expected outcomes.

You perceive that many questions are repeated or adapted so that you can gain acute insights, which may enable you to score many sure points.

You learn how to confront new questions, or types of questions, and to attack them confidently and work out the correct answers.

You note objectives and emphases, and recognize pitfalls and dangers, so that you may make positive educational adjustments.

Moreover, you are kept fully informed in relation to new concepts, methods, practices, and directions in the field.

You discover that you are actually taking the examination all the time: you are preparing for the examination by "taking" an examination, not by reading extraneous and/or supererogatory textbooks.

In short, this PASSBOOK®, used directedly, should be an important factor in helping you to pass your test.

STAFF SERVICES ANALYST

DUTIES
A Staff Services Analyst performs a variety of analytical duties such as program evaluation and planning, systems devlopment, budgeting, planning, training, management and personnel analysis and related tasks; studies the principles and techniques of the area of work to which assigned and, under supervision, applies them; participates in analytical studies of organization, procedures, budgetary requirements, and personnel management; gathers, tabulates, and analyzes data; draws organization, workload, and other charts; interviews and consults with departmental officials, employees, and others to give and secure information; prepares reports and makes recommendations on procedures, policies, and program alternatives; reviews and analyzes proposed legislation and advises management on the potential impact; makes decisions on financial, personnel, and other transactions of average complexity: works as a field representative in intergovernmental negotiations; prepares correspondence.

SCOPE OF THE EXAMINATION
The examination for Staff Services Analyst will consist of a written examination weighted 100%. The scope of the written examination will consist of Quantitative Analysis, Data Analysis, and Workload Management/Project Management Scenarios.

Hiring interviews may also evaluate the following areas:

Knowledge of: Problem-solving techniques and processes to facilitate the identification and resolution of problems and issues related to the completion of work assignments; basic statistics to calculate and interpret statistical analyses and draw appropriate conclusions.

Ability to: Work independently on projects or assignments without close supervision or detailed instructions, be flexible in adapting to changes in priorities. assignments, and other interruptions which may impact preestablished timelines and courses of action.

Skill to: Perform arithmetic computations; perform basic statistical calculations; extract specific, relevant date and information from a larger body of materials; comprehend and interpret complex information and materials, including standards, procedures, and policies; apply policies and procedures in the completion of work assignments; apply technical principles and standards in the completion of work assignments; read and interpret charts and graphs; identify all facts and implications related to a situation before drawing conclusions and determining courses of action; analyze and evaluate data and information to formulate conclusions and courses of actions; make appropriate decisions based upon the facts and information available; recognize the ramifications and possible impact of decisions and/or actions to determine the most appropriate courses of action; analyze and evaluate situations accurately and thoroughly to determine and implement effective, appropriate courses of action; organize and identify the work activities to be completed by a work team or task force completing a project; recognize the need to shift priorities and resources to complete projects and assignments within established timeframes and by expected deadlines; follow-up and ensure that the assignments and activities of work team or task force members are completed within established timelines; prioritize assignments and projects to ensure completion within established timeframes and by expected deadlines; participate in and contribute to the effectiveness of a group or team; establish and maintain cooperative relations with others.

HOW TO TAKE A TEST

I. YOU MUST PASS AN EXAMINATION

A. *WHAT EVERY CANDIDATE SHOULD KNOW*

Examination applicants often ask us for help in preparing for the written test. What can I study in advance? What kinds of questions will be asked? How will the test be given? How will the papers be graded?

As an applicant for a civil service examination, you may be wondering about some of these things. Our purpose here is to suggest effective methods of advance study and to describe civil service examinations.

Your chances for success on this examination can be increased if you know how to prepare. Those "pre-examination jitters" can be reduced if you know what to expect. You can even experience an adventure in good citizenship if you know why civil service exams are given.

B. *WHY ARE CIVIL SERVICE EXAMINATIONS GIVEN?*

Civil service examinations are important to you in two ways. As a citizen, you want public jobs filled by employees who know how to do their work. As a job seeker, you want a fair chance to compete for that job on an equal footing with other candidates. The best-known means of accomplishing this two-fold goal is the competitive examination.

Exams are widely publicized throughout the nation. They may be administered for jobs in federal, state, city, municipal, town or village governments or agencies.

Any citizen may apply, with some limitations, such as the age or residence of applicants. Your experience and education may be reviewed to see whether you meet the requirements for the particular examination. When these requirements exist, they are reasonable and applied consistently to all applicants. Thus, a competitive examination may cause you some uneasiness now, but it is your privilege and safeguard.

C. *HOW ARE CIVIL SERVICE EXAMS DEVELOPED?*

Examinations are carefully written by trained technicians who are specialists in the field known as "psychological measurement," in consultation with recognized authorities in the field of work that the test will cover. These experts recommend the subject matter areas or skills to be tested; only those knowledges or skills important to your success on the job are included. The most reliable books and source materials available are used as references. Together, the experts and technicians judge the difficulty level of the questions.

Test technicians know how to phrase questions so that the problem is clearly stated. Their ethics do not permit "trick" or "catch" questions. Questions may have been tried out on sample groups, or subjected to statistical analysis, to determine their usefulness.

Written tests are often used in combination with performance tests, ratings of training and experience, and oral interviews. All of these measures combine to form the best-known means of finding the right person for the right job.

II. HOW TO PASS THE WRITTEN TEST

A. NATURE OF THE EXAMINATION

To prepare intelligently for civil service examinations, you should know how they differ from school examinations you have taken. In school you were assigned certain definite pages to read or subjects to cover. The examination questions were quite detailed and usually emphasized memory. Civil service exams, on the other hand, try to discover your present ability to perform the duties of a position, plus your potentiality to learn these duties. In other words, a civil service exam attempts to predict how successful you will be. Questions cover such a broad area that they cannot be as minute and detailed as school exam questions.

In the public service similar kinds of work, or positions, are grouped together in one "class." This process is known as *position-classification*. All the positions in a class are paid according to the salary range for that class. One class title covers all of these positions, and they are all tested by the same examination.

B. FOUR BASIC STEPS

1) Study the announcement

How, then, can you know what subjects to study? Our best answer is: "Learn as much as possible about the class of positions for which you've applied." The exam will test the knowledge, skills and abilities needed to do the work.

Your most valuable source of information about the position you want is the official exam announcement. This announcement lists the training and experience qualifications. Check these standards and apply only if you come reasonably close to meeting them.

The brief description of the position in the examination announcement offers some clues to the subjects which will be tested. Think about the job itself. Review the duties in your mind. Can you perform them, or are there some in which you are rusty? Fill in the blank spots in your preparation.

Many jurisdictions preview the written test in the exam announcement by including a section called "Knowledge and Abilities Required," "Scope of the Examination," or some similar heading. Here you will find out specifically what fields will be tested.

2) Review your own background

Once you learn in general what the position is all about, and what you need to know to do the work, ask yourself which subjects you already know fairly well and which need improvement. You may wonder whether to concentrate on improving your strong areas or on building some background in your fields of weakness. When the announcement has specified "some knowledge" or "considerable knowledge," or has used adjectives like "beginning principles of…" or "advanced … methods," you can get a clue as to the number and difficulty of questions to be asked in any given field. More questions, and hence broader coverage, would be included for those subjects which are more important in the work. Now weigh your strengths and weaknesses against the job requirements and prepare accordingly.

3) Determine the level of the position

Another way to tell how intensively you should prepare is to understand the level of the job for which you are applying. Is it the entering level? In other words, is this the position in which beginners in a field of work are hired? Or is it an intermediate or advanced level? Sometimes this is indicated by such words as "Junior" or "Senior" in the class title. Other jurisdictions use Roman numerals to designate the level – Clerk I, Clerk II, for example. The word "Supervisor" sometimes appears in the title. If the level is not indicated by the title, check the description of duties. Will you be working under very close supervision, or will you have responsibility for independent decisions in this work?

4) Choose appropriate study materials

Now that you know the subjects to be examined and the relative amount of each subject to be covered, you can choose suitable study materials. For beginning level jobs, or even advanced ones, if you have a pronounced weakness in some aspect of your training, read a modern, standard textbook in that field. Be sure it is up to date and has general coverage. Such books are normally available at your library, and the librarian will be glad to help you locate one. For entry-level positions, questions of appropriate difficulty are chosen -- neither highly advanced questions, nor those too simple. Such questions require careful thought but not advanced training.

If the position for which you are applying is technical or advanced, you will read more advanced, specialized material. If you are already familiar with the basic principles of your field, elementary textbooks would waste your time. Concentrate on advanced textbooks and technical periodicals. Think through the concepts and review difficult problems in your field.

These are all general sources. You can get more ideas on your own initiative, following these leads. For example, training manuals and publications of the government agency which employs workers in your field can be useful, particularly for technical and professional positions. A letter or visit to the government department involved may result in more specific study suggestions, and certainly will provide you with a more definite idea of the exact nature of the position you are seeking.

III. KINDS OF TESTS

Tests are used for purposes other than measuring knowledge and ability to perform specified duties. For some positions, it is equally important to test ability to make adjustments to new situations or to profit from training. In others, basic mental abilities not dependent on information are essential. Questions which test these things may not appear as pertinent to the duties of the position as those which test for knowledge and information. Yet they are often highly important parts of a fair examination. For very general questions, it is almost impossible to help you direct your study efforts. What we can do is to point out some of the more common of these general abilities needed in public service positions and describe some typical questions.

1) General information

Broad, general information has been found useful for predicting job success in some kinds of work. This is tested in a variety of ways, from vocabulary lists to questions about current events. Basic background in some field of work, such as sociology or economics, may be sampled in a group of questions. Often these are principles which have become familiar to most persons through exposure rather than through formal training. It is difficult to advise you how to study for these questions; being alert to the world around you is our best suggestion.

2) Verbal ability

An example of an ability needed in many positions is verbal or language ability. Verbal ability is, in brief, the ability to use and understand words. Vocabulary and grammar tests are typical measures of this ability. Reading comprehension or paragraph interpretation questions are common in many kinds of civil service tests. You are given a paragraph of written material and asked to find its central meaning.

3) Numerical ability

Number skills can be tested by the familiar arithmetic problem, by checking paired lists of numbers to see which are alike and which are different, or by interpreting charts and graphs. In the latter test, a graph may be printed in the test booklet which you are asked to use as the basis for answering questions.

4) Observation

A popular test for law-enforcement positions is the observation test. A picture is shown to you for several minutes, then taken away. Questions about the picture test your ability to observe both details and larger elements.

5) Following directions

In many positions in the public service, the employee must be able to carry out written instructions dependably and accurately. You may be given a chart with several columns, each column listing a variety of information. The questions require you to carry out directions involving the information given in the chart.

6) Skills and aptitudes

Performance tests effectively measure some manual skills and aptitudes. When the skill is one in which you are trained, such as typing or shorthand, you can practice. These tests are often very much like those given in business school or high school courses. For many of the other skills and aptitudes, however, no short-time preparation can be made. Skills and abilities natural to you or that you have developed throughout your lifetime are being tested.

Many of the general questions just described provide all the data needed to answer the questions and ask you to use your reasoning ability to find the answers. Your best preparation for these tests, as well as for tests of facts and ideas, is to be at your physical and mental best. You, no doubt, have your own methods of getting into an exam-taking mood and keeping "in shape." The next section lists some ideas on this subject.

IV. KINDS OF QUESTIONS

Only rarely is the "essay" question, which you answer in narrative form, used in civil service tests. Civil service tests are usually of the short-answer type. Full instructions for answering these questions will be given to you at the examination. But in case this is your first experience with short-answer questions and separate answer sheets, here is what you need to know:

1) Multiple-choice Questions

Most popular of the short-answer questions is the "multiple choice" or "best answer" question. It can be used, for example, to test for factual knowledge, ability to solve problems or judgment in meeting situations found at work.

A multiple-choice question is normally one of three types—
- It can begin with an incomplete statement followed by several possible endings. You are to find the one ending which *best* completes the statement, although some of the others may not be entirely wrong.
- It can also be a complete statement in the form of a question which is answered by choosing one of the statements listed.

- It can be in the form of a problem – again you select the best answer.

Here is an example of a multiple-choice question with a discussion which should give you some clues as to the method for choosing the right answer:

When an employee has a complaint about his assignment, the action which will *best* help him overcome his difficulty is to
   A. discuss his difficulty with his coworkers
   B. take the problem to the head of the organization
   C. take the problem to the person who gave him the assignment
   D. say nothing to anyone about his complaint

In answering this question, you should study each of the choices to find which is best. Consider choice "A" – Certainly an employee may discuss his complaint with fellow employees, but no change or improvement can result, and the complaint remains unresolved. Choice "B" is a poor choice since the head of the organization probably does not know what assignment you have been given, and taking your problem to him is known as "going over the head" of the supervisor. The supervisor, or person who made the assignment, is the person who can clarify it or correct any injustice. Choice "C" is, therefore, correct. To say nothing, as in choice "D," is unwise. Supervisors have and interest in knowing the problems employees are facing, and the employee is seeking a solution to his problem.

2) True/False Questions

The "true/false" or "right/wrong" form of question is sometimes used. Here a complete statement is given. Your job is to decide whether the statement is right or wrong.

SAMPLE: A roaming cell-phone call to a nearby city costs less than a non-roaming call to a distant city.

This statement is wrong, or false, since roaming calls are more expensive.
This is not a complete list of all possible question forms, although most of the others are variations of these common types. You will always get complete directions for answering questions. Be sure you understand *how* to mark your answers – ask questions until you do.

V. RECORDING YOUR ANSWERS

Computer terminals are used more and more today for many different kinds of exams.
For an examination with very few applicants, you may be told to record your answers in the test booklet itself. Separate answer sheets are much more common. If this separate answer sheet is to be scored by machine – and this is often the case – it is highly important that you mark your answers correctly in order to get credit.
An electronic scoring machine is often used in civil service offices because of the speed with which papers can be scored. Machine-scored answer sheets must be marked with a pencil, which will be given to you. This pencil has a high graphite content which responds to the electronic scoring machine. As a matter of fact, stray dots may register as answers, so do not let your pencil rest on the answer sheet while you are pondering the correct answer. Also, if your pencil lead breaks or is otherwise defective, ask for another.

Since the answer sheet will be dropped in a slot in the scoring machine, be careful not to bend the corners or get the paper crumpled.

The answer sheet normally has five vertical columns of numbers, with 30 numbers to a column. These numbers correspond to the question numbers in your test booklet. After each number, going across the page are four or five pairs of dotted lines. These short dotted lines have small letters or numbers above them. The first two pairs may also have a "T" or "F" above the letters. This indicates that the first two pairs only are to be used if the questions are of the true-false type. If the questions are multiple choice, disregard the "T" and "F" and pay attention only to the small letters or numbers.

Answer your questions in the manner of the sample that follows:

32. The largest city in the United States is
    A. Washington, D.C.
    B. New York City
    C. Chicago
    D. Detroit
    E. San Francisco

1) Choose the answer you think is best. (New York City is the largest, so "B" is correct.)
2) Find the row of dotted lines numbered the same as the question you are answering. (Find row number 32)
3) Find the pair of dotted lines corresponding to the answer. (Find the pair of lines under the mark "B.")
4) Make a solid black mark between the dotted lines.

VI. BEFORE THE TEST

Common sense will help you find procedures to follow to get ready for an examination. Too many of us, however, overlook these sensible measures. Indeed, nervousness and fatigue have been found to be the most serious reasons why applicants fail to do their best on civil service tests. Here is a list of reminders:

- Begin your preparation early – Don't wait until the last minute to go scurrying around for books and materials or to find out what the position is all about.
- Prepare continuously – An hour a night for a week is better than an all-night cram session. This has been definitely established. What is more, a night a week for a month will return better dividends than crowding your study into a shorter period of time.
- Locate the place of the exam – You have been sent a notice telling you when and where to report for the examination. If the location is in a different town or otherwise unfamiliar to you, it would be well to inquire the best route and learn something about the building.
- Relax the night before the test – Allow your mind to rest. Do not study at all that night. Plan some mild recreation or diversion; then go to bed early and get a good night's sleep.
- Get up early enough to make a leisurely trip to the place for the test – This way unforeseen events, traffic snarls, unfamiliar buildings, etc. will not upset you.
- Dress comfortably – A written test is not a fashion show. You will be known by number and not by name, so wear something comfortable.

- Leave excess paraphernalia at home – Shopping bags and odd bundles will get in your way. You need bring only the items mentioned in the official notice you received; usually everything you need is provided. Do not bring reference books to the exam. They will only confuse those last minutes and be taken away from you when in the test room.
- Arrive somewhat ahead of time – If because of transportation schedules you must get there very early, bring a newspaper or magazine to take your mind off yourself while waiting.
- Locate the examination room – When you have found the proper room, you will be directed to the seat or part of the room where you will sit. Sometimes you are given a sheet of instructions to read while you are waiting. Do not fill out any forms until you are told to do so; just read them and be prepared.
- Relax and prepare to listen to the instructions
- If you have any physical problem that may keep you from doing your best, be sure to tell the test administrator. If you are sick or in poor health, you really cannot do your best on the exam. You can come back and take the test some other time.

VII. AT THE TEST

The day of the test is here and you have the test booklet in your hand. The temptation to get going is very strong. Caution! There is more to success than knowing the right answers. You must know how to identify your papers and understand variations in the type of short-answer question used in this particular examination. Follow these suggestions for maximum results from your efforts:

1) Cooperate with the monitor
The test administrator has a duty to create a situation in which you can be as much at ease as possible. He will give instructions, tell you when to begin, check to see that you are marking your answer sheet correctly, and so on. He is not there to guard you, although he will see that your competitors do not take unfair advantage. He wants to help you do your best.

2) Listen to all instructions
Don't jump the gun! Wait until you understand all directions. In most civil service tests you get more time than you need to answer the questions. So don't be in a hurry. Read each word of instructions until you clearly understand the meaning. Study the examples, listen to all announcements and follow directions. Ask questions if you do not understand what to do.

3) Identify your papers
Civil service exams are usually identified by number only. You will be assigned a number; you must not put your name on your test papers. Be sure to copy your number correctly. Since more than one exam may be given, copy your exact examination title.

4) Plan your time
Unless you are told that a test is a "speed" or "rate of work" test, speed itself is usually not important. Time enough to answer all the questions will be provided, but this does not mean that you have all day. An overall time limit has been set. Divide the total time (in minutes) by the number of questions to determine the approximate time you have for each question.

5) Do not linger over difficult questions

If you come across a difficult question, mark it with a paper clip (useful to have along) and come back to it when you have been through the booklet. One caution if you do this – be sure to skip a number on your answer sheet as well. Check often to be sure that you have not lost your place and that you are marking in the row numbered the same as the question you are answering.

6) Read the questions

Be sure you know what the question asks! Many capable people are unsuccessful because they failed to *read* the questions correctly.

7) Answer all questions

Unless you have been instructed that a penalty will be deducted for incorrect answers, it is better to guess than to omit a question.

8) Speed tests

It is often better NOT to guess on speed tests. It has been found that on timed tests people are tempted to spend the last few seconds before time is called in marking answers at random – without even reading them – in the hope of picking up a few extra points. To discourage this practice, the instructions may warn you that your score will be "corrected" for guessing. That is, a penalty will be applied. The incorrect answers will be deducted from the correct ones, or some other penalty formula will be used.

9) Review your answers

If you finish before time is called, go back to the questions you guessed or omitted to give them further thought. Review other answers if you have time.

10) Return your test materials

If you are ready to leave before others have finished or time is called, take ALL your materials to the monitor and leave quietly. Never take any test material with you. The monitor can discover whose papers are not complete, and taking a test booklet may be grounds for disqualification.

VIII. EXAMINATION TECHNIQUES

1) Read the general instructions carefully. These are usually printed on the first page of the exam booklet. As a rule, these instructions refer to the timing of the examination; the fact that you should not start work until the signal and must stop work at a signal, etc. If there are any *special* instructions, such as a choice of questions to be answered, make sure that you note this instruction carefully.

2) When you are ready to start work on the examination, that is as soon as the signal has been given, read the instructions to each question booklet, underline any key words or phrases, such as *least, best, outline, describe* and the like. In this way you will tend to answer as requested rather than discover on reviewing your paper that you *listed without describing*, that you selected the *worst* choice rather than the *best* choice, etc.

3) If the examination is of the objective or multiple-choice type – that is, each question will also give a series of possible answers: A, B, C or D, and you are called upon to select the best answer and write the letter next to that answer on your answer paper – it is advisable to start answering each question in turn. There may be anywhere from 50 to 100 such questions in the three or four hours allotted and you can see how much time would be taken if you read through all the questions before beginning to answer any. Furthermore, if you come across a question or group of questions which you know would be difficult to answer, it would undoubtedly affect your handling of all the other questions.

4) If the examination is of the essay type and contains but a few questions, it is a moot point as to whether you should read all the questions before starting to answer any one. Of course, if you are given a choice – say five out of seven and the like – then it is essential to read all the questions so you can eliminate the two that are most difficult. If, however, you are asked to answer all the questions, there may be danger in trying to answer the easiest one first because you may find that you will spend too much time on it. The best technique is to answer the first question, then proceed to the second, etc.

5) Time your answers. Before the exam begins, write down the time it started, then add the time allowed for the examination and write down the time it must be completed, then divide the time available somewhat as follows:
    - If 3-1/2 hours are allowed, that would be 210 minutes. If you have 80 objective-type questions, that would be an average of 2-1/2 minutes per question. Allow yourself no more than 2 minutes per question, or a total of 160 minutes, which will permit about 50 minutes to review.
    - If for the time allotment of 210 minutes there are 7 essay questions to answer, that would average about 30 minutes a question. Give yourself only 25 minutes per question so that you have about 35 minutes to review.

6) The most important instruction is to *read each question* and make sure you know what is wanted. The second most important instruction is to *time yourself properly* so that you answer every question. The third most important instruction is to *answer every question*. Guess if you have to but include something for each question. Remember that you will receive no credit for a blank and will probably receive some credit if you write something in answer to an essay question. If you guess a letter – say "B" for a multiple-choice question – you may have guessed right. If you leave a blank as an answer to a multiple-choice question, the examiners may respect your feelings but it will not add a point to your score. Some exams may penalize you for wrong answers, so in such cases *only*, you may not want to guess unless you have some basis for your answer.

7) Suggestions
    a. Objective-type questions
        1. Examine the question booklet for proper sequence of pages and questions
        2. Read all instructions carefully
        3. Skip any question which seems too difficult; return to it after all other questions have been answered
        4. Apportion your time properly; do not spend too much time on any single question or group of questions

5. Note and underline key words – *all, most, fewest, least, best, worst, same, opposite,* etc.
6. Pay particular attention to negatives
7. Note unusual option, e.g., unduly long, short, complex, different or similar in content to the body of the question
8. Observe the use of "hedging" words – *probably, may, most likely,* etc.
9. Make sure that your answer is put next to the same number as the question
10. Do not second-guess unless you have good reason to believe the second answer is definitely more correct
11. Cross out original answer if you decide another answer is more accurate; do not erase until you are ready to hand your paper in
12. Answer all questions; guess unless instructed otherwise
13. Leave time for review

b. Essay questions
1. Read each question carefully
2. Determine exactly what is wanted. Underline key words or phrases.
3. Decide on outline or paragraph answer
4. Include many different points and elements unless asked to develop any one or two points or elements
5. Show impartiality by giving pros and cons unless directed to select one side only
6. Make and write down any assumptions you find necessary to answer the questions
7. Watch your English, grammar, punctuation and choice of words
8. Time your answers; don't crowd material

8) Answering the essay question

Most essay questions can be answered by framing the specific response around several key words or ideas. Here are a few such key words or ideas:

M's: manpower, materials, methods, money, management
P's: purpose, program, policy, plan, procedure, practice, problems, pitfalls, personnel, public relations

a. Six basic steps in handling problems:
1. Preliminary plan and background development
2. Collect information, data and facts
3. Analyze and interpret information, data and facts
4. Analyze and develop solutions as well as make recommendations
5. Prepare report and sell recommendations
6. Install recommendations and follow up effectiveness

b. Pitfalls to avoid
1. *Taking things for granted* – A statement of the situation does not necessarily imply that each of the elements is necessarily true; for example, a complaint may be invalid and biased so that all that can be taken for granted is that a complaint has been registered

2. *Considering only one side of a situation* – Wherever possible, indicate several alternatives and then point out the reasons you selected the best one
3. *Failing to indicate follow up* – Whenever your answer indicates action on your part, make certain that you will take proper follow-up action to see how successful your recommendations, procedures or actions turn out to be
4. *Taking too long in answering any single question* – Remember to time your answers properly

IX. AFTER THE TEST

Scoring procedures differ in detail among civil service jurisdictions although the general principles are the same. Whether the papers are hand-scored or graded by machine we have described, they are nearly always graded by number. That is, the person who marks the paper knows only the number – never the name – of the applicant. Not until all the papers have been graded will they be matched with names. If other tests, such as training and experience or oral interview ratings have been given, scores will be combined. Different parts of the examination usually have different weights. For example, the written test might count 60 percent of the final grade, and a rating of training and experience 40 percent. In many jurisdictions, veterans will have a certain number of points added to their grades.

After the final grade has been determined, the names are placed in grade order and an eligible list is established. There are various methods for resolving ties between those who get the same final grade – probably the most common is to place first the name of the person whose application was received first. Job offers are made from the eligible list in the order the names appear on it. You will be notified of your grade and your rank as soon as all these computations have been made. This will be done as rapidly as possible.

People who are found to meet the requirements in the announcement are called "eligibles." Their names are put on a list of eligible candidates. An eligible's chances of getting a job depend on how high he stands on this list and how fast agencies are filling jobs from the list.

When a job is to be filled from a list of eligibles, the agency asks for the names of people on the list of eligibles for that job. When the civil service commission receives this request, it sends to the agency the names of the three people highest on this list. Or, if the job to be filled has specialized requirements, the office sends the agency the names of the top three persons who meet these requirements from the general list.

The appointing officer makes a choice from among the three people whose names were sent to him. If the selected person accepts the appointment, the names of the others are put back on the list to be considered for future openings.

That is the rule in hiring from all kinds of eligible lists, whether they are for typist, carpenter, chemist, or something else. For every vacancy, the appointing officer has his choice of any one of the top three eligibles on the list. This explains why the person whose name is on top of the list sometimes does not get an appointment when some of the persons lower on the list do. If the appointing officer chooses the second or third eligible, the No. 1 eligible does not get a job at once, but stays on the list until he is appointed or the list is terminated.

X. HOW TO PASS THE INTERVIEW TEST

The examination for which you applied requires an oral interview test. You have already taken the written test and you are now being called for the interview test – the final part of the formal examination.

You may think that it is not possible to prepare for an interview test and that there are no procedures to follow during an interview. Our purpose is to point out some things you can do in advance that will help you and some good rules to follow and pitfalls to avoid while you are being interviewed.

What is an interview supposed to test?

The written examination is designed to test the technical knowledge and competence of the candidate; the oral is designed to evaluate intangible qualities, not readily measured otherwise, and to establish a list showing the relative fitness of each candidate – as measured against his competitors – for the position sought. Scoring is not on the basis of "right" and "wrong," but on a sliding scale of values ranging from "not passable" to "outstanding." As a matter of fact, it is possible to achieve a relatively low score without a single "incorrect" answer because of evident weakness in the qualities being measured.

Occasionally, an examination may consist entirely of an oral test – either an individual or a group oral. In such cases, information is sought concerning the technical knowledges and abilities of the candidate, since there has been no written examination for this purpose. More commonly, however, an oral test is used to supplement a written examination.

Who conducts interviews?

The composition of oral boards varies among different jurisdictions. In nearly all, a representative of the personnel department serves as chairman. One of the members of the board may be a representative of the department in which the candidate would work. In some cases, "outside experts" are used, and, frequently, a businessman or some other representative of the general public is asked to serve. Labor and management or other special groups may be represented. The aim is to secure the services of experts in the appropriate field.

However the board is composed, it is a good idea (and not at all improper or unethical) to ascertain in advance of the interview who the members are and what groups they represent. When you are introduced to them, you will have some idea of their backgrounds and interests, and at least you will not stutter and stammer over their names.

What should be done before the interview?

While knowledge about the board members is useful and takes some of the surprise element out of the interview, there is other preparation which is more substantive. It *is* possible to prepare for an oral interview – in several ways:

1) Keep a copy of your application and review it carefully before the interview

This may be the only document before the oral board, and the starting point of the interview. Know what education and experience you have listed there, and the sequence and dates of all of it. Sometimes the board will ask you to review the highlights of your experience for them; you should not have to hem and haw doing it.

2) Study the class specification and the examination announcement

Usually, the oral board has one or both of these to guide them. The qualities, characteristics or knowledges required by the position sought are stated in these documents. They offer valuable clues as to the nature of the oral interview. For example, if the job involves supervisory responsibilities, the announcement will usually indicate that knowledge of modern supervisory methods and the qualifications of the candidate as a supervisor will be tested. If so, you can expect such questions, frequently in the form of a hypothetical situation which you are expected to solve. NEVER go into an oral without knowledge of the duties and responsibilities of the job you seek.

3) Think through each qualification required

Try to visualize the kind of questions you would ask if you were a board member. How well could you answer them? Try especially to appraise your own knowledge and background in each area, *measured against the job sought*, and identify any areas in which you are weak. Be critical and realistic – do not flatter yourself.

4) Do some general reading in areas in which you feel you may be weak

For example, if the job involves supervision and your past experience has NOT, some general reading in supervisory methods and practices, particularly in the field of human relations, might be useful. Do NOT study agency procedures or detailed manuals. The oral board will be testing your understanding and capacity, not your memory.

5) Get a good night's sleep and watch your general health and mental attitude

You will want a clear head at the interview. Take care of a cold or any other minor ailment, and of course, no hangovers.

What should be done on the day of the interview?

Now comes the day of the interview itself. Give yourself plenty of time to get there. Plan to arrive somewhat ahead of the scheduled time, particularly if your appointment is in the fore part of the day. If a previous candidate fails to appear, the board might be ready for you a bit early. By early afternoon an oral board is almost invariably behind schedule if there are many candidates, and you may have to wait. Take along a book or magazine to read, or your application to review, but leave any extraneous material in the waiting room when you go in for your interview. In any event, relax and compose yourself.

The matter of dress is important. The board is forming impressions about you – from your experience, your manners, your attitude, and your appearance. Give your personal appearance careful attention. Dress your best, but not your flashiest. Choose conservative, appropriate clothing, and be sure it is immaculate. This is a business interview, and your appearance should indicate that you regard it as such. Besides, being well groomed and properly dressed will help boost your confidence.

Sooner or later, someone will call your name and escort you into the interview room. *This is it.* From here on you are on your own. It is too late for any more preparation. But remember, you asked for this opportunity to prove your fitness, and you are here because your request was granted.

What happens when you go in?

The usual sequence of events will be as follows: The clerk (who is often the board stenographer) will introduce you to the chairman of the oral board, who will introduce you to the other members of the board. Acknowledge the introductions before you sit down. Do not be surprised if you find a microphone facing you or a stenotypist sitting by. Oral interviews are usually recorded in the event of an appeal or other review.

Usually the chairman of the board will open the interview by reviewing the highlights of your education and work experience from your application – primarily for the benefit of the other members of the board, as well as to get the material into the record. Do not interrupt or comment unless there is an error or significant misinterpretation; if that is the case, do not hesitate. But do not quibble about insignificant matters. Also, he will usually ask you some question about your education, experience or your present job – partly to get you to start talking and to establish the interviewing "rapport." He may start the actual questioning, or turn it over to one of the other members. Frequently, each member undertakes the questioning on a particular area, one in which he is perhaps most competent, so you can expect each member to participate in the examination. Because time is limited, you may also expect some rather abrupt switches in the direction the questioning takes, so do not be upset by it. Normally, a board member will not pursue a single line of questioning unless he discovers a particular strength or weakness.

After each member has participated, the chairman will usually ask whether any member has any further questions, then will ask you if you have anything you wish to add. Unless you are expecting this question, it may floor you. Worse, it may start you off on an extended, extemporaneous speech. The board is not usually seeking more information. The question is principally to offer you a last opportunity to present further qualifications or to indicate that you have nothing to add. So, if you feel that a significant qualification or characteristic has been overlooked, it is proper to point it out in a sentence or so. Do not compliment the board on the thoroughness of their examination – they have been sketchy, and you know it. If you wish, merely say, "No thank you, I have nothing further to add." This is a point where you can "talk yourself out" of a good impression or fail to present an important bit of information. Remember, *you close the interview yourself.*

The chairman will then say, "That is all, Mr. _____, thank you." Do not be startled; the interview is over, and quicker than you think. Thank him, gather your belongings and take your leave. Save your sigh of relief for the other side of the door.

How to put your best foot forward
Throughout this entire process, you may feel that the board individually and collectively is trying to pierce your defenses, seek out your hidden weaknesses and embarrass and confuse you. Actually, this is not true. They are obliged to make an appraisal of your qualifications for the job you are seeking, and they want to see you in your best light. Remember, they must interview all candidates and a non-cooperative candidate may become a failure in spite of their best efforts to bring out his qualifications. Here are 15 suggestions that will help you:

1) Be natural – Keep your attitude confident, not cocky
If you are not confident that you can do the job, do not expect the board to be. Do not apologize for your weaknesses, try to bring out your strong points. The board is interested in a positive, not negative, presentation. Cockiness will antagonize any board member and make him wonder if you are covering up a weakness by a false show of strength.

2) Get comfortable, but don't lounge or sprawl
Sit erectly but not stiffly. A careless posture may lead the board to conclude that you are careless in other things, or at least that you are not impressed by the importance of the occasion. Either conclusion is natural, even if incorrect. Do not fuss with your clothing, a pencil or an ashtray. Your hands may occasionally be useful to emphasize a point; do not let them become a point of distraction.

3) Do not wisecrack or make small talk
This is a serious situation, and your attitude should show that you consider it as such. Further, the time of the board is limited – they do not want to waste it, and neither should you.

4) Do not exaggerate your experience or abilities

In the first place, from information in the application or other interviews and sources, the board may know more about you than you think. Secondly, you probably will not get away with it. An experienced board is rather adept at spotting such a situation, so do not take the chance.

5) If you know a board member, do not make a point of it, yet do not hide it

Certainly you are not fooling him, and probably not the other members of the board. Do not try to take advantage of your acquaintanceship – it will probably do you little good.

6) Do not dominate the interview

Let the board do that. They will give you the clues – do not assume that you have to do all the talking. Realize that the board has a number of questions to ask you, and do not try to take up all the interview time by showing off your extensive knowledge of the answer to the first one.

7) Be attentive

You only have 20 minutes or so, and you should keep your attention at its sharpest throughout. When a member is addressing a problem or question to you, give him your undivided attention. Address your reply principally to him, but do not exclude the other board members.

8) Do not interrupt

A board member may be stating a problem for you to analyze. He will ask you a question when the time comes. Let him state the problem, and wait for the question.

9) Make sure you understand the question

Do not try to answer until you are sure what the question is. If it is not clear, restate it in your own words or ask the board member to clarify it for you. However, do not haggle about minor elements.

10) Reply promptly but not hastily

A common entry on oral board rating sheets is "candidate responded readily," or "candidate hesitated in replies." Respond as promptly and quickly as you can, but do not jump to a hasty, ill-considered answer.

11) Do not be peremptory in your answers

A brief answer is proper – but do not fire your answer back. That is a losing game from your point of view. The board member can probably ask questions much faster than you can answer them.

12) Do not try to create the answer you think the board member wants

He is interested in what kind of mind you have and how it works – not in playing games. Furthermore, he can usually spot this practice and will actually grade you down on it.

13) Do not switch sides in your reply merely to agree with a board member

Frequently, a member will take a contrary position merely to draw you out and to see if you are willing and able to defend your point of view. Do not start a debate, yet do not surrender a good position. If a position is worth taking, it is worth defending.

14) Do not be afraid to admit an error in judgment if you are shown to be wrong

The board knows that you are forced to reply without any opportunity for careful consideration. Your answer may be demonstrably wrong. If so, admit it and get on with the interview.

15) Do not dwell at length on your present job

The opening question may relate to your present assignment. Answer the question but do not go into an extended discussion. You are being examined for a *new* job, not your present one. As a matter of fact, try to phrase ALL your answers in terms of the job for which you are being examined.

Basis of Rating

Probably you will forget most of these "do's" and "don'ts" when you walk into the oral interview room. Even remembering them all will not ensure you a passing grade. Perhaps you did not have the qualifications in the first place. But remembering them will help you to put your best foot forward, without treading on the toes of the board members.

Rumor and popular opinion to the contrary notwithstanding, an oral board wants you to make the best appearance possible. They know you are under pressure – but they also want to see how you respond to it as a guide to what your reaction would be under the pressures of the job you seek. They will be influenced by the degree of poise you display, the personal traits you show and the manner in which you respond.

ABOUT THIS BOOK

This book contains tests divided into Examination Sections. Go through each test, answering every question in the margin. We have also attached a sample answer sheet at the back of the book that can be removed and used. At the end of each test look at the answer key and check your answers. On the ones you got wrong, look at the right answer choice and learn. Do not fill in the answers first. Do not memorize the questions and answers, but understand the answer and principles involved. On your test, the questions will likely be different from the samples. Questions are changed and new ones added. If you understand these past questions you should have success with any changes that arise. Tests may consist of several types of questions. We have additional books on each subject should more study be advisable or necessary for you. Finally, the more you study, the better prepared you will be. This book is intended to be the last thing you study before you walk into the examination room. Prior study of relevant texts is also recommended. NLC publishes some of these in our Fundamental Series. Knowledge and good sense are important factors in passing your exam. Good luck also helps. So now study this Passbook, absorb the material contained within and take that knowledge into the examination. Then do your best to pass that exam.

EXAMINATION SECTION

EXAMINATION SECTION
TEST 1

DIRECTIONS: Each question or incomplete statement is followed by several suggested answers or completions. Select the one that BEST answers the question or completes the statement. *PRINT THE LETTER OF THE CORRECT ANSWER IN THE SPACE AT THE RIGHT.*

1. The PRIMARY purpose of program analysis as it is used in government is to
    A. replace political judgments with rational programs and policies
    B. help decision-makers to sharpen their judgments about program choices
    C. analyze the impact of past programs on the quality of public services
    D. reduce costs by eliminating waste in public programs and services

1.____

2. While there is no complete method for program analysis that is agreed to by all the experts and is relevant to all types of problems, the MOST important element in program analysis involves the
    A. development of alternatives and the definition of objectives or criteria
    B. collection of information and the construction of a mathematical model
    C. design of experiments and procedures to validate results
    D. collection of expert opinion and the combination of their views

2.____

3. Electronic data processing is a particularly valuable tool of analysis in situations where the analyst has a processing problem involving
    A. *small* input, *few* operations, and *small* output
    B. *large* input, *many* operations, and *small* output
    C. *large* input, *few* operations, and *large* output
    D. *small* input, *many* operations, and *small* output

3.____

4. In order for an analyst to use electronic data processing to solve an analytic problem, the problem must be clearly defined.
The BEST way to prepare material for such definition in electronic data processing is to
    A. discuss the problem with computer programmers in a meeting
    B. prepare a flow diagram outlining the steps in the analysis
    C. write a memorandum with a list of the relevant program issues
    D. write a computer program using FORTRAN, BASIC, or another language

4.____

5. The "growth rate" referred to in current political and economic discussion refers to change from year to year in a country's
    A. investments   B. population
    C. gross national product D. sale of goods

5.____

6. Interactive or conversational programming is important to the program analyst ESPECIALLY for
   A. preparing analyses leading to management information systems
   B. communicating among analysts in different places
   C. using canned programs in statistical analysis
   D. testing trial solutions in rapid sequence

7. Program analysts often calls for recommendation of a choice between competing program possibilities that differ in the timing of major costs. Analysts using the present value technique by setting an interest or discount rate are in effect arguing that, other things being equal,
   A. it is inadvisable to defer the start of projects because of rising costs
   B. projects should be completed within a short time period to save money
   C. expenditures should be made out of tax revenues to avoid payment of interest
   D. postponing expenditures is advantageous at some measurable rate

8. Of the following, the formula which is MOST appropriately used to estimate the net need for a given type of service is that net need equals
   A. current clients – anticipate losses + anticipated gains
   B. $\frac{\text{current supply}}{\text{standard}}$ + current clients
   C. (client population x standard) – current supply
   D. current supply – anticipated losses + anticipated gains

9. The purpose of feasibility analysis is to protect the analyst from naïve alternatives and, MOST generally, to
   A. identify and quantify technological constraints
   B. carry out a preliminary stage of analysis
   C. anticipate potential blocks to implementation
   D. line up the support of political leadership

Questions 10-11.

DIRECTIONS: Questions 10 and 11 are to be answered on the basis of the following chart. In a hypothetical problem involving four criteria and four alternatives, the following data have been assembled.

Cost Criterion	Effectiveness Criterion	Timing Criterion	Feasibility Criterion
Alternative A $500,000	50 units	3 months	probably feasible
Alternative B $300,000	100 units	6 months	probably feasible
Alternative C $400,000	50 units	12 months	probably infeasible
Alternative D $200,000	75 units	3 months	probably infeasible

10. On the basis of the above data, it appears that the one alternative which is dominated by another alternative is Alternative
    A. A   B. B   C. C   D. D

11. If the feasibility constraint is absolute and fixed, then the critical trade-off is between lower cost
    A. on the one hand and faster timing and higher effectiveness on the other
    B. and higher effectiveness on one hand and faster timing on the other
    C. and faster timing on the one hand and higher effectiveness on the other
    D. on the one hand and higher effectiveness on the other

12. A classification of an agency's activities in a program structure is MOST useful if it highlights
    A. trade-offs that might not otherwise be considered
    B. ways to improve the efficiency of each activity
    C. the true organizational structure of an agency
    D. bases for insuring that expenditures stay within limits

13. CPM, like PERT, is a useful tool for scheduling large-scale, complex processes. In CPM, the critical path is the
    A. path composed of important links
    B. path composed of uncertain links
    C. longest path through the network
    D. shortest path through the network

14. Classical evaluative research calls for the use of control groups. However, there are practical difficulties in collecting data on individuals to be used as "controls" in program evaluations.
    Researchers may attempt to overcome these difficulties by
    A. using control groups that have no choice such as prison inmates or inmates of other public institutions or facilities
    B. developing better measures of the inputs, processes, and outputs relevant to public programs and services
    C. using experimental demonstration projects with participants in the different projects serving as comparison groups for one another
    D. abandoning attempts at formal evaluation in favor of more qualitative approaches employing a journalistic style of analysis

15. During the course of an analysis of the remaining "life" of a certain city's landfill for refuse disposal, there was a great deal of debate about the impact of changing rates of garbage generation on the amount of landfill needed and about what rates of garbage generation to expect over the next decade. Faced with the need to attempt to resolve this debate, an analyst would construct a simple model of the refuse disposal system and
    A. project landfill needs without considering refuse generation in the future
    B. conduct a detailed household survey in order to estimate future garbage generation rates
    C. ask the experts to continue to debate the issue until the argument is won by one view
    D. do a sensitivity analysis to test the impact of alternative assumptions about refuse generation

16. The limitations of traditional surveys have fostered the development and use of panels.
A panel is a
    A. group of respondents that serves as a continuous source of survey information
    B. group of advisors expert in the design and implementation of surveys
    C. representative sample of respondents at a single point in time
    D. post-survey discussion group composed of former respondents

16.____

17. The difference between sensitivity analysis and risk analysis is that risk analysis
    A. is applicable only to profit and loss situations where the concept of risk is operable
    B. includes an estimate of probabilities of different values of input factors
    C. is applicable to physical problems while sensitivity analysis is applicable to social ones
    D. requires a computer simulation while sensitivity analysis does not

17.____

18. A decision tree, although initially applied to business problems, is a graphic device which is useful to public analysts in
    A. scheduling complex processes
    B. doing long-range forecasting
    C. formulating the structure of alternatives
    D. solving production-inventory problems

18.____

19. The purpose of a management information system in an agency is to
    A. structure data relevant to managerial decision-making
    B. put all of an agency's data in machine-processing form
    C. simplify the record-keeping operations in an agency
    D. keep an ongoing record of management's activities

19.____

20.

20.____

Assume that an analyst is presented with the above chart for a fire department and supplied also with information indicating a stable size firefighting staff over this time.
The analyst could REASONABLY conclude regarding productivity that
    A. productivity over this time period was essentially stable for this firefighting force because the number of responses to real fires during this period was stable, as was the work force
    B. productivity was essentially increasing for this force because the number of total responses was increasing relative to a stable force

C. productivity was declining because a greater proportion of the total work effort was wasted effort in responding to false alarms
D. it is impossible to make a judgment about the productivity of the firefighting staff without a judgment about the value of a response to a false alarm

21. In the design of a productivity program for the sanitary department, the BEST measure of productivity would be
    A. tons of refuse collected annually
    B. number of collections made per week
    C. tons of refuse collected per truck shift
    D. number of trucks used per shift

21.____

22. The cohort-survival method for estimating future population has been widely employed.
    In this method,
    A. migration is assumed to be constant over time
    B. net migration within cohorts is assumed to be zero
    C. migration is included as a multiplier factor
    D. net migration within cohorts is assumed to be constant

22.____

23. Cost-effectiveness and cost-benefit analysis represent a systematic approach to balancing potential losses against potential gains as a prelude to public action.
    In addition to limitations based on difficulties of measurement and inadequacies in data that are typical of systematic program analysis, cost-benefit analysis suffers from a serious conceptual flaw in that
    A. the definition of benefit or cost does not typically distinguish to whom benefits or costs accrue
    B. a full-scale cost benefit analysis takes too long to do, is too expensive, and needs too much data
    C. it has been shown that such analyses are more suitable for defense or water resources problems
    D. such analyses are not useful in any problem involving capital and operating costs or benefits

23.____

24. If you were asked to develop a total cost estimate for one year for a program involving both a capital improvement and operating costs, the BEST way to estimate the capital cost component would be to
    A. divide the estimated cost of the capital improvement by the projected operating costs over the life of the improvement
    B. multiply the annual operating cost by the projected life of the capital improvement
    C. divide the amortized cost of the capital improvement by the projected life of the improvement
    D. multiply the portion of the capital improvement to be completed within the year by the cost of the improvement

24.____

25. In comparing the costs of two or more alternative programs, it is important to consider all relevant costs.
The MOST important principle in defining "relevant cost" is that
   A. only marginal or incremental cost should be considered in the estimate
   B. only recurring costs should be considered for each alternative
   C. estimates should include the sunk costs for each alternative
   D. cost estimates need to be as precise as in budget preparation

26. Different techniques for projecting future costs may be suitable in different situations. Assume that it is necessary to estimate the future costs of maintaining garbage collection vehicles.
Under which of the following conditions would it be advisable to develop a cost-estimating equation rather than to use unadjusted current data?
   A. When it is expected that more complex equipment will replace simpler equipment
   B. Whether or not it is expected that the nature of future garbage collection will change
   C. When the current unadjusted data still has to be verified
   D. When the nature of future garbage collection equipment is unknown

27. The following data has been collected on the costs of two pilot programs, each representing a different approach to the same problem.

	Total Cost	Fixed Cost	Variable Cost	Average Unit Cost	Number of Users
Program A	$45,000	$20,000	$50 per user	$90 Per User	500
Program B	$42,000	$7,000	$100 Per User	$120 Per User	350

Assume that the pilot programs are extended city-wide and other factors are constant.
Using the above data, what would a cost analysis conclude about the relative costs of the two programs?
Program
   A. B would be less costly with fewer than 300 users and Program A would be less costly with more than 300 users
   B. B would be less costly with fewer than 260 users and Program A would be less costly with more than 260 users
   C. A would be less costly without regard to the size of the program
   D. B would be less costly without regard to the size of the program

Questions 28-30.

DIRECTIONS: Questions 28 through 30 are to be answered on the basis of the following data assembled for a cost-benefit analysis.

	Cost	Benefit
No program	0	0
Alternative W	$3,000	$6,000
Alternative X	$10,000	$17,000
Alternative Y	$17,000	$25,000
Alternative Z	$30,000	$32,000

28. From the point of view of pushing public expenditure to the point where marginal benefit equals or exceeds marginal cost, the BEST alternative is Alternative 28.____
    A. W   B. X   C. Y   D. Z

29. From the point of view of selecting the alternative with the best cost-benefit ratio, the BEST alternative is Alternative 29.____
    A. W   B. X   C. Y   D. Z

30. From the point of view of selecting the alternative with the best measure of net benefit, the BEST alternative is Alternative 30.____
    A. W   B. X   C. Y   D. Z

Questions 31-35.

DIRECTIONS: The set of answers listed below applies to Questions 31 through 35. Each answer is a type of statistical test.

    A. Analysis of variance
    B. Pearson Product-Moment Correlation (r)
    C. t-test
    D. x^2 test (Chi-squared)

Pick the test which is MOST appropriate to the situation described. An answer may be used more than once.

31. A comparison between two correlated means obtained from a small sample. 31.____
    The CORRECT answer is:
    A. A   B. B   C. C   D. D

32. A comparison of three or more means. 32.____
    The CORRECT answer is:
    A. A   B. B   C. C   D. D

33. A comparison of the divergence of observed frequencies with those expected on the hypothesis of equal probability of occurrence. 33.____
    The CORRECT answer is:
    A. A   B. B   C. C   D. D

34. A comparison of the divergence of observed frequencies with those expected on the hypothesis of a normal distribution. 34.____
    The CORRECT answer is:
    A. A   B. B   C. C   D. D

35. A comparison between two uncorrelated means obtained from small samples. 35.____
    The CORRECT answer is:
    A. A   B. B   C. C   D. D

36. There are many different models for evaluative research.
A time-series design is an example of a _____ experimental design.
   A. field
   B. true
   C. quasi-
   D. pre-

37. In policy research, as in all kinds of research, it is important to develop research hypotheses early.
The MAIN purpose of a research hypothesis is to
   A. include the kind of statistical procedures to be used in the research
   B. provide a ready answer in case data is not available for doing research
   C. serve as a guide to the kind of data that must be collected in order to answer the research question
   D. clarify what is known and what is not known in the research problem

38. While descriptive and causal research are not completely separable, there has been a distinct effort to move in the direction of causal research.
Such an effort is epitomized by the use of
   A. predictive models and measures of deviation from predictions
   B. option and attitudinal surveys in local neighborhoods
   C. community studies and area profiles of localities
   D. individual case histories and group case studies

39. The one of the following which BEST describes a periodic report is that it
   A. provides a record of accomplishments for a given time span and a comparison with similar time spans in the past
   B. covers the progress made in a project that has been postponed
   C. integrates, summarizes, and perhaps interprets published data on technical or scientific material
   D. describes a decision, advocates a policy or action, and presents facts in support of the writer's position

40. The PRIMARY purpose of including pictorial illustrations in a formal report is usually to
   A. amplify information which has been adequately treated verbally
   B. present detail that are difficult to describe verbally
   C. provide the reader with a pleasant, momentary distraction
   D. present supplementary information incidental to the main ideas developed in the report

KEY (CORRECT ANSWERS)

1.	B	11.	B	21.	C	31.	C
2.	A	12.	A	22.	B	32.	A
3.	B	13.	C	23.	A	33.	D
4.	B	14.	C	24.	C	34.	D
5.	C	15.	D	25.	A	35.	C
6.	D	16.	A	26.	A	36.	C
7.	D	17.	B	27.	B	37.	C
8.	C	18.	C	28.	C	38.	A
9.	C	19.	A	29.	A	39.	A
10.	C	20.	D	30.	C	40.	B

TEST 2

DIRECTIONS: Each question or incomplete statement is followed by several suggested answers or completions. Select the one that BEST answers the question or completes the statement. *PRINT THE LETTER OF THE CORRECT ANSWER IN THE SPACE AT THE RIGHT.*

1. A measurement procedure is considered to be RELIABLE to the extent that 1.____
   A. independent applications under similar conditions yield consistent results
   B. independent applications under different conditions yield similar results
   C. scores reflect true differences among individuals or situations
   D. scores reflect true differences in the same individual over time

2. Different scales of measurement are distinguished by the feasibility of various empirical operations. 2.____
   An ordinal scale of measurement
   A. is not as useful as a ratio or interval scale
   B. is useful in rank-ordering or priority setting
   C. provides the data for addition or subtraction
   D. provides the data for computation of means

3. A widely used approach to sampling is systematic sampling, i.e., selecting every Kth element in a listing. 3.____
   Even with a random start, a DISADVANTAGE in this approach is that
   A. the listing used may contain a cyclical pattern
   B. it is too similar to a simple random sample
   C. the system does not insure a probability sample
   D. it yield an unpredictable sample size

4. A rule of thumb sometimes used in sample size selection it to set sample size equal to five percent of the population size. 4.____
   Other things being equal, this rule
   A. tends to oversample small populations
   B. tends to oversample large populations
   C. provides an accurate rule for sampling
   D. is a relatively inexpensive basis for sampling

5. With regard to a stratified random sample, it may be APPROPRIATE to sample the various strata in different proportions in order to 5.____
   A. approximate the characteristics of a true random sample
   B. establish classes that are internally heterogenous in each case
   C. avoid the necessity of subdividing the cases within each stratum
   D. adequately cover important strata that have small numbers of cases

6. One possible response to the "unknown" or "no answer" category in a tabulation of survey information is to "allocate" the unknown responses, i.e., to estimate the missing data on the basis of other known information about the respondents. 6.____

This technique is APPROPRIATE when the unknown category
- A. is very small and is randomly distributed within all subgroups of respondents
- B. is very large and is randomly distributed within all subgroups of respondents
- C. reflects an interviewing failure and a subgroup in the sample ends to produce more unknowns
- D. is a legitimate category and a subgroup in the sample tends to produce more unknowns

7. In presenting cross-tabulated data showing the relationship between two variables, it is MOST meaningful to compute percentages
    - A. in both directions in all instances
    - B. of each cell in relation to the grand total
    - C. in the direction of the smaller number of cells
    - D. in the direction of the causal factor

8. In portraying data based on a sampling operation, it is MOST meaningful and comprehensible to the reader to present
    - A. percentages for the sample and the universe
    - B. percentages by themselves
    - C. percentages and the base figures
    - D. numbers by themselves

9. A new bridge spanning a river is expected to carry 60,000 cars a day on a rainy day and 80,000 cars a day on other kinds of days.
   If there is a $5 toll and one chance in four of a rainy day, the expected value of a day's revenue is
   A. $175,000   B. $375,000   C. $475,000   D. $700,000

10. The analyst who is asked to estimate the probability of a relatively rare event occurring cannot use the classical frequency measures of probability but rather should
    - A. use a random-numbers table to pick a probability
    - B. project historical data into the future
    - C. indicate that no probabilistic judgment is possible
    - D. make the best possible judgment as to the subjective probability

11. A useful source of census data for computing annual indicators is the
    - A. Public Use Sample
    - B. Continuing Population Survey
    - C. Census of Population
    - D. Census of Governments

12. An analyst presented with a set of household records showing age, ethnicity, income, and family status and wishing to study the inter-relationship of all of these variables simultaneously will probably equal
    - A. one four-way cross-tabulation
    - B. four three-way cross-tabulation
    - C. six two-way cross-tabulations
    - D. four single tabulations

13. Downward communication, from high management to lower levels in an organization, will often not be fully accepted at the lowest levels of an organization unless high-level management
    A. communicates through several levels of mid-level management, where the message can be properly modified and interpreted
    B. communicates directly with the level of the organization it wishes to reach, bypassing any intermediate levels
    C. first establishes an atmosphere in which upward communication is encouraged and listened to
    D. establishes penalties for non-compliance with its communications

13._____

14. A top-level manager sometimes has an inaccurate view of the actual lower-level operations of his agency, particularly of those operations which are not running well.
    Of the following, the MOST frequent cause of this is the
    A. general unconcern of top-level management with the way an agency actually operates
    B. tendency of the people at the lowest level in an agency to lie about their actual performance
    C. unwillingness of top-level management to deal with unfavorable information when it is presented
    D. tendency of mid-level management to edit bad news and unpleasant information from reports directed to top management

14._____

15. In the conduct of productivity analyses, work measurement is a USEFUL technique for
    A. substantiating executive decisions
    B. designing a research study
    C. developing performance yardsticks
    D. preparing a manual of procedure

15._____

16. Issue analysis is closely identified with the "fire-fighting" function of management. As such, issue analysis is a(n)
    A. systematic assessment over time of an agency's strategic options
    B. annual review of the issues that have come up during the past year
    C. basis for a set of procedures to be followed in an emergency
    D. analysis of a specific policy question often performed in a crisis environment

16._____

17. The transportation agency in a large city wishes to study the impact of fare increases on ridership in buses. Ridership data for peak hours has been assembled for the same time period for three geographic subareas (A, B, and C) with approximately the same socio-economic characteristics, residential density, and distance from the central business district (CBD). Subarea A had experienced a moderate fare increase on its bus line; Subarea B had had no fare increase; and Subarea C had experienced a major fare increase during the time period

17._____

In the design of this study, the analysis should be framed:
A. Ridership = f (fare level)
B. Ridership = f (fare level), distance from CBD)
C. Fare level = f (ridership)
D. Ridership = f (fare level, socio-economic characteristics, residential density)

18. What organizational concept is illustrated when a group is organized on an *ad hoc* basis to accomplish a specific goal? 18.____
    A. Functional Teamwork   B. Line/staff
    C. Task Force   D. Command

19. The concept of "demand" provides an appropriate theoretical basis for estimating the needs for public services or programs where the service will be on a _____ basis and _____ life-sustaining necessities. 19.____
    A. fee; involves   B. free; involves
    C. free; does not involve   D. fee; does not involve

20. Analysts should be wary of relying exclusively on traditional service standards (e.g., one acre of playground per 1,000 population). 20.____
    Such standards are often DEFICIENT because they tend to overstate
    A. the consumer view and understate behavior and values of producers
    B. the producer view and understate behavior and values of users or consumers
    C. local conditions and understate national conditions
    D. behavioral factors and understate practical effects

21. The BEST measure of the performance of a manpower program would be 21.____
    A. percentage reduction in unemployment by impacted population groups
    B. number of trainees placed in jobs at the beginning of the training program
    C. percentage of students completing a training program
    D. cost per student of the training program and the job placement effort

22. Indices are single figures that measure multi-dimensional concepts. 22.____
    The critical judgment in the construction of an index involves
    A. the trade-off between accuracy and simplicity
    B. determination of enough data to do the measurement
    C. avoidance of all possible error
    D. developing a theoretical basis for it

23. Evaluation of public programs is complicated by the reality that programs tend to reflect negotiated compromises among conflicting objectives. 23.____
    The absence of clear, unitary objectives PARTICULARLY complicates the
    A. assessment of program input or effort
    B. development of effectiveness criteria
    C. design of new programs to replace the old
    D. diagnosis of a program's processes

24. The BASIC purpose of the "Super-Agencies" is to
    A. reduce the number of departments and agencies in the city government
    B. reduce the number of high-level administrators
    C. coordinate agencies reporting to the mayor and supervise agencies in related fields
    D. supervise departments and agencies in unrelated fields

25. In most municipal budgeting systems involving capital and operating budgets, the leasing or renting of facilities is usually shown in
    A. the operating budget
    B. the capital budget
    C. a separate schedule
    D. either budget

26. New York City's budgeting procedure is unusual in that budget appropriations are considered in two parts, as follows:
    A. Capital budget and income budget
    B. Expense budget and income budget
    C. Revenue budget and expense budget
    D. Expense budget and capital budget

27. The "growth rate" referred to in current political and economic discussion refers to change from year to year in a country's
    A. gross national product
    B. population
    C. available labor force
    D. capital goods investment

Questions 28-29.

DIRECTIONS: Questions 28 and 29 are to be answered on the basis of the following illustration. Assume that the figures in the chart are cubes.

28. In the illustration above, how many times GREATER is the quantity represented by Figure III than the quantity represented by Figure II?
    A. 2   B. 4   C. 8   D. 16

29. The above illustration illustrates a progression in quantity BEST described as
    A. arithmetic   B. geometric   C. discrete   D. linear

Questions 30-35.

DIRECTIONS: Questions 30 through 35 are to be answered on the basis of the following chart.

In a national study of poverty trends, the following data have been assembled by interpretation.

Item	Persons Below Poverty, By Residence			
	Number (millions)		Percent	
	U.S.	Metropolitan Areas	U.S.	Metropolitan Areas
2010				
Total	38.8	17.0	22.0	15.3
Under 25 years	20.0	8.8	25.3	18.1
65 years & over	5.5	2.5	35.2	26.9
Black	9.9	5.0	55.1	42.8
Other	28.3	11.8	18.1	12.0
2020				
Total	24.3	12.3	12.2	9.5
Under 25 years	12.2	6.4	13.2	10.4
65 years & over	4.8	2.3	25.3	20.2
Black	7.2	3.9	32.3	24.4
Other	16.7	8.2	9.5	7.3

30. If no other source of data were available, which of the following groups would you expect to have the HIGHEST rate of poverty?
    A. Others over 65
    B. Others under 65
    C. Blacks over 65
    D. Blacks under 65

30._____

31. Between 2010 and 2020, the percentage of poor in the United States who were Black
    A. increased from 25.5% to 29.6%
    B. decreased from 55.1% to 32.3%
    C. decreased from 9.9% to 7.2%
    D. stayed the same

31._____

32. The data in the second column of the table indicate that, in the metropolitan areas, the number of poor declined by 4.7 million or 36.2% between 2010 and 2020. Yet, the fourth column shows a corresponding decline from 15.3% to 9.5%, or only 5.8%.
    This apparent discrepancy reflects the fact that
    A. metropolitan areas are growing while the number of poor is contracting
    B. two columns in question are based on different sources of information
    C. difference between two percentages is not the same as the percent change in total numbers
    D. tables have inherent errors and must be carefully checked

32._____

33. The percentages in each of the last two columns of the table for 2010 and 2020 don't add up to 100%. This is for the reason that
   A. rounding off each entry to the nearest decimal place caused an error in the total such that the total is not equal to 100%
   B. these columns show the percentage of Blacks, aged, etc. who are poor rather than the percentage of poor who are Black, aged, etc.
   C. there was an error in the construction of the table which was not noticed until the table was already in print
   D. there is double counting in the entries in the table; some people ae counted more than once

34. Data such as that presented in the table on persons below poverty level are shown to a single decimal place because
   A. data in every table should always be shown to a single decimal place
   B. it is the minimal number of decimal places needed to distinguish among table entries
   C. there was no room for more decimal places in the table without crowding
   D. the more accurately a figure is shown the better it is for the user

35. In comparing the poverty of the young (under 25 years) with that of the older population (65 years and over) in 2010 and 2020, one could REASONABLY conclude that
   A. more young people than old people were poor but older people had a higher rate of poverty
   B. more older people than young people were poor but young people had a higher rate of poverty
   C. there is a greater degree of poverty among the younger population than among the older people

Questions 36-37.

DIRECTIONS: Questions 36 and 37 are to be answered ONLY on the basis of the information given in the following passage.

Two approaches are available in developing criteria for the evaluation of plans. One approach, designated Approach A, is a review and analysis of characteristics that differentiate successful plans from unsuccessful plans. These criteria are descriptive in nature and serve as a checklist against which the plan under consideration may be judged. These characteristics have been observed by many different students of planning, and there is considerable agreement concerning the characteristics necessary for a plan to be successful.

A second approach to the development of criteria for judging plans, designated Approach B is the determination of the degree to which the plan under consideration is economic. The word "economic" is used here in its broadest sense, i.e., effective in its utilization of resources. In order to determine the economic worth of a plan, it is necessary to use a technique that permits the description of any plan in economic terms and to utilize this technique to the extent that it becomes a "way of thinking" about plans.

36. According to Approach B, the MOST successful plan is generally one which
   A. costs least to implement
   B. gives most value for resources expended
   C. uses the least expensive resources
   D. utilizes the greatest number of resources

37. According to Approach A, a successful plan is one which is
   A. descriptive in nature
   B. lowest in cost
   C. similar to other successful plans
   D. agreed upon by many students of planning

Questions 38-40.

DIRECTIONS: Questions 38 through 40 are to be answered ONLY on the basis of the information provided in the following passage.

The primary purpose of control reports is to supply information intended to serve as the basis for corrective action if needed. At the same time, the significance of control reports must be kept in proper perspective. Control reports are only a part of the planning-management information system. Control information includes non-financial as well as financial data that measure performance and isolate variances from standard. Control information also provides feedback so that planning information may be updated and corrected. Whenever possible, control reports should be designed so that they provide feedback for the planning process as well as provide information of immediate value to the control process.

Since the culmination of the control process is the taking of necessary corrective action to bring performance in line with standards, it follows that control information must be directed to the person who is organizationally responsible for taking the required action. Usually the same information, though in a somewhat abbreviated form, is given to the responsible manager's superior. A district sales manager needs a complete daily record of the performance of each of his salesmen; yet, the report forwarded to the regional sales manager summarizes only the performance of each sales district in his region. In preparing reports for higher echelons of management, summary statements and recommendations for action should appear on the first page; substantiating data, usually the information presented to the person directly responsible for the operation, may be include if needed.

38. A control report serves its primary purpose as part of the process which leads DIRECTLY to
   A. better planning for future action
   B. increasing the performance of district salesmen
   C. the establishment of proper performance standards
   D. taking corrective action when performance is poor

39. The one of the following which would be the BEST description of a control report is that a control report is a form of
   A. planning   B. communication
   C. direction   D. organization

40. If control reports are to be effective, the one of the following which is LEAST essential to the effectiveness of control reporting is a system of
    A. communication
    B. standards
    C. authority
    D. work simplification

KEY (CORRECT ANSWERS)

1.	A	11.	B	21.	A	31.	B
2.	B	12.	A	22.	A	32.	C
3.	A	13.	C	23.	B	33.	B
4.	B	14.	D	24.	C	34.	D
5.	D	15.	C	25.	A	35.	A
6.	C	16.	D	26.	D	36.	B
7.	D	17.	A	27.	A	37.	C
8.	C	18.	C	28.	C	38.	D
9.	B	19.	D	29.	B	39.	B
10.	D	20.	B	30.	C	40.	D

EXAMINATION SECTION
TEST 1

DIRECTIONS: Each question or incomplete statement is followed by several suggested answers or completions. Select the one that BEST answers the question or completes the statement. *PRINT THE LETTER OF THE CORRECT ANSWER IN THE SPACE AT THE RIGHT.*

1. An analyst is writing a report dealing with the distribution of deaths caused by various types of cardiovascular diseases. He decides to facilitate the reader's grasp of the information presented by including in the report a device that permits comparison of parts to each other, and to the whole at the same time.
   Of the following, the MOST appropriate and efficient device he should use for this purpose is the

   A. graph
   B. pie diagram
   C. flow sheet
   D. line chart with one series

   1._____

2. In carrying out a cost-effectiveness analysis, the analyst should follow certain guidelines. The MOST important of these guidelines involves the

   A. utilization of both the fixed utility approach and the fixed budget approach
   B. proper structuring of the problem and design of the analysis
   C. necessity of building a model that is highly formal and mathematical
   D. provision for implicit treatment of uncertainty

   2._____

3. In a decision which involves fairness -- such as assigning new office equipment to workers when the agency does not receive enough new office equipment for the entire group -- the PRIMARY determinant of the decision's effectiveness will be the

   A. systematic or traditional approach which is emphasized in reaching the decision
   B. random nature of the assignment
   C. feedback a decisionmaker receives concerning the decision
   D. acceptance of the decision by the persons who have to execute it

   3._____

4. In order to give line personnel some insight into staff problems and vice versa it has been suggested that line and staff assignments within a particular city agency be rotated. Which of the following criticisms would be MOST valid for opposing such a proposal?

   A. Generally speaking, line and staff personnel have different perspectives on organizational structures which makes rotation in assignments extremely difficult.
   B. Since their educational backgrounds are often quite diverse, staff personnel are often at a disadvantage when serving in line assignments.
   C. Line personnel frequently resent having to perform the more difficult tasks that staff assignments entail.
   D. Serving in a rotating assignment may not necessarily provide the personnel with any significant degree of insight as anticipated.

   4._____

5. Which one of the following approaches to criticism of a subordinate or associate is *generally* the MOST appropriate and effective?
   Criticize

   A. by making a comparison with a more exemplary employee

   5._____

B. the act, not the person
C. in a humorous vein
D. in general rather than specific terms

6. Assume that two policy units have been formed to study the impact of Federal programs in the city. The two units operate in an essentially similar manner, except for their communications procedures. In unit A any member may communicate and exchange information with any other member of the unit; in unit B a member may only communicate information with the unit supervisor.
In evaluating the effect that these communications procedures have on the level of productivity, it will *generally* be found that

   A. unit A's level of productivity will be greater than unit B's level of productivity for simple problems
   B. unit B's level of productivity will be greater than unit A's level of productivity for simple problems
   C. initial levels of profuctivity are higher in unit A than unit B for complex problems
   D. initial levels of productivity are higher in unit B than in unit A for complex problems

7. In the process of communicating an idea, the following five distinct steps are generally involved:
   I. Selection of a media and transmission of the message
   II. Decoding of a message, i.e., meaning is extracted from the message
   III. Message is received
   IV. Idea is organized into a series of symbols designed to give meaning
   V. Action is taken and/or feedback is given

   In what logical, sequential order should these steps be arranged for effective two-way communications to take place?

   A. V, I, II, III, IV
   B. II, I, III, IV, V
   C. IV, I, III, II, V
   D. I, III, IV, II, V

8. Informal employee groups that share certain norms and strive for member satisfaction through the achievement of group goals are known as work groups.
Which of the following statements can *generally* be considered as being *FALSE* in describing work groups in a moderate size organization?

   A. Formation of work groups is ubiquitous and inevitable.
   B. Work groups strongly influence the overall behavior and performance of their members.
   C. An organization can reap positive and negative consequences as a result of work groups.
   D. Elimination of work groups can be easily achieved by management pressure.

9. Under the management approach known as *management by objectives* which of the following criteria is *generally* used to determine whether the manager has been successful?

   A. Activities performed
   B. Results achieved
   C. Production schedules completed
   D. Financial savings accomplished

10. Of the following, the MOST accurate statement relative to job attitudes is that they

   A. cannot be influenced by only one person
   B. are always the result of work groups
   C. have no relationship to productivity
   D. are strongly influenced by work situation

11. Assume that measures to overcome a budget deficit, including attrition and a hiring freeze, have significantly decreased the work-output of a city agency. The agency administrator desires to develop a plan to restore production to its former level by increasing the work-load and responsibility of the agency's employees.
In order to obtain *maximum* employee cooperation and *minimize* employee resistance, it would be MOST advisable for the

   A. administrator of the agency to personally describe to the employees the new work changes that they are to follow
   B. employees to decide what the optimal changes in the work load should be
   C. management representatives to consult with employee representatives on these matters
   D. immediate supervisor of the employees to decide on the work changes to be implemented

12. Eliciting the support and cooperation of others often requires a great deal of persuasion. Which one of the following persuasive techniques or practices is generally the LEAST desirable for you, an analyst, to use?

   A. Establish your expertness and authority
   B. Present your arguments without emotion
   C. In presenting your arguments, express yourself in the manner to which you are accustomed
   D. Try to find a face-saving way for your opponent to change his/her mind

13. The following illustration depicts the structure of a municipal agency.

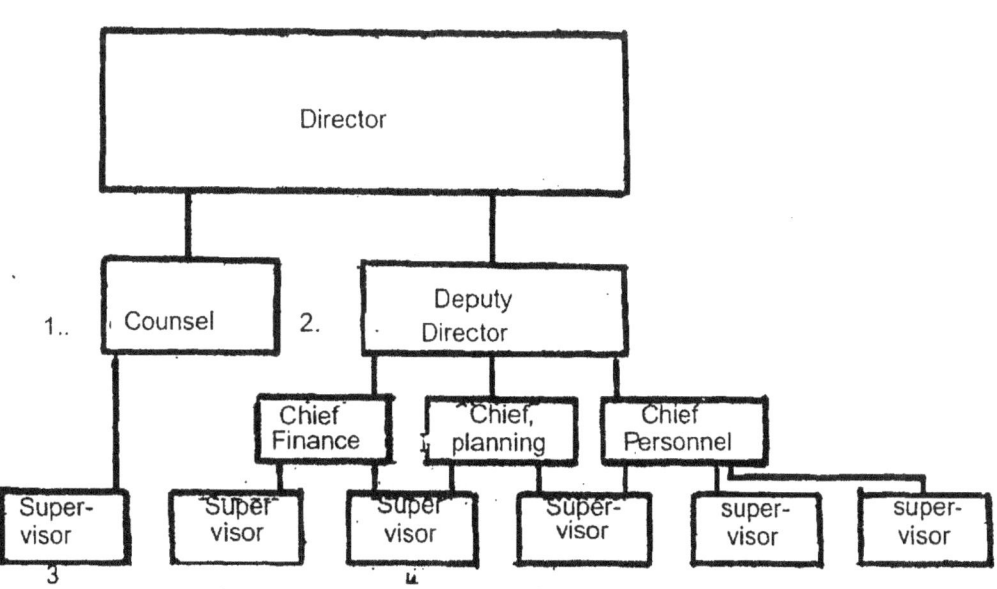

In the above illustration, which individual would generally be expected to encounter the MOST difficulty in carrying out his organizational functions?

   A. 1 B. 2 C. 3 D. 4

14. An agency in which a free flow of communication exists is an agency in which no barriers or structures are erected to control or bar the flow of information and messages between and among management and staff, horizontally or vertically.
Of the following, the GREATEST disadvantage that would be most likely to occur in an agency in which such a free flow of communication exists, is that

    A. it would be difficult to determine which information is important and which is irrelevant
    B. there would be a lesser degree of staff-employee participation and cooperation in communicating
    C. more restrictive controls would be placed on managerial employees
    D. important communications would tend to be eliminated, and and trivial communications over-emphasized

15. Feedback is generally considered an essential factor in oral communication MAINLY because

    A. it enables the speaker to know whether he is understood
    B. the speed of communication is accelerated
    C. it eliminates the necessity of the speaker to use gestures and facial expressions when speaking
    D. the listener is unable to immediately respond to the speaker until the latter is finished

16. Assume that two employees are working on a joint project and they have a difference of opinion on the methodology to be used. Each employee not only listens to the other's opinion on methodology but projects him-self into the other's position.
This type of listening is *usually* considered

    A. *ineffective*, mainly because it will be impossible for the employees to reach a satisfactory agreement
    B. *effective*, mainly because each employee will then be more critical of the other's argument
    C. *ineffective*, mainly because each worker will unconsciously and unintentionally accept the other's viewpoint
    D. *effective*, mainly because each speaker can understand the other's viewpoint and can then respond intelligently to his remarks

17. The arithmetic mean is commonly used in describing data. Which one of the following statements is NOT true about the arithmetic mean?

    A. It is a measure of dispersion.
    B. The sum of the deviations around it is zero.
    C. It is easy to compute, understand and recognize.
    D. It may be treated alegebraically.

Questions 18 - 20.

DIRECTIONS: Answer Questions 18 through 20 on the basis of the following data. Assume that you are using these data in assessing the impact of Federal and State income taxes on New York City residents, and comparing it to the effect of Federal and State taxes in other areas.

EFFECT OF DEDUCTIBILITY (i.e., deductibility of taxes levied by other jurisdictions in calculating the net base of the tax in the taxing jurisdiction.)

Net income before personal exemption	Effective rate of tax				
	Federal (assuming no state tax)	State		Combined Federal and State	
		New York*	Minnesota (assuming no federal tax)	New York	Minnesota
	(1)	(2)	(3)	(4)	(5)
$20,000	25.0	4.1	6.9	27.6	27.9
50,000	42.2	5.4	9.1	44.0	43.9
100,000	56.0	5.9	9.8	57.5	57.1
200,000	69.2	6.1	10.1	69.9	69.5
1,500,000	88.0	6.3	10.5	89.3	88.9

*New York has no deductibility; the Federal government has deductibility.

18. In which of the following columns is the tax rate shown to be the LEAST progressive?

    A. 1   B. 2   C. 4   D. 5

19. Which of the following statements is TRUE about the reasons why Columns 1 and 2 do not equal Column 4 for each salary level?

    A. Personal deductions are taken into account in Column 4 but not in Columns 1 and 2.
    B. Federal deducibility of state taxes only is taken into account in Column 4 but not in Columns 1 and 2.
    C. Reciprocal deductibility is taken into account in Column 4 but not in Columns 1 and 2.
    D. State deductibility of federal taxes only is taken into account in Column 4 but not in Columns 1 and 2.

20. The EFFECT of the State's introducing deductibility, given that the Federal government maintains deductibility, is to

    A. *increase* Federal and State income
    B. *decrease* Federal and State income
    C. *decrease* Federal income and increase State income
    D. *increase* Federal income and decrease State income

21. Assume that you have been made project coordinator for a study concerning the implementation of casino gambling in the city. You have assigned each of the professional staff members simple tasks in specialized areas for the duration of the project. For you to make such job assignments would *generally* be

    A. *desirable;* the performance of simple tasks will motivate individuals to work diligently
    B. *desirable;* specialized tasks induce a sense of accomplishment to individuals
    C. *undesirable;* specialized tasks are more difficult to learn
    D. *undesirable;* specialized tasks may lead to a loss of feeling of accomplishment

22. Assume that you have been asked to submit a proposal for the reorganization of a unit that is charged with performing difficult nonroutine work. Frequently decisions must be made quickly and concurrence obtained from high-level agency heads.
    Given the above conditions, of the following it would be MOST logical to structure the organization

    A. on the basis of a relatively wide span of control
    B. on the basis of a relatively narrow span of control
    C. with many organizational levels with a wide span of control
    D. with more emphasis on line than staff units

23. Assume that a study has indicated that a recently created city *superagency* has had formal communication difficulties among various component agencies. It appears that jurisdictional overlapping among those agencies has caused frequent rerouting and unnecessary duplication of communications within the organization. Which one of the following proposals would MOST effectively deal with the communications problem encountered by this *superagency?*

    A. Create a central communications office to handle all communications for this *superagency.*
    B. Duplicate and distribute all communications to each component within this *superagency.*
    C. Reduce the overlapping areas of jurisdiction among the component agencies
    D. Decentralize the *superagency* on a *borough* basis to expedite mail delivery

24. The utilization of input-output concepts in connection with the application of the systems concept to government raises the problem of the quantification of objectives and performance (the value of the public benefit). The one of the following which is MOST easily *quantifiable* is

    A. education
    B. police service
    C. subway car maintenance
    D. the effectiveness of a welfare administrator

25. When an analyst tries to conceive of a city management problem as a *systems* problem, he is, first of all, confronted with establishing the boundaries of the system. Of the following, the city problem which can *most likely* be conceived of within a system whose boundaries are roughly equivalent to those of the city is

    A. taxation
    B. welfare
    C. fire protection
    D. transportation

25.____

KEY (CORRECT ANSWERS)

1. B	11. C
2. B	12. B
3. D	13. D
4. D	14. A
5. B	15. A
6. C	16. D
7. C	17. A
8. D	18. B
9. B	19. B
10. D	20. D

21. D
22. B
23. C
24. C
25. C

TEST 2

DIRECTIONS: Each question or incomplete statement is followed by several suggested answers or completions. Select the one that *BEST* answers the question or completes the statement. *PRINT THE LETTER OF THE CORRECT ANSWER IN THE SPACE AT THE RIGHT.*

1. When installing a new *system,* an analyst may choose among several types of installation plans - the *all-at-once type,* the *piecemeal type,* or the *parallel type* each suited to a particular problem or degree of complexity in the system.
   The one of the following situations in which the *parallel type* would be MOST appropriate is a situation

   A. in which a minimum installation cost is required
   B. involving a small volume of transactions
   C. in which the change is not radical or does not involve new machines
   D. involving large installation projects and intricate processing

   1.___

2. Many decision situations involve a great deal of uncertainty about the future, which is difficult to take into account in the analysis of alternatives. One technique developed for treating such uncertainty is designed to measure the possible effects on alternatives under analysis resulting from variations in uncertain elements. The analyst uses several *expected values* for uncertain parameters in an attempt to ascertain how the results vary (i.e., the relative ranking of the alternatives under consideration) in light of variations in the uncertain parameters. The analyst attempts to determine the alternative (or feasible combination of alternatives) likely to achieve a specified objective, gain or utility at the lowest cost. The one of the following which *BEST* describes the above technique is:

   A. Contingency analysis employing the fixed-budget approach
   B. Contingency analysis employing the fixed-benefits approach
   C. Sensitivity analysis employing the fixed-budget approach
   D. Sensitivity analysis employing the fixed-benefits approach

   2.___

3. In general, the analytical techniques of management science are of the *LEAST* value when

   A. the effects of a small number of controlled variables must be considered
   B. the number of relevant uncontrolled variables is small
   C. relevant causes and effects are factual in nature and can be stated and measured numerically or symbolically
   D. There are reasons to believe that past relationships will continue to hold in the future

   3.___

4. During the installation period of a new system, tight controls must be maintained over every phase of the operation. To do this, an analyst may set up a *warning system* within the system which forecasts potential bottle-necks and affords sufficient clues for correcting any problems, errors or fall-downs.
   The one of the following control devices or techniques which would be *most likely* to involve extra effort during the installation, and slow down the processing time is

   4.___

26

A. paper flow controls - log sheets, numerical controls, etc. (a system of logging input and output)
B. timing controls - to inform the analyst about the proper time interval between certain activities with-in the systems
C. program check points - a periodic review of processing to date at each check point
D. accounting control totals, to accumulate invoice numbers as the first and last steps in the system and compare the totals

5. Which of the following types of work measurement techniques would be MOST appropriate for obtaining details of a particular job for cost analysis purposes, such as the operating costs of various types of duplicating machines?

A. Work sampling
B. Predetermined time standards
C. The time study (stop-watch timing)
D. Historical

6. It is anticipated that a certain cancer detection program will be capable of detecting many cases at an early stage and that society will be thus enabled to cure twice as many cases as it cures currently. The benefits to society include the reduction in cost of hospitalization, etc., that would have been incurred otherwise.
Benefits such as a reduction in the cost of hospitalization are *most usually* called

A. direct benefits
B. secondary benefits
C. intergenerational benefits
D. external benefits

7. The results of departmental and agency programs can be measured in terms of EFFECTIVENESS or BENEFITS. Thus, careful budget preparation will permit the calculation of costs which can then be compared, or equated, to these results. Which one of the following statements pertaining to cost-effectiveness measurements is MOST valid?

A. In cost-effectiveness measurements, a dollar value is assigned to the output.
B. The measurement is expressed in terms of quality of output for a given cost.
C. Cost effectiveness ratios express the relationship between the costs of programs
D. A cost-effectiveness measurement will show the number of outputs which can be achieved for the expenditure of a given amount of money.

8. Assume that you have been asked to evaluate personnel programs in four city agencies The statistical test that would be MOST appropriate for testing the significance of the differences in the mean number of days absent (normality may be assumed) during the year 2004 in four different agencies is the

A. one-way analysis of variance
B. standard deviation
C. regression analysis
D. Chi-square test (x^2-test)

9. Assume that you have been asked to evaluate differences in the children just enrolled in two youth programs. In reviewing the relevant published material you find that in one particular study involving two groups, N = 9 and N = 13, there is a significant difference in the mean scores of the two groups on a characteristic which you believe to be normally distributed.
   The statistical test *most likely* used in this study to determine the significance of the difference in the means of the two groups on this characteristic is the

   A. Chi-square test (x2-test)
   B. Pearson Product-Moment correlation (r)
   C. t-test
   D. two-way analysis of variance

10. In statistics, three common measures of central tendency are the mean, median and mode.
    For which of the following conditions would the median generally be the *BEST* choice to use? When the

    A. distribution of scores is skewed
    B. scores are distributed symmetrically around a central point
    C. standard deviation must also be calculated
    D. most frequently occurring value is required

11. Nonparametric statistical tests are *usually* employed when

    A. large samples are used
    B. a very powerful or exact test is needed
    C. data cannot be expressed in ranks
    D. a normally distributed population cannot be assumed

12. Assume that in a report presented to you by an employee under your supervision, a coefficient of correlation of +1.73 is reported between the age at which one first smokes cigarettes and the age at which one first smokes marijuana.
    You should *most reasonably* interpret this figure to mean there is a

    A. strong positive correlation
    B. weak positive correlation
    C. weak negative correlation
    D. typographical error

13. One of the major research techniques most often used in studies of organizational behavior problems is the survey. An analyst who utilizes the survey technique should be aware that its *MAJOR* drawback is

    A. the lack of depth obtained from the two major data-collection tolls used in surveys: the mailed question-naire and the personal interview
    B. its impracticality in assessing or estimating the present state of affairs with regard to a variable that changes over time for a large group of subjects
    C. the restriction of this technique to a single, or very few, units of analysis
    D. its absence of dependence upon the collection of empirical data

14. In order for an analyst to understand and interpret statistical data he/she must understand which types of data tend to approximate the normal probability curve, i.e., are normally distributed.
Which of the following types of data falls into this category?
Frequency of

   A. educational test scores for students of a given age, plotted against test score
   B. filing of income tax returns for citizens of a given age, plotted against date of filing
   C. deaths due to childhood disease plotted against age
   D. deaths due to degenerative diseases, plotted against age

14.____

15. Which of the following terms describes a line or curve formed by plotting employees salaries that increase yearly by a fixed percentage over the previous year? (In answering the question, assume that time is on the horizontal axis (abscissa) and salary is on the vertical axis (ordinate) - both axes are marked linearly.)

   A. Linear (increasing at a constant rate)
   B. Positively accelerating (increasing at an increasing rate)
   C. Negatively accelerating (increasing at a decreasing rate)
   D. Negatively decelerating (decreasing at a decreasing rate)

15.____

Questions 16 - 17

DIRECTIONS: Answer Questions 16 and 17 on the basis of the following groups, both of which depict the same information in different ways.

The x and y axes in graphs A and B are not necessarily drawn in the same scale. The points along the curves on both graphs represent corresponding points, and are the upper limits of class intervals.

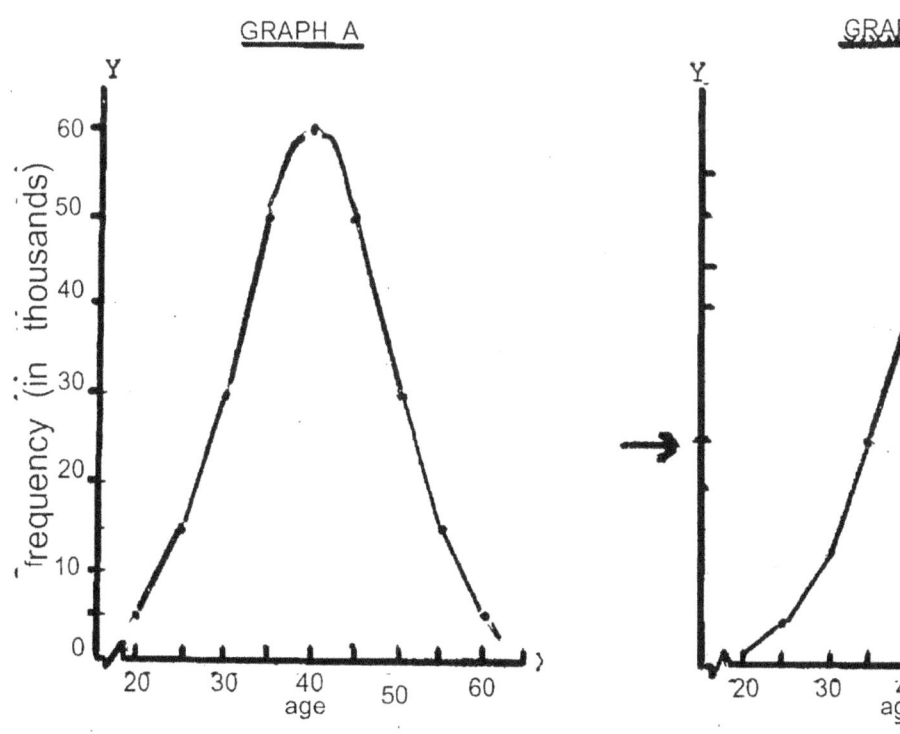

16. The ordinate (y-axis) in graph B is

    A. frequency
    B. cumulative frequency
    C. average frequency
    D. log frequency

17. The arrow on the y-axis in graph B indicates a particular number. That number is, *most nearly*

    A. 100   B. 50,000   C. 100,000   D. 150,000

Questions 18 - 19

DIRECTIONS: Answer Questions 18 and 19 on the basis of the graphs that appear on the following page.

18. In Graph I, the vertical distance between lines E and T within the crosshatched area represents the

    A. savings to the city if work of less than 50 miles is performed by the city
    B. loss to the city if work of less than 50 miles is performed by the city
    C. savings to the city if work of more than 50 miles is performed by the city
    D. loss to the city if work of more than 50 miles is performed by the city

19. Graph II is identical to Graph I except that contractor costs have been eliminated. Total costs (line E) are the sum of fixed costs (line F) and variable costs. Variable costs are represented by line

    A. A   B. B   C. C   D. D

ROAD REPAIR COSTS IF PERFORMED BY
CITY STAFF OR AN OUTSIDE CONTRACTOR

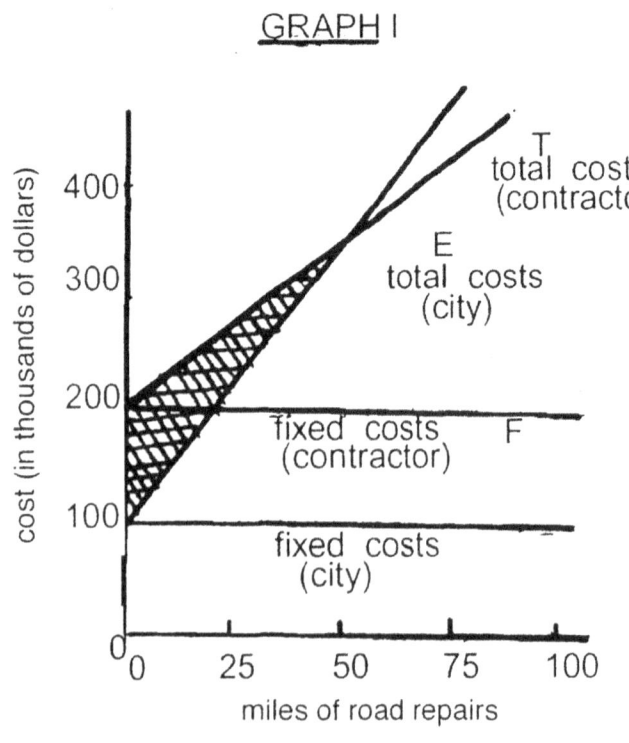
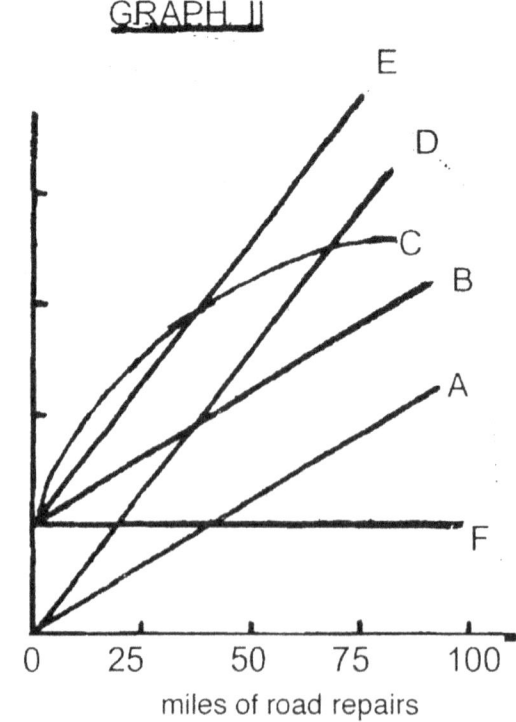

20. Fiscal experts in municipal affairs have contended that the most acute problem facing the city today seems to be the growth of the city's short-term debt.
Of the following, the LEAST likely reason for the city to engage in short-term borrowing is that the city

    A. expects money from long-term borrowing that it plans to undertake
    B. needs to be tided over until funds due from the Federal or State government arrive
    C. needs money to finance big construction outlays
    D. anticipates money from future tax collections

20.____

21. A MAJOR criticism of the *superagency* has been the

    A. additional layers of control and additional lines of command
    B. merger of departmental functions
    C. political manipulation
    D. professional incompetence in administration

21.____

22. The management of a large urban city is different in many ways from the management of other systems, particularly large business organizations.
The one of the following which does NOT exemplify these differences is:

    A. A mayor, in contrast to a manager of a large business, is often held responsible for services, etc., over which he has little authority.
    B. Top management of a large urban city must deal with a greater number of different pressures from diverse interest groups.
    C. The city government, in contrast to a large business organization, often lacks adequate management controls, and goals are often ill-defined.
    D. The multiplicity of alternatives available to city government as opposed to large businesses, are substantially greater, making decision-making haphazard.

22.____

23. The function called internal control applies to those measures taken by a government agency to protect its assets. Internal control has a role to play as an enforcer of administrative edicts as well as for purposes of asset protection.
Of the following statements relating to internal control, as described above, select the *one* usually considered to be LEAST valid.

    A. Internal control makes auditing by an external agency more difficult.
    B. The function of internal control often involves the auditing process.
    C. That people cannot be trusted to act wisely and honestly seems to be implicit in all the principles of internal control.
    D. Internal control is simply a form of self-audit by the agency itself.

23.____

24. In addition to the new effect on workers who are unskilled and undereducated, the severe effect of the high unemployment rate in the city has recently become MOST apparent among

    A. skilled craftsmen in the building trades
    B. clerical employees
    C. middle management personnel
    D. architects and engineers

24.____

25. The fact that the city has the second highest jobless rate of any major U.S. city except Detroit is considered particularly significant because, compared to Detroit, unemployment in the city

    A. is caused by city government fiscal measures rather than private business conditions
    B. exists in more than one industry
    C. results in an increase in welfare expenditures to a greater extent
    D. more seriously affects the world-wide economy

25.___

KEY (CORRECT ANSWERS)

1.	D	11.	D
2.	D	12.	D
3.	A	13.	A
4.	A	14.	A
5.	C	15.	B
6.	A	16.	B
7.	D	17.	C
8.	A	18.	A
9.	C	19.	D
10.	A	20.	C

21. A
22. D
23. A
24. A
25. B

EXAMINATION SECTION
TEST 1

DIRECTIONS: Each question or incomplete statement is followed by several suggested answers or completions. Select the one that BEST answers the question or completes the statement. *PRINT THE LETTER OF THE CORRECT ANSWER IN THE SPACE AT THE RIGHT.*

1. The MOST important factor in establishing a disciplinary policy in an organization is

    A. consistency of application
    B. strict supervisors
    C. strong enforcement
    D. the degree of toughness or laxity

2. The FIRST step in planning a program is to

    A. clearly define the objectives
    B. estimate the costs
    C. hire a program director
    D. solicit funds

3. The PRIMARY purpose of control in an organization is to

    A. punish those who do not do their job well
    B. get people to do what is necessary to achieve an objective
    C. develop clearly stated rules and regulations
    D. regulate expenditures

4. After a procedures manual has been written and distributed,

    A. continuous maintenance work is necessary to keep the manual current
    B. it is best to issue new manuals rather than make changes in the original manual
    C. no changes should be necessary
    D. only major changes should be considered

5. Of the following, the MOST important criterion of effective report writing is

    A. eloquence of writing style
    B. the use of technical language
    C. to be brief and to the point
    D. to cover all details

6. The use of electronic data processing

    A. has proven unsuccessful in most organizations
    B. has unquestionable advantages for all organizations
    C. is unnecessary in most organizations
    D. should be decided upon only after careful feasibility studies by individual organizations

7. Of the following methods, which would normally be MOST appropriate to validate a new aptitude test?

    A. Concurrent   B. Construct
    C. Content   D. Predictive

1.____

2.____

3.____

4.____

5.____

6.____

7.____

33

8. The PRIMARY purpose of work measurement is to

   A. design and install a wage incentive program
   B. determine who should be promoted
   C. establish a yardstick to determine extent of progress
   D. set up a spirit of competition among employees

9. A hypothetical construct is BEST defined as an(any)

   A. speculation that a researcher wishes to articulate
   B. entity or process presumed to exist but currently unable to be observed
   C. explanation of what antecedent conditions lead to various consequences
   D. expression of the relationship between stimulus and response variables

10. Representative samples are

    A. always drawn from finite populations
    B. always drawn from infinite populations
    C. drawn in a random, unbiased manner and have the characteristics of the larger universe
    D. larger than stratified samples

11. Interval or equal-interval scales have

    A. an absolute or natural zero that has empirical meaning
    B. none of the characteristics of nominal and ordinal scales
    C. no validity
    D. the property that numerically equal distances on the scale represent equal distances in the property being measured

12. Protective techniques of obtaining and analyzing information from respondents are

    A. designed so that subjects will respond as frankly as possible
    B. easier to analyze than objective techniques
    C. forms of structured scales
    D. to be avoided at all costs

13. Of the following, which is NOT a descriptive research design? _____ study.

    A. Case
    B. Correlation
    C. Developmental
    D. Pretest-posttest

14. One method of testing hypotheses using available materials produced by institutions, organizations, and individuals is

    A. content analysis
    B. distance-cluster analysis
    C. semantic differential
    D. sociometric analysis

15. The MOST important difference between experimental research and ex post facto research is   15.____

    A. analysis of data required
    B. control of the variables
    C. cost of the study
    D. length of time required to conduct the study

16. *The public health department of a large city wishes to study the effect of different chemicals on the retardation of tooth decay in children. Three groups of children ranging in age from 10 to 15 are selected randomly. One group of children is given toothpaste containing chemical X and another group is given toothpaste with chemical Y. A third group is given toothpaste with no chemical added. All three groups are given the same kind of toothbrush and are asked to brush their teeth twice a day for one year using the toothpaste and toothbrushes they have received. Periodic dental check-ups are made of the children in all three groups to determine the amount of tooth decay.*   16.____
    In the above study, the independent and dependent variables may BEST be defined as follows:

    A. chemicals X and Y and toothbrushes are independent variables and the amount of tooth decay is the dependent variable
    B. chemicals X and Y are independent variables and the amount of tooth decay is the dependent variable
    C. chemicals X and Y, toothbrushes, and the number of times a day the children brush their teeth are dependent variables and the amount of tooth decay is the independent variable
    D. chemicals X and Y, toothbrushes, and the number of times a day the children brush their teeth are independent variables and the amount of tooth decay is the dependent variable

17. A research hypothesis may BEST be defined as a(n)   17.____

    A. problem statement concerning two or more unknown variables
    B. speculation based on the researcher"s experience
    C. statement of expectation concerning the relations between variables which can be tested
    D. expository statement of the statistical procedure to be used in the research

18. A review of the literature is included in the research report PRIMARILY in order to   18.____

    A. demonstrate the scope of the investigator's knowledge about the research problem
    B. develop the theoretical foundation of the study
    C. indicate the literature reviewed by the investigator in planning the study
    D. save the reader time

19. The null hypothesis is a statistical proposition which states that   19.____

    A. no explanation of differences between variables should be accepted completely
    B. no differences exist between two or more sample means
    C. no variable can be accurately measured
    D. the real difference between the variables of the problem is greater than one would expect by chance

20. The following scores were obtained by an elementary mathematics class at the end of one year of instruction:

    | 11 | 19 | 17 |
    | 2 | 15 | 6 |
    | 5 | 6 | 8 |

    If the score of 8 were changed to 10, the mean(,)
    A. and median of this group of data would change but the mode would remain the same
    B. median, and mode would change
    C. median, and mode would remain the same
    D. of this group of data would change but the median would remain the same

21. The normal distribution which is represented by a theoretical bell-shaped curve has the following property:

    A. Exactly .6826 of the total area will fall between an ordinate of two standard deviations above the mean
    B. It is a fictional curve having no real function
    C. The mean and median will coincide and have exactly the same value
    D. The total area under the curve is equal to 2.98

22. In the case of variables that are linearly related, the correlation coefficient is a measure of

    A. the causal relationship present between variables
    B. the difference between the mean and the standard deviation
    C. the direction and degree of the relationship between variables
    D. which variable is independent and which is dependent

23. If a student's score on the final examination in a chemistry class is at the 72nd percentile, one can SAFELY assume that

    A. the student answered 7 more questions correctly than did a student whose score was at the 65th percentile
    B. 72% of the class scored lower than this student
    C. the student answered 72 out of 100 questions correctly
    D. the student is above average in chemistry

24. The significance level of a statistic is the probability that

    A. a Type II error has been committed
    B. the obtained result of the statistic could occur by chance
    C. the outcome of the experiment is $\bar{X}_1 \neq \bar{X}_2$
    D. there is a positive relationship between the variables being measured

25. The standard error of the mean is an estimate of

    A. how far the sample mean is likely to differ from the population mean
    B. how far two sample means differ from each other
    C. the amount of error committed in computation
    D. the amount of error inherent in the population mean

26. Nonparametric statistics are different from parametric statistics in that 26.____

   A. conditions about the population parameters are not specified in nonparametric tests
   B. nonparametric statistics are easier and faster to compute
   C. the measures to be analyzed by nonparametric tests must be continuous
   D. the measures to be analyzed by parametric statistics must be discrete

27. The Chi square test CANNOT be used reliably when the 27.____

   A. population distribution is not assumed to be normal
   B. population distribution is positively skewed
   C. samples are very large
   D. samples are very small

28. Of the following, the MOST critical problem faced by metropolitan educational systems is 28.____

   A. inadequate physical facilities
   B. parental indifference
   C. the lack of motivation to learn among urban youth
   D. the rapidity and magnitude of population change

29. In reference to educational systems, the concept of community control 29.____

   A. advocates that parents should take the place of professional educators
   B. implies that all educational decisions should be voted upon in open community meetings
   C. is essentially the same as decentralization
   D. represents the idea that the ultimate authority to make policy decisions rests with community representatives

30. Of the following, the MOST serious drawback to the *grant-in-aid* approach to support community services is that 30.____

   A. grants are difficult to obtain
   B. it encourages overcentralization of services
   C. it has had little or no provision for coordination of services
   D. it is too expensive

31. Of the following, the BEST definition of records management is 31.____

   A. storage of all types of records at minimum expense
   B. planned control of all types of records
   C. storage of records for maximum accessibility
   D. systematic filing of all types of records

32. The title of a contemporary best-selling book by Robert Townsend is . 32.____

   A. MANAGEMENT ANALYSIS: WAVE OF THE FUTURE
   B. MANAGEMENT FOR RESULTS
   C. THE HUMAN SIDE OF ENTERPRISE
   D. UP THE ORGANIZATION

33. A summary punched card containing totals of a group of similar detail cards is GENERALLY called a _____ card.

    A. master unit record
    B. summary unit record
    C. total
    D. unit record

34. One of the more famous studies of organizations is called the Hawthorne study. This work was one of the first to point out the importance of

    A. employees' benefit and retirement programs
    B. informal organization among employees
    C. job engineering
    D. styles of position classification

35. In organization theory, the type of position in which an individual is appointed to give technical aid to management on a particular problem area is generally BEST termed a(n)

    A. administrative assistant
    B. *assistant to*
    C. staff assistant
    D. staff specialist

36. In analyzing data for the acquisition of new equipment, a methods analyst gathers the facts, analyzes them, and develops new procedures which will be required when the new equipment arrives.
    In analyzing the factors involved, which one of the following is normally LEAST important in the evaluation of new equipment?

    A. Cost factors
    B. Layout and installation factors
    C. Production planning
    D. Operational experience of manufacturers of allied equipment

37. The one of the following which is NOT a primary objective of a records retention and disposal system is to

    A. assure appropriate preservation of records having permanent value
    B. dispose of records not warranting further preservation
    C. establish retention standards for archives
    D. provide an opportunity to use miniaturization techniques to simplify filing systems

38. In organizing, doing what *works* in the particular situation, with due regard to both short and long range objectives, is BEST termed

    A. ambivalence
    B. authoritarianism
    C. decentralization
    D. pragmatism

39. If an effort were made to reduce the number of private offices in a new layout, the LEAST effective substitute in offering privacy would be the use of

    A. an open area, with lower movable partitions or railings separating each individual
    B. conference rooms
    C. larger desks
    D. modular desk units

40. The term *administrative substation* NORMALLY refers to 40.____
    A. a work station handling a number of office services for an office organization
    B. a work station where middle level supervisors are located
    C. an office for handling management trainees
    D. the functions allocated to particular levels of administrative managers

KEY (CORRECT ANSWERS)

1.	A	11.	D	21.	C	31.	B
2.	A	12.	A	22.	C	32.	D
3.	B	13.	D	23.	B	33.	B
4.	A	14.	A	24.	B	34.	B
5.	C	15.	B	25.	A	35.	D
6.	D	16.	B	26.	A	36.	D
7.	D	17.	C	27.	D	37.	D
8.	C	18.	B	28.	D	38.	D
9.	B	19.	B	29.	D	39.	C
10.	C	20.	A	30.	C	40.	A

TEST 2

DIRECTIONS: Each question or incomplete statement is followed by several suggested answers or completions. Select the one that BEST answers the question or completes the statement. *PRINT THE LETTER OF THE CORRECT ANSWER IN THE SPACE AT THE RIGHT.*

1. A research technique which would be applied to determine the optimum number of window clerks or interviewers to have in an agency serving the public would MOST likely be the use of

    A. line of balance
    B. queuing theory
    C. simulation
    D. work sampling

2. A type of file which permits the operator to remain seated while the file can be moved backward and forward as required is BEST termed a ___ file.

    A. lateral
    B. movable
    C. reciprocating
    D. rotary

3. The technique of work measurement in which the analyst observes the work at random times of the day is BEST termed

    A. indirect observation
    B. logging
    C. ratio delay
    D. wristwatch

4. Examples of predetermined time systems generally should include all of the following EXCEPT

    A. Master Clerical Data
    B. Methods Time Measurement
    C. Short Interval Data
    D. Work Factor

5. A technique by which the supervisor or an assistant distributes a predetermined batch of work to the employees at periodic intervals of the day is generally BEST known as

    A. backlog control scheduling
    B. production control scheduling
    C. short interval scheduling
    D. workload balancing

6. Wright Bakke defined his *fusion process* as the

    A. work environment to some degree remakes the organization and the organization to some degree remakes the work environment
    B. fusing of the interests of both management and labor unions
    C. community of interest between first line supervisors and top management
    D. organization to some degree remakes the individual and the individual to some degree remakes the organization

7. If a staff analyst is required to recommend the selection of a machine for an office operation, he can BEST judge the expected output of a particular machine by pursuing which of the following courses of action?
Obtaining

    A. an actual test run of the machine in his office
    B. data from the manufacturer of the machine
    C. information on the percentage of working time the machine will be used
    D. the experience of actual users of similar machines elsewhere

8. In planning office space for a newly established bureau, it would usually be LEAST desirable to

   A. concentrate, rather than disperse, the chief sources of office noises
   B. design an office environment with about the same brightness as the office desk
   C. designate as reception rooms, washrooms, and other service areas those areas that will receive lesser amounts of illumination than those areas in which private office work will be performed
   D. eliminate natural light in cases where it is not the major light source

9. A private office should be used when its use is dictated by facts and unbiased judgment. It should never be provided simply because requests and sometimes pressure have been brought to bear.
   Of the following reasons used to justify use of a private office, the one that requires the MOST care in determining whether a private office is actually warranted is

   A. an office has always been provided for a particular job
   B. prestige considerations
   C. the confidential nature of the work
   D. the work involves high concentration

10. Theoretically, an ideal organization structure can be set up for each enterprise. In actual practice, the ideal organization structure is seldom, if ever, obtained.
    Of the following, the one that normally is of LEAST influence in determining the organization structure is the

    A. existence of agreements and favors among members of the organization
    B. funds available
    C. opinions and beliefs of top executives
    D. tendency of management to discard established forms in favor of new forms

11. An IMPORTANT aspect to keep in mind during the decision-making process is that

    A. all possible alternatives for attaining goals should be sought out and considered
    B. considering various alternatives only leads to confusion
    C. once a decision has been made, it cannot be retracted
    D. there is only one correct method to reach any goal

12. Implementation of accountability requires

    A. a leader who will not hesitate to take punitive action
    B. an established system of communication from the bottom to the top
    C. explicit directives from leaders
    D. too much expense to justify it

13. Of the following, the MAJOR difference between systems and procedures analysis and work simplification is

    A. the former complicates organizational routine and the latter simplifies it
    B. the former is objective and the latter is subjective
    C. the former generally utilizes expert advice and the latter is a *do-it-yourself* improvement by supervisors and workers
    D. there is no difference other than in name

14. Systems development is concerned with providing

    A. a specific set of work procedures
    B. an overall framework to describe general relationships
    C. definitions of particular organizational functions
    D. organizational symbolism

15. Organizational systems and procedures should be

    A. developed as problems arise as no design can anticipate adequately the requirements of an organization
    B. developed jointly by experts in systems and procedures and the people who are responsible for implementing them
    C. developed solely by experts in systems and procedures
    D. eliminated whenever possible to save unnecessary expense

16. The CHIEF danger of a decentralized control system is that

    A. excessive reports and communications will be generated
    B. problem areas may not be detected readily
    C. the expense will become prohibitive
    D. this will result in too many *chiefs*

17. Of the following, management guides and controls clerical work PRINCIPALLY through

    A. close supervision and constant checking of personnel
    B. spot checking of clerical procedures
    C. strong sanctions for clerical supervisors
    D. the use of printed forms

18. Which of the following is MOST important before conducting fact-finding interviews?

    A. Becoming acquainted with all personnel to be interviewed
    B. Explaining the techniques you plan to use
    C. Explaining to the operating officials the purpose and scope of the study
    D. Orientation of the physical layout

19. Of the following, the one that is NOT essential in carrying out a comprehensive work improvement program is

    A. standards of performance
    B. supervisory training
    C. work count/task list
    D. work distribution chart

20. Which of the following control techniques is MOST useful on large, complex systems projects?

    A. A general work plan
    B. Gantt Chart
    C. Monthly progress report
    D. PERT Chart

21. The action which is MOST effective in gaining acceptance of a study by the agency which is being studied is

    A. a directive from the agency head to install a study based on recommendations included in a report
    B. a lecture-type presentation following approval of the procedures
    C. a written procedure in narrative form covering the proposed system with visual presentations and discussions
    D. procedural charts showing the *before* and *after* situation, forms, steps, etc. to the employees affected

22. Which of the following is NOT an advantage in the use of oral instructions as compared with written instructions? Oral instruction(s)

    A. can easily be changed
    B. is superior in transmitting complex directives
    C. facilitate exchange of information between a superior and his subordinate
    D. without discussions make it easier to ascertain understanding

23. Which organization principle is MOST closely related to procedural analysis and improvement?

    A. Duplication, overlapping, and conflict should be eliminated.
    B. Managerial authority should be clearly defined.
    C. The objectives of the organization should be clearly defined.
    D. Top management should be freed of burdensome detail.

24. Which of the following is the MAJOR objective of operational audits?

    A. Detecting fraud
    B. Determining organization problems
    C. Determining the number of personnel needed
    D. Recommending opportunities for improving operating and management practices

25. Of the following, the formalization of organization structure is BEST achieved by

    A. a narrative description of the plan of organization
    B. functional charts
    C. job descriptions together with organization charts
    D. multi-flow charts

26. Budget planning is MOST useful when it achieves

    A. cost control
    B. forecast of receipts
    C. performance review
    D. personnel reduction

27. The underlying principle of sound administration is to

    A. base administration on investigation of facts
    B. have plenty of resources available
    C. hire a strong administrator
    D. establish a broad policy

28. Although questionnaires are not the best survey tool the management analyst has to use, there are times when a good questionnaire can expedite the *fact-finding* phase of a management survey.
Which of the following should be AVOIDED in the design and distribution of the questionnaire?   28.____

    A. Questions should be framed so that answers can be classified and tabulated for analysis.
    B. Those receiving the questionnaire must be knowledgeable enough to accurately provide the information desired.
    C. The questionnaire should enable the respondent to answer in a narrative manner.
    D. The questionnaire should require a minimum amount of writing.

29. Of the following, the formula which is used to calculate the arithmetic mean from data grouped in a frequency distribution is   29.____

    A. $M = \dfrac{N}{\Sigma fX}$ B. $M = N(\Sigma fX)$
    C. $M = \dfrac{\Sigma fX}{N}$ D. $M = \dfrac{\Sigma X}{fN}$

30. Arranging large groups of numbers in frequency distributions   30.____

    A. gives a more composite picture of the total group than a random listing
    B. is misleading in most cases
    C. is unnecessary in most instances
    D. presents the data in a form whereby further manipulation of the group is eliminated

31. After a budget has been developed, it serves to   31.____

    A. assist the accounting department in posting expenditures
    B. measure the effectiveness of department managers
    C. provide a yardstick against which actual costs are measured
    D. provide the operating department with total expenditures to date

32. Of the following, which formula is used to determine staffing requirements?   32.____

    A. $\dfrac{\text{Hours per man-day}}{\text{Volume X Standard}} = \text{Employees Needed}$
    B. $\dfrac{\text{Hours per man-day X Standard}}{\text{Volume}} = \text{Employees Needed}$
    C. $\dfrac{\text{Hours per man-day X Volume}}{\text{Standard}} = \text{Employees Needed}$
    D. $\dfrac{\text{Volume X Standard}}{\text{Hours per man-day}} = \text{Employees Needed}$

33. Of the following, which formula is used to determine the number of days required to process work?   33.____

A. $\dfrac{\text{Employees X Daily Output}}{\text{Volume}}$ =Days to Process Work

B. $\dfrac{\text{Employees X Volume}}{\text{Daily Output}}$ =Days to Process Work

C. $\dfrac{\text{Volume}}{\text{Employees X Daily Output}}$ =Days to Process Work

D. $\dfrac{\text{Volume X Daily Output}}{\text{Employees}}$ =Days to Process Work

34. Identify this symbol, as used in a Systems Flow Chart.
    A. Document
    B. Decision
    C. Preparation
    D. Process

34._____

35. Of the following, the MAIN advantage of a form letter over a dictated letter is that a form letter

    A. is more expressive
    B. is neater
    C. may be mailed in a window envelope
    D. requires less secretarial time

35._____

36. The term that may be defined as a systematic analysis of all factors affecting work being done or all factors that will affect work to be done, in order to save effort, time or money is

    A. flow process charting
    B. work flow analysis
    C. work measurement
    D. work simplification

36._____

37. Generally, the LEAST important basic factor to be considered in developing office layout improvements is to locate

    A. office equipment, reference facilities, and files as close as practicable to those using them
    B. persons as close as practicable to the persons from whom they receive their work
    C. persons as close as practicable to windows and/or adequate ventilation
    D. persons who are friendly with each other close together to improve morale

37._____

38. Of the following, the one which is LEAST effective in reducing administrative costs is

    A. applying objective measurement techniques to determine the time required to perform a given task
    B. establishing budgets on the basis of historical performance data
    C. motivating supervisors and managers in the importance of cost reduction
    D. selecting the best method - manual, mechanical, or electronic - to process the essential work

38._____

39. *Fire-fighting* is a common expression in management terminology.
Of the following, which BEST describes *fire-fighting* as an analyst's approach to solving paperwork problems?

    A. A complete review of all phases of the department's processing functions
    B. A studied determination of the proper equipment to process the work
    C. An analysis of each form that is being processed and the logical reasons for its processing
    D. The solution of problems as they arise, usually at the request of operating personnel

39.____

40. Assume that an analyst with a proven record of accomplishment on many projects is having difficulties on his present assignment.
Of the following, the BEST course of action for his superior to take is to

    A. assume there is a personality conflict involved and transfer the analyst to another project
    B. give the analyst some time off
    C. review the nature of the project to determine whether or not the analyst is equipped to handle the assignment
    D. suggest that the analyst seek counseling

40.____

KEY (CORRECT ANSWERS)

1. B	11. A	21. C	31. C
2. C	12. B	22. B	32. D
3. C	13. C	23. A	33. C
4. C	14. B	24. D	34. A
5. C	15. B	25. C	35. D
6. D	16. B	26. A	36. D
7. A	17. D	27. A	37. D
8. D	18. C	28. C	38. B
9. A	19. B	29. C	39. D
10. D	20. D	30. A	40. C

READING COMPREHENSION
UNDERSTANDING AND INTERPRETING WRITTEN MATERIAL

STRATEGIES

<u>SURVEYING PASSAGES, SENTENCES AS CUES</u>

While individual readers develop unique reading styles and skills, there are some known strategies which can assist any reader in improving his or her reading comprehension and performance on the reading subtest. These strategies include understanding how single paragraphs and entire passages are structured, how the ideas in them are ordered, and how the author of the passage has connected these ideas in a logical and sequential way for the reader.

The section that follows highlights the importance of reading a passage through once for meaning, and provides instruction on careful reading for context cues within the sentences before and after the missing word.

SURVEY THE ENTIRE PASSAGE

To get a sense of the topic and the organization of ideas in a passage, it is important to survey each passage initially in its entirety and to identify the main idea. (The first sentence of a paragraph usually states the main idea.) Do not try to fill in the blanks initially. The purpose or surveying a passage is to prepare for the more careful reading which will follow. You need a sense of the big picture before you start to fill in the details; for example, a quick survey of the passage on page 11 indicate that the topic is the early history of universities. The paragraphs are organized to provide information on the origin of the first universities, the associations formed by teachers and students, the early curriculum, and graduation requirements.

READ PRECEDING SENTENCES CAREFULLY

The missing words in a passage cannot be determined by reading and understanding only the sentences in which the deletions occur. Information from the sentences which precede or follow can provide important cues to determine the correct choice. For example, if you read the first sentence from the passage about universities which contains a blank, you will notice that all the alternatives make sense if this one sentence is read in isolation:

Nobody actually _____ them.
  A. started   B. guarded   C. blamed
  D. compared   E. remembered

The only way that you can make the correct word choice is to read the preceding sentences. In the excerpt below, notice that the first sentence tells the reader what the passage will be about: how universities developed. A key word in the first sentence is *emerged*, which is closely related in meaning to one of the five choices for the first blank. The second sentence explains the key word *emerged*, by pointing out that we have no historical record of a decree or a date indicating when the first university was established. Understanding the ideas in the first two sentences makes it possible to select the correct word for the blank. Look at the sentence with the deleted word in the context of the preceding sentences and think about why you are now able to make the correct choice.

The first universities emerged at the end of the 11th century and beginning of the 12th. These institutions were not founded on any particular date or created by any formal action. Nobody actually _____ them.
- A. started
- B. guarded
- C. blamed
- D. compared
- E. remembered

Started is the best choice because it fits the main idea of the passage and is closely related to the key word *emerged*.

READ THE SENTENCE WHICH FOLLOWS TO VERIFY YOUR CHOICE

The sentences which follow the one from which a word has been deleted may also provide cues to the correct choice. For example, look at an excerpt from the passage about universities again, and consider how the sentence which follows the one with the blank helps to reinforce the choice of the word *started*.

The first universities emerged at the end of the 11th century and the beginning of the 12th. These institutions were not founded on any particular date or created by any formal action. Nobody actually _____ them. Instead, they developed gradually in places like Paris, Oxford, and Bologna, where scholars had long been teaching students.
- A. started
- B. guarded
- C. blamed
- D. compared
- E. remembered

The words *developed gradually* mean the same as the key word *emerged*. The signal word *instead* helps to distinguish the difference between starting on a specific date as a result of some particular act or event and emerging over a period of time as a result of various factors.

Here is another example of how the sentence which follows the one from which a word is deleted might help you decide which of two good alternatives is the correct choice. This excerpt is from the practice passage about bridges (page 10).

Bridges are built to allow a continuous flow of highway and railway traffic across water lying in their paths. But engineers cannot forget that river traffic, too, is essential to our economy. The role of _____ is important. To keep these vessels moving freely, bridges are built big enough, when possible, to let them pass underneath.
- A. wind
- B. boats
- C. weight
- D. wires
- E. experience

After the first two sentences, the reader may be uncertain about the direction the writer intended to take in the rest of the paragraph. If the writer intended to continue the paragraph with information concerning how engineers make choices about the relative importance and requirements of land traffic and rive traffic, *experience* might be the appropriate choice for the missing word. However, the sentence following the one in which the deletion occurs makes it clear that *boats* is the correct choice. It provides the synonym *vessels*, which in the noun phrase *these vessels* must refer back to the previous sentence or sentences. The phrase *to let them pass underneath* also helps make it clear that *boats* is the appropriate choice. *Them* refers back to *these vessels* which, in turn, refers back to *boats* when the word *boats* is placed in the previous sentence. Thus, the reader may use these cohesive ties (the pronoun referents) to verify the final choice.

Even when the text following a sentence with a deletion is not necessary to choose the best alternative, it may be helpful in other ways. Specifically, complete sentences provide important transitions into a related topic which is developed in the rest of the paragraph or in the next paragraph of the same passage. For example, the first paragraph in the passage about universities ends with a sentence which introduces the term *guilds*: *But, over time, they joined together to form guilds.* Prior to this sentence, information about the slow emergence of universities and about how independently scholars had acted was introduced. The next paragraph begins with two sentences about guilds in general. Someone who had not read the last sentence in the first paragraph might have missed the link between guilds and scholars and universities and, thus, might have been unnecessarily confused.

COHESIVE TIES AS CUES

Sentences in a paragraph may be linked together by several devices called cohesive ties. Attention to these ties may provide further cues about missing words. This section will describe the different types of cohesive ties and show how attention to them can help you to select the correct word.

PERSONAL PRONOUNS

Personal pronouns (e.g., he, she, they, it, its) are often used in adjoining sentences to refer back to an already mentioned person, place, thing, or idea. The word to which the pronoun refers is called the antecedent.

Tools used in farm work changed very slowly from ancient times to the eighteenth century, and the changes were minor. Since the eighteenth century *they* have changed quickly and dramatically.

The word *they* refers back to *tools* in the example above.

In the examination reading subtest, a deleted word sometimes occurs in a sentence in which the sentence subject is a pronoun that refers back to a previously mentioned noun. You must correctly identify the referent for the particular pronoun in order to interpret the sentence and select the correct answer. Here is an example from the passage about bridges.

An ingenious engineer designed the bridge so that it did not have to be raised above traffic. Instead it was _____.
  A. burned   B. emptied   C. secured
  D. shared   E. lowered

Q. What is the antecedent of *it* in both cases in the example?
A. The antecedent, of course, is *bridge*.

DEMONSTRATIVE PRONOUNS

Demonstrative pronouns (e.g., this, that, these) are also used to refer to a specific, previously mentioned noun. They may occur alone as noun replacements, or they may accompany and modify nouns.

I like jogging, swimming, and tennis. *These* are the only sports I enjoy.

In the sentence above, the word *these* is a replacement noun. However, demonstrative pronouns may also occur as adjectives modifying nouns.

I like jogging, swimming, and tennis. *These* sports are the only ones I enjoy.

The word *these* in the example above is an adjective modifier. The word *these* in each of the two previous examples refers to *jogging, swimming,* and *tennis*.

Here is an example from the passage about universities on page 11.

Undergraduates took classes in Greek philosophy, Latin grammar, arithmetic, music, and astronomy. These were the only _____ available.
  A. rooms   B. subjects   C. clothes
  D. pens   E. company

Q. Which word is a noun replacement?
A. The word *these* is the replacement for *Greek philosophy, Latin grammar, arithmetic, music,* and *astronomy*.

Here is another example from the same passage.

The concept of a fixed program of study leading to a degree first evolved in Medieval Europe. This _____ had not appeared before.
  A. idea   B. desk   C. library   D. capital

Q. What is the antecedent of *this*?
A. The antecedent is *the concept of a fixed program of study leading to a degree*.

COMPARATIVE ADJECTIVES AND ADVERBS

When comparative adjectives and adverbs (e.g., so, such, better, more) occur, they refer to something else in the passage, otherwise a comparison could not be made.

The hotels in the city were all full; so were the motels and boarding houses.

Q. To what in the first sentence does the word *so* refer?
A. So tells us to compare the *motels* and *boarding houses* to the *hotels in the city*.

Q. In what way are the *hotels, motels,* and *boarding houses* similar to each other?
A. The *hotels, motels,* and *boarding houses* are similar in that they were all *full*.

Look at an example from the passage about universities.

Guilds were groups of tradespeople, somewhat akin to modern trade unions. In the Middle Ages, all the crafts had such
   A. taxes   B. secrets   C. products
   D. problems   E. organizations

Q. To what in the first sentence does the word *such* refer?
A. *Such* refers to *groups of tradespeople*.

SUBSTITUTIONS

Substitution is another form of cohesive tie. A substitution occurs when one linguistic item (e.g., a noun) is replaced by another. Sometimes the substitution provides new or contrasting information. The substitution is not identical to the original, or antecedent, idea. A frequently occurring substitution involves the use of *one*. A noun substitution may involve another member of the same class as the original one.

My car is falling apart. I need a new one.

Q. What in the first sentence is replaced in the second sentence with *one*?
A. *One* is a substitute for the specific car mentioned in the first sentence. The contrast comes from the fact that the *new one* isn't the writer's current car.

The substitution may also pinpoint a specific member of a general class.

1. There are many unusual courses available at the university this summer. The *one* I am taking is called *Death and Dying.*
2. There are many unusual courses available at the university this summer. *Some* have never been offered before.

Q. In these examples, what is the general class in the first sentence that is replaced by *one* and by *some*?
A. In both cases the words *one* and *some* replace *many unusual* courses.

SYNONYMS

Synonyms are words that have similar meaning. In the examination reading subtest, a synonym of a deleted word is sometimes found in one of the sentences before and/or after the sentence with the deletion. Examine the following excerpt from the passage about bridges again.

But engineers cannot forget that river traffic, too, is essential to our economy. The role of _____ is important. To keep these vessels moving freely, bridges are built high enough, when possible, to let them pass underneath.
   A. wind   B. boats   C. weight
   D. wires   E. experience

Q. Can you identify synonyms in the sentences, before and after the sentence containing the deletion, which are cues to the correct deleted word?
A. If you identified the correct words, you probably noticed that *river traffic* is not exactly a synonym since it is a slightly more general term than the word *boats* (the correct choice). But the word *vessels* is a direct synonym. Demonstrative pronouns (this, that, these, those) are sometimes used as modifiers for synonymous nouns in sentences which follow those containing deletions. The word *these* in *these vessels* is the demonstrative pronoun (modifier) for the synonymous noun *vessels*.

ANTONYMS

Antonyms are words of opposite meaning. In the examination reading subtest passages, antonyms may be cues for missing words. A contrasting relationship, which calls for the use of an antonym, is often signaled by the connective words *instead*, *however*, *but*, etc. Look at an excerpt from the passage about bridges.

An ingenious engineer designed the bridges so that it did not have to be raised above traffic. Instead it was
  A. burned   B. emptied   C. secured
  D. shared   E. lowered

Q: Can you identify an antonym in the first sentence for one of the five alternatives?
A. The word *raised* is an antonym for the word *lowered*.

SUBORDINATE-SUBORDINATE WORDS

In the examination reading subtest, a passage sometimes contains a general term which provides a cue that a more specific term is the appropriate alternative. At other times, the passage may contain a specific term which provides cues that a general term is the appropriate alternative for a particular deletion. The general and more specific words are said to have superordinate-subordinate relationships.

Look at Example 1 below. The more specific word *boy* in the first sentence serves as the antecedent for the more general word *child* in the second sentence. In Example 2, the relationship is reversed. In both examples, the words *child* and *boy* reflect a superordinate-subordinate relationship.

1. The *boy* climbed the tree. Then the *child* fell.
2. The *child* climbed the tree. Then the *boy* fell.

In the practice passage about bridges on Page 11, the phrase *river traffic* is a general term that is superordinate to the alternative *boats* (Item 1). Later in the passage about bridges the following sentences also contain superordinate-subordinate words:

A lift bridge was desired, but there were wartime shortages of steel and machinery needed for the towers. It was hard to find enough _____.
  A. work   B. material   C. time
  D. power   E. space

Q. Can you identify two words in the first sentence that are specific examples for the correct response in the second sentence?
A. Of course, the words *steel* and *machinery* are the specific examples for the more general term *material*.

WORDS ASSOCIATED BY ENTAILMENT

Sometimes the concept described by one word within the context of the passage entails, or implies, the concept described by another word. For example, consider again Item 7 in the practice passage about bridges. Notice how the follow-up sentence to Item 7 provides a cue to the correct response.

An ingenious engineer designed the bridge so that it did not have to be raised above traffic. Instead it was _____. It could be submerged seven meters below the surface of the river.
A. burned   B. emptied   C. secured
D. shared   E. lowered

Q. What word in the sentence after the blank implies the concept of an alternative?
A. *Submerged* implies *lowered*. The concept of submerging something implies the idea of lowering the object beneath the surface of the water.

WORDS ASSOCIATED BY PART-WHOLE RELATIONSHIPS

Words may be related because they involve part of a whole and the whole itself; for example, *nose* and *face*. Words may also be related because they involve two parts of the same whole; for example, *radiator* and *muffler* both refer to parts of a car.

The captain of the ship was nervous. The storm was becoming worse and worse. The hardened man paced the _____.
A. floor   B. hall   C. deck   D. court

Q. Which choice has a part-whole relationship with a word in the sentences above?
A. A *deck* is a part of a *ship*. Therefore, *deck* has a part-whole relationship with *ship*.

CONJUNCTIVE AND CONNECTIVE WORDS AND PHRASES

Conjunctions or connectives are words or phrases that connect parts of sentences or parts of a passage to each other. Their purpose is to help the reader understand the logical and conceptual relationships between ideas and events within a passage. Examples of these words and phrases include coordinate conjunctions (e.g., and, but, yet), subordinate conjunctions (e.g., because, although, since, after), and other connective words and phrases (e.g., too, also, on the other hand, as a result).

Listed below are types of logical relationships expressed by conjunctive, or connective words. Also listed are examples of words used to cue relationships to the reader.

Additive and comparative words and phrases: and, in addition to, too, also, furthermore, similarly.

Adversative and contrastive words and phrases: yet, though, only, but, however, instead, rather, on the other hand, conversely.

Causal words or phrases: so, therefore, because, as a result, if…then, unless, except, in that case, under the circumstances.

Temporal words and phrases: before, after, when, while, initially, lastly, finally, until.

<u>Examples</u>

1. I enjoy fast-paced sports like tennis and volleyball, but my brother prefers _____ sports.
   A. running   B. slower   C. team   D. active

   Q. What is the connective word that tells you to look for a contrast relationship between the two parts of the sentence?
   A. The connective word *but* signals that a contrast relationship exists between the two parts of the sentence.

   Q. Of the four options, what is the best choice for the blank?
   A. The word *slower* is the best response here.

2. The child stepped to close to the edge of the brook. As a result, he _____ in.
   A. fell   B. waded   C. ran   D. jumped

   Q. What is the connective phrase that links the two sentences?
   A. The connective phrase *as a result* links the two sentences.

   Q. Of the four relationships of words and phrases listed previously, what kind of relationship between the two sentences does the connective phrase in the example signal to the reader?
   A. The phrase *as a result* signals that a cause and effect relationship exists between the two sentences.

   Q. Identify the correct response which makes the second sentence reflect and cause and effect relationship.
   A. The correct response is *fell*.

Understanding connectives is very important to success on the examination reading subtest. Sentences with deletions are often very closely related to adjacent sentences in meaning, and the relationships often signaled by connective words or phrases. Here is an example from the practice passage about universities.

At first, these tutors had not been associated with one another. Rather, they had been _____. But, over time, they joined together to form guilds.
   A. curious   B. poor   C. religious
   D. ready   E. independent

Q. Identify the connective and contrastive words and phrases in the example.
A. *At first* and *over time* are connective phrases that set up temporal progression. *Rather* and *but* are contrastive items. The use of *rather* in the sentence with the deletion tells the reader that the missing word has to convey a meaning in contrast to *associated with one another*. (Notice also that *rather* occurs after a negative statement.) The use of *but* in the sentence after the one with the deletion indicates that the deleted word in the previous sentence has to reflect a meaning that contrasts with *joined together*. Thus, the reader is given two substantial cues to the meaning of the missing word. *Independent* is the only choice that meets the requirement for contrastive meaning.

SAMPLE QUESTIOINS

DIRECTIONS: There are two passages on the following pages. In each passage some words are missing. Wherever a word is missing, there is a blank line with a number on it. Below the passage you will find the same number and five words. Choose the word that makes the best sense in the blank. You may not be sure of the answer to a question until you read the sentences that come after the blank, so be sure to read enough to answer the questions. As you work on these passages, you will find that the second passage is harder to read than the first. Answer as many questions as you can.

Bridges are built to allow a continuous flow of highway and railway traffic across water lying in their paths. But engineers cannot forget that river traffic, too, is essential to our economy. The role of __1__ is important. To keep these vessels moving freely, bridges are built high enough, when possible, to let them pass underneath. Sometimes, however, channels must accommodate very tall ships. It may be uneconomical to build a tall enough bridge. The __2__ would be too high. To save money, engineers build movable bridges.

In the swing bridge, the middle part pivots or swings open. When the bridge is closed, this section joins the two ends of the bridge, blocking tall vessels. But this section __3__. When swung open, it is perpendicular to the ends of the bridge, creating two free channels for river traffic. With swing bridges channel width is limited by the bridge's piers. The largest swing bridge provides only a 75-meter channel. Such channels are sometimes __4__. In such cases, a bascule bridge may be built.

Bascule bridges are drawbridges with two arms that swing upward. They provide an opening as wide as the span. They are also versatile. These bridges are not limited to being fully opened or fully closed. They can be __5__ in many ways. They can be fixed at different angles to accommodate different vessels.

In vertical lift bridges, the center remains horizontal. Towers at both ends allow the center to be lifted like an elevator. One interesting variation of this kind of bridge was built during World War II. A lift bridge was desired, but there were wartime shortages of the steel and machinery needed for the towers. It was hard enough to find enough __6__. An ingenious engineer designed the bridge so that it did not have to be raised above traffic. Instead it was __7__. It could be submerged seven meters below the surface of the river. Ships sailed over it.

1. A. wind B. boats C. experience 1.____
   D. wires E. experience

2. A. levels B. cost C. standards 2.____
   D. waves E. deck

3. A. stands B. floods C. wears 3.____
   D. turns E. supports

4. A. narrow B. rough C. long 4.____
   D. deep E. straight

5. A. crossed B. approached C. lighted 5.____
   D. planned E. positioned

6. A. work B. material C. time 6.____
    D. power E. space

7. A. burned B. emptied C. secured 7.____
    D. shared E. lowered

The first universities emerged at the end of the 11th century and beginning of the 12th. These institutions were not founded on any particular date or created by any formal action. Nobody actually __8__ them. Instead, they developed gradually in places like Paris, Oxford, and Bologna, where scholars had long been teaching students. At first, these tutors had not been associated with one another. Rather, they had been __9__. But, over time, they joined together to form guilds.

Guilds were groups of tradespeople, somewhat akin to modern unions. In the Middle Ages, all the crafts had such __10__. The scholars' guilds built school buildings and evolved an administration which charged fees and set standards for the curriculum. It set prices for members' services and fixed requirements for entering the profession.

Professors were not the only schoolpeople forming associations. In Italy, students joined guilds to which teachers had to swear obedience. The students set strict rules, fining professors for beginning class a minute late. Teachers had to seek their students' permission to marry, and such permission was not always granted. Sometimes the students __11__. Even if they said yes, the teacher got only one day's honeymoon.

Undergraduates took classes in Greek philosophy, Latin grammar, arithmetic, music, and astronomy. These were the only __12__ available. More advanced study was possible in law, medicine, and theology, but one could not earn such postgraduate degrees quickly. It took a long time to __13__. Completing the requirements in theology, for example, took at least 13 years.

The concept of a fixed program of study leading to a degree first evolved in medieval Europe. This __14__ had not appeared before, in earlier academic settings, notions about *meeting requirements meeting requirements* and *graduating* had been absent. Since the middle ages, though, we have continued to view education as a set curriculum culminating in a degree.

8. A. started B. guarded C. blamed 8.____
    D. compared E. remembered

9. A. curious B. poor C. religious 9.____
    D. ready E. independent

10. A. taxes B. secrets C. products 10.____
    D. problems E. organizations

11. A. left B. copied C. refused 11.____
    D. paid E. prepared

12. A. rooms B. subjects C. clothes 12.____
    D. pens E. markets

13. A. add B. answer C. forget 13.____
    D. finish E. travel

14. A. idea   B. desk   C. library   14._____
    D. capital   E. company

KEY (CORRECT ANSWERS)

1.	B	6.	B	11.	C
2.	B	7.	E	12.	B
3.	D	8.	A	13.	D
4.	A	9.	E	14.	A
5.	E	10.	E		

WORD SUBSTITUTION
EXAMINATION SECTION
TEST 1

DIRECTIONS: Each question or incomplete statement is followed by several suggested Answers or completions. Select the one that BEST answers the question or completes the statement. *PRINT THE LETTER OF THE CORRECT ANSWER IN THE SPACE AT THE RIGHT.*

Questions 1-5.

DIRECTIONS: Questions 1 through 5 consist of one sentence each. Each sentence contains an incorrectly used word. First, decide which is the incorrectly used word. Then, from among the options given, decide which word, when substituted for the incorrectly used word, makes the meaning of the sentence clear.

SAMPLE QUESTION
The U.S. national income exhibits a pattern of long term deflation.
  A. reflection
  B. subjection
  C. rejoicing
  D. growth

The word deflation in the sentence does not convey the meaning the sentence evidently intended to convey. The word growth (Answer D) when substituted for the word deflation makes the meaning of the sentence clear. Accordingly, the answer to the question is D.

1. The study commissioned by the joint committee fell compassionately short of the mark and would have to be redone.
   A. successfully
   B. insignificantly
   C. experimentally
   D. woefully

   1.____

2. He will not idly exploit any violation of the provisions of the order.
   A. tolerate
   B. refuse
   C. construe
   D. guard

   2.____

3. The defendant refused to be virile and bitterly protested service.
   A. irked
   B. feasible
   C. docile
   D. credible

   3.____

4. As today's violence has no single cause, so its causes have no single scheme.　　　4.____
    A. deference
    B. cure
    C. flaw
    D. relevance

5. He took the position that the success of the program was insidious on getting additional　　　5.____
   revenue.
    A. reputed
    B. contingent
    C. failure
    D. indeterminate

KEY (CORRECT ANSWERS)

1. D
2. A
3. C
4. B
5. B

TEST 2

DIRECTIONS: Each question or incomplete statement is followed by several suggested answers or completions. Select the one that BEST answers the question or completes the statement. *PRINT THE LETTER OF THE CORRECT ANSWER IN THE SPACE AT THE RIGHT.*

Questions 1-5.

DIRECTIONS: Questions 1 through 5 each consist of a statement which contains one word that is incorrectly used because it is not in keeping with the meaning that the quotation is evidently intended to convey. Of the words underlined in each statement, determine which word is incorrectly used. Then select from among the words lettered A, B, C, and D the word which, when substituted for the incorrectly used word, would BEST help to convey the meaning of the quotation. (Do not indicate a change for an underlined word unless the underlined word is incorrectly used.)

1. Unless unreasonable managerial supervision is exercised over office supplies, it is certain that there will be extravagance, rejected items out of stock, excessive prices paid for certain items, and obsolete material in the stock room.
    A. overlooked
    B. immoderate
    C. needed
    D. instituted

1._____

2. Since office supplies are in such common use, an attitude. of indifference about their handling is not unusual. Their importance is often recognized only when they are utilized or out of stock, for office employees must have proper supplies if maximum productivity is to be attained.
    A. plentiful
    B. unavailable
    C. reduced
    D. expected

2._____

3. Anyone effected by paperwork, interested in or engaged in office work, or desiring to improve informational activities can find materials keyed to his needs.
    A. attentive
    B. available
    C. affected
    D. ambitious

3._____

4. Information is homogeneous and must therefore be properly classified so that each type may be employed in ways appropriate to its own peculiar properties.
    A. apparent
    B. heterogeneous
    C. consistent
    D. idiosyncratic

4._____

5. <u>Intellectual</u> training may seem a <u>formidable</u> phrase, but it means nothing more than the <u>deliberate</u> cultivation of the ability to think, and there is no <u>dark</u> contrast between the intellectual and the practical.   5._____
       A. subjective
       B. objective
       C. sharp
       D. vocational

KEY (CORRECT ANSWERS)

1. C
2. B
3. C
4. B
5. C

EXAMINATION SECTION
TEST 1

DIRECTIONS: Each of Questions 1 through 15 consists of a passage which contains one word that is incorrectly used because it is not in keeping with the meaning that the passage is evidently intended to convey. Determine which word is incorrectly used. Then select from the words lettered A, B, C, or D the word which, when substituted for the incorrectly used word, would BEST help to convey the meaning of the passage.

1. A manager must often operate systems that are quite complex, but these systems are an effective vehicle for management. Each system has an input, a process, and an output, and is a self-contained unit, but it is also related to a system of a wider and higher order as well as to its own sub-systems that represent the integration of several systems of the lower order. Thinking in terms of systems restricts his understanding of the multitudinous activities with which he must work, and it also enables him to see better the nature of the complex problems that he faces.

    A. isolation   B. simplifies
    C. perpetuating   D. constrains

2. Planning involves, first, the conceiving of goals and the development of alternative courses of future action to achieve the goals. Second, it involves the reduction of these alternatives from a very large number to a small number and finally to one approved course of action, the program. Budgeting probably plays a slight part in the first phase but an increasingly important and decisive part in the second. It facilitates the choice-making process by providing a basis for systematic comparisons among alternatives which take into account their total impacts on both the debit and the credit sides. It thus encourages, and provides some of the tools for, an increasing degree of precision in the planning process. Budgeting is the ingredient of planning which precedes the entire process.

    A. achievement   B. improved
    C. immediate   D. disciplines

3. In every instance the burden of proving each of the charges against the employee, which constitute the claimed misconduct or incompetence, must be upon the agency alleging the same. This simply means that it is incumbent upon the agency to establish each of the charges by a fair preponderance of the entire evidence. Unless the Hearing Officer is satisfied that the evidence has fairly and reasonably established the facts asserted by the agency, the agency has not sustained the burden of proof. The Hearing Officer must determine the admissibility of evidence where there is an objection to a question. Although at disciplinary hearings the presentation of the testimony is not limited by strict and technical rules of evidence as in a court, nevertheless the Hearing Officer should at all times consider its relevance and materiality, and then make his determination on the basis of fairness.

    A. corroborate   B. incredible
    C. disinterested   D. obligatory

2 (#1)

4. The examination of alternative means available for the accomplishment of a given program must proceed along lines somewhat different from the review of alternative programs. In the former, the budget officer should possess sufficient knowledge of operations, and of methods and procedures, to be able to challenge badly conceived projects and to ask the kinds of questions which call forth the orderly processes of administration. This is where budget review and organization and method analysis tend to conflict, and it is here that the reviewing officer who has had operating experience can be most effective in questioning and criticizing management techniques.

   A. personnel
   B. problems
   C. public
   D. merge

4.___

5. The employee is not required to submit a written answer to the charges of incompetency or misconduct. The fact that an employee does not choose to submit a written answer should not be taken to mean that he admits guilt. However, the answer provides a means for the accused employee, in writing and for the record, to plead guilty or not guilty to the various charges and specifications, to allege matters tending to disprove the charges, including his good character and reputation, to allege any incriminating circumstances and also to plead a favorable record of service and conduct which might tend to lessen the penalty. Upon receipt of the employee's written answer to the charges, the answer should be carefully analyzed and any allegations therein verified. It may also be necessary to gather new evidence for the hearing in relation to allegations contained in the answer.

   A. confidential
   B. mitigative
   C. particularize
   D. procedural

5.___

6. In an article in the Harvard Business Review ("Human Relations or Human Resources"), Raymond E. Miles expounded a human resources theory of management. He declared that a manager's job cannot be viewed as merely one of giving direction and obtaining cooperation; rather, it is one of creating an environment in which the total resources of his department can be utilized. In this environment, the manager shares information and modifies departmental decisions with his employees and encourages their self-direction, not to improve their role satisfactions but to improve the decision making and the total performance efficiency of the organization. Many decisions are made more efficiently by those directly involved in and affected by them. In fact, Miles added, the more important the decisions, the greater the manager's obligation to encourage subordinate self-direction.

   A. actuate
   B. appearance
   C. compulsion
   D. discusses

6.___

7. Each organization follows a particular philosophy of management selected from a spectrum ranging from authoritarian to participative. If it adopts an approach in which the manager makes all the decisions and passes them on to subordinates for consideration, it follows an authoritarian philosophy that determines its organization structure and climate. Its structure will follow closely the pattern of many levels of management, tight spans of control, and formal channels of communication. The direction of information flow will be downward, supervisors will have little trust in subordinates, and a high degree of emphasis will be placed on management controls.

   A. approve
   B. concentrated
   C. discretionary
   D. execution

7.___

8. Besides the ability to comprehend the magnitude of decisions the ability to deal with decision complexity also differs from person to person. Most human beings are discouraged only with a two-option decision, seeing reality in terms of black or white and hardly ever noticing the gray. Even when there is a choice of three or four pretty well-defined options, a human being will consciously or unconsciously reduce them to two. It takes a good deal of training and education plus a highly developed intellectual structure to handle multi-option decisions and to actively seek a third or fourth alternative.   8.____

   A. comfortable   B. enlarging
   C. narrowly   D. passive

9. Manpower planning, like finance; is a management function that cannot be delegated or decentralized. What has often been overlooked in studies of decentralization is that no successful firm has ever decentralized the financial function. Since there has rarely been more than one treasurer in a firm, the centralized, control of finances exercises an auxiliary power over all members in a decentralized organization. Just as the management of financial resources is regularly centralized, so the management of human and, in particular, managerial resources must be centralized and the primary responsibility accepted by the chief executive. In fact, he should consider the direction of the managerial manpower plan to be his top responsibility.   9.____

   A. concentration   B. external
   C. subsidiary   D. ultimate

10. One drawback of the participative-management approach is the lack of solid research to document its contentions. What has been collected is either inconclusive or negative. Laboratory experiments have repeatedly demonstrated that groups that are organized to counter interpersonal comfort, openness, familiarity, and cohesiveness perform poorly. At least one study, in a large insurance company, of different styles of management revealed that while greater acceptance of leadership and high morale were present in the division led by the manager who believes in democratic supervision, this division's performance results were no better than those achieved by the authoritarian leaders.   10.____

    A. disputed   B. emphasise
    C. inconsistency D. resistance

11. An organization experiences continuous changes which, taken together, tend to follow a course that can be defined and projected as a trend. Thus, after a company has accumulated sufficient historical data, it is fairly simple to project certain manpower trends. For example, to estimate within a fairly close margin the number of managers who will retire, die, resign, or be discharged in the succeeding 12 months is not so difficult. What is much more difficult and should not even be tried is to predict the number of those individuals who will die, retire, or resign. Simply knowing that, according to present trends, the company must replace 23 managers in the next 12 months is a distinct advantage, and knowing within certain confidence limits how many must be replaced within the next five years affords an even greater advantage   11.____

    A. handicap   B. names
    C. terminated D. withheld

12. To assess another person, one must first obtain an accurate description of him in relation to the task for which he is being considered, But, to describe a person accurately, we must obtain relevant information about him and this is the sensitive area. Precisely what information is relevant to the role he is asked to play? If it is relevant, have we the right to it? Are there not some personal areas that are open for public inspection? These quite difficult questions are made even more difficult by the unfortunate way they have been raised recently by government agencies. The mishandling of inquiries into the personal background of applicants for positions has been so widespread that it has been necessary to pass laws at all levels restricting the amount and the quality of information that an employer may seek to obtain from a job applicant.   12.___

    A. disclosure
    B. processing
    C. prohibition
    D. unavailable

13. An organization's goals must be based on an accurate appraisal of its manpower resources, otherwise they will be like the objectives announced by a last-place baseball-team manager in the spring no more than pious hopes set down for their inspirational value. Public officials are quite guilty in this respects establishing targets for full employment, tax reduction, and urban renewal that are totally attainable and hardly within the capacities of those on the payroll. Many businesses follow the same practice, establishing market-penetration or sales goals that are quite beyond the competence and the energy of their employees. Setting goals, therefore, must take into account the probable course of events that is likely to unfold inside and outside the organization. This prediction of future events is known as forecasting.   13.___

    A. estimates
    B. laxity
    C. tendency
    D. unrealistic

14. In some organizations, a silent conspiracy can prevail that masks the facts about the managerial situation. Older managers who feel threatened by their advancing age, their creeping obsolescence, or their rapidly changing environment may try to hide their heads in the sands of yesterday. To support themselves, they may try many maneuvers — hiding promising young men, promoting incompetence, or making a farce out of the performance evaluation program. Out of this mass anxiety an "establishment" is born, a highly structured "in" group that invalidates manpower rules designed to insure its own security. This is the system that old men cherish and young men rail a gainst, that blights an organization like a creeping cancer and slowly destroys it as, all the while, its presence remains unfelt until it is fatal.   14.___

    A. enforces
    B. erosion
    C. manipulate
    D. terminating

15. Z. Pietrowski found that the successful top executive strives more intensively for personal achievement, sets more difficult work goals for himself, can adapt emotionally to a variety of people, is more original, and has less insecurity and self-doubt. E. Ghiselli found in his study of 287 managers that the effective manager showed less need for job security than did less effective managers. The effective managers showed the strongest desire for self-actualization, for the opportunity to utilize their talents in customary ways. In summary, the studies indicate quite clearly that the successful manager has a total life pattern of successful endeavor.   15.___

    A. conspicuously
    B. creative
    C. effacement
    D. ineffectual

KEY (CORRECT ANSWERS)

1. B
2. D
3. A
4. D
5. B

6. D
7. D
8. A
9. D
10. B

11. B
12. D
13. D
14. A
15. B

TEST 2

DIRECTIONS: Each of the following questions consists of a paragraph which contains one word that is incorrectly used because it is not in keeping with the meaning that the paragraph is evidently intended to convey. Determine which word is incorrectly used. Select from the choices lettered A, B, C, and D the word which, when substituted for the incorrectly used work, would BEST help to convey the meaning of the paragraph.

1. Among the Housing Manager's over-all responsibilities in administering a project is the prevention of the development of conditions which might lead to termination of tenancy and eviction of a tenant. Where there appears to be doubt that a tenant is fully aware of his responsibilities and is thus jeopardizing his tenancy, the Housing Manager should acquaint him with these responsibilities. Where a situation involves behavior of a tenant or a member of his family, the Housing Manager should confirm, through discussions and referrals to social agencies, correction of the conditions before they reach a stage where there is no alternative but termination proceedings.

   A. coordinate B. identify
   C. assert D. attempt

2. There is one almost universal administrative complaint. The budget is inadequate, Now, between adequacy and inadequacy lie all degrees of adequacy. Further, human wants are modest in relation to human resources. From these two facts we may conclude that the fundamental criterion of administrative decision must be a criterion Of efficiency (the degree to which the goals have been reached relative to the available resources) rather than a criterion of adequacy (the degree to which its goals have been reached). The task of the administrator is to maximize social values relative to limited resources.

   A. improve B. simple
   C. limitless D. optimize

3. Leadership is a personality characteristic based to a large extent on the charisma the leader possesses for his followers. Thus his appeal must be to the emotional and the personal life of the group. A manager, on the other hand, has been entrusted with the responsibility of decision making, which has nothing whatsoever to do with leadership. It is not a personal trait, it is a role that is not administrative and based upon the process of choosing a course of action and committing the group's resources to it. The manager's function is to define goals and objectives, to select a course of action to achieve them, and to evaluate realistically the results of that action. There is little charisma in such a role. Leaders depend for their success on personality, a characteristic that has nothing to do with management. Consequently, leadership and management are most appropriately treated as separate phenomena that are effectively handled simultaneously but not necessarily by the same person.

   A. initiates B. limit
   C. purely D. rational

4. Where it appears that any City employee may be guilty of corruption or wrongdoing, the Department of Investigation should be informed. The agency itself should then conduct the inquiry immediately only if the Department of Investigation so determines. If during an inquiry it appears that the corruption or wrongdoing may be more serious or widespread than originally suspected, the Department of Investigation should be recontacted immediately. In some instances, it may be necessary to hold the disciplinary hearing prior to the criminal proceedings and it is essential that the conduct of the criminal case not be unnecessarily warranted by the department trial. The transcript and all papers should be kept in a secure place and there should be no disclosure or publicity about what transpired without the approval of the Corpora- tion Counsel and the Commissioner of Investigation.

    A. superseded
    B. prejudiced
    C. premature
    D. concurrently

4.____

5. It is often easy to enumerate reasons why a housing enterprise succeeds or fails. With so many variables that appear to have a make-or-break impact upon the outcome, there is a natural tendency to over-emphasize the importance of the man, particularly the man in charge. Society subscribes to the idea that housing leadership is important, but society doesn't really believe it. Even top housing managers are dubious about the significance of their own roles in the success or failure of a public enterprise. When things go wrong, they tend to blame the system; when things go right, they modestly give credit to "the team." The only way to manage a housing organization effectively is to give managers authority to run it and then hold them strictly accountable for the results. This idea is hardly new to anyone, however rarely it is carried out in practice. But the idea breaks down because we know so little about picking men who have the capacity to manage large housing enterprises.

    A. coalesce
    B. disavows
    C. overlook
    D. wavering

5.____

6. The technological and social changes that have occurred in American economy during the rise of the Managerial Society have not only required much more highly trained managers, they have created intense competition for these same men from other sectors of the economy: from the government, from education, and from the nonprofit areas. In the decade between 1954 and 1964, the number of employees in the executive classes of the federal government jumped 58 percent. The result is an unprecedented demand for managers that is likely to continue unabated for the next three decades. If we assume that the shortage has been met in the same way as in technical fields, it is probable that a substantial number of managerial positions are filled by people not fully qualified or that the positions have been reinforced by the inclusion of duties incompatible with those of a manager. Since this latter strategy is most commonly employed, it is possible to assert that many managers are managers in name only.

    A. conflicting
    B. diluted
    C. eliminate
    D. incumbent

6.____

7. There is also a suspicion in some quarters that admin- istrators have a tendency to be imperialistic, that government officials have an inborn desire to spend more of the tax- payers' money, to hire more people, to build more buildings. Sometimes this charge is couched in more gentle terms, it is suggested that administrators tend to overestimate simply to be on the safe side, so that they will be able to retain some leeway in program administration. Again, there is no doubt that these charges and suspicions are justified in particular cases. The overzealous and overambitious are not unknown in our society, or in any society. But it would be difficult to demonstrate that these tendencies are more widespread in government than elsewhere. Very often, what looks like an overweening ambition may turn out to be regressive administration. The government official who seeks to expand his program may do so because he sees the need, because he would like to do a better job, because he is close to the beneficiaries of his program operations. 7.___

    A. responsive   B. fewer
    C. freedom   D. targets

KEY (CORRECT ANSWERS)

1. D
2. C
3. C
4. B
5. C
6. B
7. A

READING COMPREHENSION
UNDERSTANDING AND INTERPRETING WRITTEN MATERIAL
EXAMINATION SECTION
TEST 1

DIRECTIONS: Each question or incomplete statement is followed by several suggested answers or completions. Select the one that BEST answers the question or completes the statement. *PRINT THE LETTER OF THE CORRECT ANSWER IN THE SPACE AT THE RIGHT.*

1. The National Assessment of Educational Progress recently released the results of the first statistically valid national sampling of young adult reading skills in the United States. According to the survey, ninety-five percent of United States young adults (aged 21-25) can read at a fourth-grade level or better. This means they can read well enough to apply for a job, understand a movie guide or join the Army. This is a higher literacy rate than the eighty to eighty-five percent usually estimated for all adults. The study also found that ninety-nine percent can write their names, eighty percent can read a map or write a check for a bill, seventy percent can understand an appliance warranty or write a letter about a billing error, twenty-five percent can calculate the amount of a tip correctly, and fewer than ten percent can correctly figure the cost of a catalog or understand a complex bus schedule.
Which statement about the study is BEST supported by the above passage?
   A. United States literacy rates among young adults are at an all-time high.
   B. Forty percent of young people in the United States cannot write a letter about a billing error.
   C. Twenty percent of United States teenagers cannot read a map,
   D. More than ninety percent of United States young adults cannot correctly calculate the cost of a catalog order.

1.____

2. It is now widely recognized that salaries, benefits, and working conditions have more of an impact on job satisfaction than on motivation. If they aren't satisfactory, work performance and morale will suffer. But even when they are high, employees will not necessarily be motivated to work well. For example, THE WALL STREET JOURNAL recently reported that as many as forty or fifty percent of newly hired Wall Street lawyers (whose salaries start at upwards of $50,000) quit within the first three years, citing long hours, pressures, and monotony as the prime offenders. It seems there's just not enough of an intellectual challenge in their jobs. An up and coming money-market executive concluded: *Whether it was $1 million or $100 million, the procedure was the same. Except for the tension, a baboon could do my job.* When money and benefits are adequate, the most important additional determinants of job satisfaction are: more responsibility, a sense of achievement, recognition, and a chance to advance. All of these factors have a more significant influence on employee motivation and performance. As a footnote, several studies have found that the absence of these non-monetary factors can lead to serious stress-related illnesses.

2.____

Which statement is BEST supported by the above passage?
- A. A worker's motivation to perform well is most affected by salaries, benefits, and working conditions.
- B. Low pay can lead to high levels of job stress.
- C. Work performance will suffer if workers feel they are not paid well.
- D. After satisfaction with pay and benefits, the next most important factor is more responsibility.

3. The establishment of joint labor-management production committees occurred in the United States during World War I and again during World War II. Their use was greatly encouraged by the National War Labor Board in World War I and the War Production Board in 1942. Because of the war, labor-management cooperation was especially desired to produce enough goods for the war effort, to reduce conflict, and to control inflation. The committees focused on how to achieve greater efficiency, and consulted on health and safety, training, absenteeism, and people issues in general. During the second world war, there were approximately five thousand labor-management committees in factories, affecting over six million workers. While research has found that only a few hundred committees made significant contributions to productivity, there were additional benefits in many cases. It became obvious to many that workers had ideas to contribute to the running of the organization, and that efficient enterprises could become even more so. Labor-management cooperation was also extended to industries that had never experienced it before. Directly after each war, however, few United States labor-management committees were in operation.
Which statement is BEST supported by the above passage?
- A. The majority of United States labor-management committees during the second world war accomplished little.
- B. A major goal of United States labor-management committees during the first and second world wars was to increase productivity.
- C. There were more United States labor-management committees during the second world war than during the first world war.
- D. There are few United States labor-management committees in operation today.

4. Studies have found that stress levels among employees who have a great deal of customer contact or a great deal of contact with the public can be very high. There are many reasons for this. Sometimes stress results when the employee is caught in the middle—an organization wants things done one way, but the customer wants them done another way. The situation becomes even worse for the employee's stress levels when he or she knows was to more effectively provide the service, but isn't allowed to, by the organization. An example is the bank teller who is required to ask a customer for two forms of identification before he or she can cash a check, even though the teller knows the customer well. If organizational mishaps occur or if there are problems with job design, the employee may be powerless to satisfy the customer, and also powerless to protect himself or herself from the customer's wrath. An example of this is the waitress who is forced to serve poorly prepared food. Studies have also found,

however, that if the organization and the employee design the positions and the service encounter well, and encourage the use of effective stress management techniques, stress can be reduced to levels that are well below average.
Which statement is BEST supported by the above passage?
- A. It is likely that knowledgeable employees will experience greater levels of job-related stress.
- B. The highest levels of occupational stress are found among those employees who have a great deal of customer contact.
- C. Organizations can contribute to the stress levels of their employees by poorly designing customer contact situations.
- D. Stress levels are generally higher in banks and restaurants.

5. It is estimated that approximately half of the United States population suffers from varying degrees of adrenal malfunction. When under stress for long periods of time, the adrenals produce extra cortisol and norepinephrine. By producing more hormones than they were designed to comfortably manufacture and secrete, the adrenals can *burn out* over time and then decrease their secretion. When this happens, the body loses its capacity to cope with stress, and the individual becomes sicker more easily and for longer periods of time. A result of adrenal malfunction may be a diminished output of cortisol. Symptoms of diminished cortisol output include any of the following: craving substances that will temporarily raise serum glucose levels such as caffeine, sweets, soda, juice, or tobacco; becoming dizzy when standing up too quickly; irritability; headaches; and erratic energy levels. Since cortisol is an anti-inflammatory hormone, a decreased output over extended periods of time can make one prone to inflammatory disease such ass arthritis, bursitis, colitis, and allergies. (Many food and pollen allergies disappear when adrenal function is restored to normal.) The patient will have no reserve energy, and infections can spread quickly. Excessive cortisol production, on the other hand, can decrease immunity, leading to frequent and prolonged illnesses.
Which statement is BEST supported by the above passage?
- A. Those who suffer from adrenal malfunction are most likely to be prone to inflammatory diseases such as arthritis and allergies.
- B. The majority of Americans suffer from varying degrees of adrenal malfunction.
- C. It is better for the health of the adrenals to drink juice instead of soda.
- D. Too much cortisol can inhibit the body's ability to resist disease.

5.____

6. Psychologist B.F. Skinner pointed out long ago that gambling is reinforced either by design or accidentally, by what he called a variable ratio schedule. A slot machine, for example, is cleverly designed to provide a payoff after it has been played a variable number of times. Although the person who plays it and wins while playing receives a great deal of monetary reinforcement, over the long run the machine will take in much more money than it pays out. Research on both animals and humans has consistently found that such variable reward schedules maintain a very high rate of repeat behavior, and that this behavior is particularly resistant to extinction.

6.____

Which statement is BEST supported by the above passage?
A. Gambling, because it is reinforced by the variable ratio schedule, is more difficult to eliminate than most addictions.
B. If someone is rewarded or wins consistently, even if it is not that often, he or she is likely to continue that behavior.
C. Playing slot machines is the safest form of gambling because they are designed so that eventually the player will indeed win.
D. A cat is likely to come when called if its owner has trained it correctly.

7. Paper entrepreneurialism is an offshoot of scientific management that has become so extreme that it has lost all connection to the actual workplace. It generates profits by cleverly manipulating rules and numbers that only in theory represent real products and real assets. At its worst, paper entrepreneurialism involves very little more than imposing losses on others for the sake of short-term profits. The others may be taxpayers, shareholders who end up indirectly subsidizing other shar holders, consumers, or investors. Paper entrepreneurialism has replaced product entrepreneurialism, is seriously threatening the United States economy, and is hurting our necessary attempts to transform the nation's industrial and productive economic base. An example is the United States company that complained loudly in 1979 that it did not have the $200 million needed to develop a video-cassette recorder, though demand for them had been very high. The company, however, did not hesitate to spend $1.2 billion that same year to buy a mediocre finance company. The video recorder market was handed over to other countries, who did not hesitate to manufacture them.
Which statement is BEST supported by the above passage?
A. Paper entrepreneurialism involves very little more than imposing losses on others for the sake of short-term profits.
B. Shareholders are likely to benefit most from paper entrepreneurialism.
C. Paper entrepreneurialism is hurting the United States economy.
D. The United States could have made better video-cassette recorders than the Japanese but we ceded the market to them in 1979.

7.____

8. The *prisoner's dilemma* is an almost 40-year-old game-theory model psychologists, biologists, economists, and political scientists use to try to understand the dynamics of competition and cooperation. Participants in the basic version of the experiment are told that they and their *accomplice* have been caught red-handed. Together, their best strategy is to cooperate by remaining silent. If they do this, each will get off with a 30-day sentence. But either person can do better for himself or herself. If you double-cross your partner, you will go scot free while he or she serves ten years. The problem is, if you each betray the other, you will both go to prison for eight years, not thirty days. No matter what your partner chooses, you are logically better off choosing betrayal. Unfortunately, your partner realizes this too, and so the odds are good that you will both get eight years. That's the dilemma. (The length of the prison sentences is always the same for each variation.) Participants at a recent symposium on behavioral economics at Harvard University discussed the many variations on the game that have been used

8.____

over the years. In one standard version, subjects are paired with a supervisor who pays them a dollar for each point they score. Over the long run, both subjects will do best if they cooperate every time. Yet in each round, there is a great temptation to betray the other because no one knows what the other will do. The best overall strategy for this variation was found to be *tit for tat*, doing unto your opponent as he or she has just done unto you. It is a simple strategy, but very effective. The partner can easily recognize it and respond. It is retaliatory enough not to be easily exploited, but forgiving enough to allow a pattern of mutual cooperation to develop.
Which statement is BEST supported by the above passage?
  A. The best strategy for playing *prisoner's dilemma* is to cooperate and remain silent.
  B. If you double-cross your partner, and he or she does not double-cross you, your partner will receive a sentence of eight years.
  C. When playing *prisoner's dilemma*, it is best to double-cross your partner.
  D. If you double-cross your partner, and he or she double-crosses you, you will receive an eight-year sentence.

9. After many years of experience as the vice president and general manager of a large company, I feel that I know what I'm looking for in a good manager. First, the manager has to be comfortable with himself or herself, and not be arrogant or defensive. Secondly, he or she has to have a genuine interest in people. There are some managers who love ideas—and that's fine—but to be a manager, you must love people, and you must make a hobby of understanding them, believing in them and trusting them. Third, I look for a willingness and a facility to manage conflict. Gandhi defined conflict as a way of getting at the truth. Each person brings his or her own grain of truth and the conflict washes away the illusion and fantasy. Finally, a manager has to have a vision, and the ability and charisma to articulate it. A manager should be seen as a little bit crazy. Some eccentricity is an asset. People don't want to follow vanilla leaders. They want to follow chocolate-fudge-ripple leaders.
Which statement is BEST supported by the above passage?
  A. It is very important that a good manager spend time studying people.
  B. It is critical for good managers to love ideas.
  C. Managers should try to minimize or avoid conflict.
  D. Managers should be familiar with people's reactions to different flavors of ice cream.

10. Most societies maintain a certain set of values and assumptions that make their members feel either good or bad about themselves, and either better or worse than other people. In most developed countries, these values are based on the assumption that we are all free to be what we want to be, and that differences in income, work, and education are a result of our own efforts. This may make us believe that people with more income work that is more skilled, more education, and more power are somehow *better* people. We may view their achievements as proof that they have more intelligence, more motivation, and more initiative than those with lower status. The myth tells us that power, income, and education are freely and equally available to all, and that our

failure to achieve them is due to our own personal inadequacy. This simply is not the case.

The possessions we own may also seem to point to our real worth as individuals. The more we own, the more worthy of respect we may feel we are. Or, the acquisition of possessions may be a way of trying to fulfill ourselves, to make up for the loss of community and/or purpose. It is a futile pursuit because lost community and purpose can never be compensated for by better cars or fancier houses. And too often, when these things fail to satisfy, we believe it is only because we don't have enough money to buy better quality items, or more items. We feel bad that we haven't been successful enough to get all that we think we need. No matter how much we do have, goods never really satisfy for long. There is always something else to acquire, and true satisfaction eludes many, many of us.
Which statement is BEST supported by the above passage?
- A. The author would agree with the theory of *survival of the fittest*.
- B. The possessions an individual owns are not a proper measure of his or her real worth.
- C. Many countries make a sincere attempt to ensure equal access to quality education for their citizens.
- D. The effect a society's value system has on the lives of its members is greatly exaggerated.

11. *De nihilo nihil* is Latin for *nothing comes from nothing*. In the first century, the Roman poet Persius advised that if anything is to be produced of value, effort must be expended. He also said, *In nihilum nil posse revorti*—anything once produced cannot become nothing again. It is thought that Persius was parodying Lucretius, who expounded the 500-year-old physical theories of Epicurus. *De nihilo nihil* can also be used as a cynical comment, to negatively comment on something that is of poor quality produced by a person of little talent. The implication here is: *What can you expect from such a source?*
Which statement is BEST supported by the above passage?
- A. *In nihilum nil posse revorti* can be interpreted as meaning, *If anything is to be produced of value, then effort must be expended.*
- B. *De nihilo nihil* can be understood in two different ways,
- C. Lucretius was a great physicist.
- D. Persius felt that Epicurus put in little effort while developing his theories.

11.____

12. A Cornell University study has found that less than one percent of the billion pounds of pesticides used in this country annually strike their intended targets. The study found that the pesticides, which are somewhat haphazardly applied to 370 million acres, or about sixteen percent of the nation's total land area, end up polluting the environment and contaminating almost all 200,000 species of plants and animals, including humans. While the effect of indirect contamination on human cancer rates was not estimated, the study found that approximately 45,000 human pesticide poisonings occur annually, including about 3,000 cases admitted to hospitals and approximately 200 fatalities.

12.____

Which statement is BEST supported by the above passage?
- A. It is likely that indirect pesticide contamination affects human health.
- B. Pesticides are applied to over one-quarter of the total United States land area.
- C. If pesticides were applied more carefully, fewer pesticide-resistant strains of pests would develop.
- D. Human cancer rates in this country would drop considerably if pesticide use was cut in half.

13. The new conservative philosophy presents a unified, coherent approach to the world. It offers to explain much of our experience since the turbulent 1960s, and it shows what we've learned since about the dangers of indulgence and permissiveness. But it also warns that the world has become more ruthless, and that as individuals and as a nation, we must struggle for survival. It is necessary to impose responsibility and discipline in order to defeat those forces that threaten us. This lesson is dramatically clear, and can be applied to a wide range of issues.
    Which statement is BEST supported by the above passage?
    - A. The 1970s were a time of permissiveness and indulgence.
    - B. The new conservative philosophy may help in imposing discipline and a sense of responsibility in order to meet the difficult challenges facing this country.
    - C. The world faced greater challenges during the second world war than it faces at the present time.
    - D. More people identify themselves today as conservative in their political philosophy.

13.____

14. One of the most puzzling questions in management in recent years has been how usually honest, compassionate, intelligent managers can sometimes act in ways that are dishonest, uncaring, and unethical. How could top-level managers at the Manville Corporation, for example, suppress evidence for decades that proved beyond all doubt that asbestos inhalation was killing their own employees? What drove the managers of a Midwest bank to continue to act in a way that threatened to bankrupt the institution, ruin its reputation, and cost thousands of employees and investors their jobs and their savings? It's been estimated that about two out of three of America's five hundred largest corporations have been involved in some form of illegal behavior. There are, of course, some common rationalizations used to justify unethical conduct: believing that the activity is in the organization's or the individual's best interest, believing that the activity is not *really* immoral or illegal, believing that no one will ever know, or believing that the organization will sanction the behavior because it helps the organization. Ambition can distort one's sense of *duty*.
    Which statement is BEST supported by the above passage?
    - A. Top-level managers of corporations are currently involved in a plan to increase ethical behavior among their employees.
    - B. There are many good reasons why a manager may act unethically.
    - C. Some managers allow their ambitions to override their sense of ethics,
    - D. In order to successfully compete, some organizations may have to indulge in unethical or illegal behavior from time to time.

14.____

15. Some managers and supervisors believe that they are leaders because they occupy positions of responsibility and authority. But leadership is more than holding a position. It is often defined in management literature as *the ability to influence the opinions, attitudes and behaviors of others.* Obviously, there are some managers that would not qualify as leaders, and some leaders that are not *technically* managers. Research has found that many people overrate their own leadership abilities. In one recent study, seventy percent of those surveyed rated themselves in the top quartile in leadership abilities, and only two percent felt they were below average as leaders.
Which statement is BEST supported by the above passage?
    A. In a recent study, the majority of people surveyed rated themselves in the top twenty-five percent in leadership abilities.
    B. Ninety-eight percent of the people surveyed in a recent study had average or above-average leadership skills.
    C. In order to be a leader, one should hold a management position.
    D. Leadership is best defined as the ability to be liked by those one must lead.

15.____

KEY (CORRECT ANSWERS)

1.	D	6.	B	11.	B
2.	C	7.	C	12.	A
3.	B	8.	D	13.	B
4.	C	9.	A	14.	C
5.	D	10.	B	15.	A

READING COMPREHENSION
UNDERSTANDING AND INTERPRETING WRITTEN MATERIAL
EXAMINATION SECTION
TEST 1

DIRECTIONS: Each question or incomplete statement is followed by several suggested answers or completions. Select the one that BEST answers the question or completes the statement. *PRINT THE LETTER OF THE CORRECT ANSWER IN THE SPACE AT THE RIGHT.*

Questions 1-3.

DIRECTIONS: Questions 1 through 3 are to be answered SOLELY on the basis of the following passage.

Every organization needs a systematic method of checking its operations as a means to increase efficiency and promote economy. Many successful private firms have instituted a system of audit or internal inspections to accomplish these ends. Law enforcement organizations, which have an extremely important service to *sell*, should be no less zealous in developing efficiency and economy in their operations. Periodic, organized, and systematic inspections are one means of promoting the achievement of these objectives. The necessity of an organized inspection system is perhaps greatest in those law enforcement groups which have grown to such a size that the principal officer can no longer personally supervise or be cognizant of every action taken. Smooth and effective operation demands that the head of the organization have at hand some tool with which he can study and enforce general policies and procedure and also direct compliance with day-to-day orders, most of which are put into execution outside his sight and hearing. A good inspection system can serve as that tool.

1. The central thought of the above passage is that a system of inspections within a police department
    A. is unnecessary for a department in which the principal officer can personally supervise all official actions taken
    B. should be instituted at the first indication that there is any deterioration in job performance by the force
    C. should be decentralized and administered by first-line supervisory officers
    D. is an important aid to the police administrator in the accomplishment of law enforcement objectives

1.____

2. The MOST accurate of the following statements concerning the need for an organized inspection system in a law enforcement organization is: It is
    A. never needed in an organization of small size where the principal officer can give personal supervision
    B. most needed where the size of the organization prevents direct supervision by the principal officer
    C. more needed in law enforcement organizations than in private firms
    D. especially needed in an organization about to embark upon a needed expansion of services

2.____

3. According to the above passage, the head of the police organization utilizes the internal inspection system
   A. as a tool which must be constantly re-examined in the light of changing demands for police service
   B. as an administrative technique to increase efficiency and promote economy
   C. by personally visiting those areas of police operation which are outside his sight and hearing
   D. to augment the control of local commanders over detailed field operations

Questions 4-10.

DIRECTIONS: Questions 4 through 10 are to be answered SOLELY on the basis of the following passage.

Job evaluation and job rating systems are intended to introduce scientific procedures. Any type of approach, when properly used, will give satisfactory results. The Point System, when properly validated by actual use, is more likely to be suitable for general use than the ranking system. In many aspects, the Factor Comparison Plan is a point system tied to money values. Of course, there may be another system that combines the ranking system with the point system, especially during the initial stages of the development of the program. After the program has been in use for some time, the tendency is to drop off the ranking phase and continue the use of the point system.

In the ranking system of rating of jobs, every job within the plant is arranged in some order, either from the one with the simplest qualifications to the one with maximum requirements, or in the reverse order. This system should be preceded by careful job analysis and the writing of accurate job descriptions before the rating process is undertaken. It is possible, of course, to take the jobs as they are found in the business enterprise and use the names as they are without any attempt at standardization, and merely rank them according to the general overall impression of the raters. Such a procedure is certain to fall short of what may reasonably be expected of job rating. Another procedure that is in reality merely a modification of the simple rating described above is to establish a series of grades or zones and arrange all he jobs in the plant into groups within these grades and zones. The practice in most common use is to arrange all the jobs in the plant according to their requirements by rating them and then to establish the classification or groups.

The actual ranking of jobs may be done by one individual, several individuals, or a committee. If several individuals are working independently on the task, it will usually be found that, in general, they agree but that their rankings vary in certain details. A conference between the individuals, with each person giving his reasons why he rated one way or another, usually produces agreement. The detailed job descriptions are particularly helpful when there is disagreement among raters as to the rating of certain jobs. It is not only possible but desirable to have workers participate in the construction of the job description and in rating the job.

4. The MAIN theme of this passage is
   A. the elimination of bias in job rating
   B. the rating of jobs by the ranking system
   C. the need or accuracy in allocating points in the point system
   D. pitfalls to avoid in selecting key jobs in the Factor Comparison Plan

5. The ranking system of rating jobs consists MAINLY of
   A. attaching a point value to each ratable factor of each job prior to establishing an equitable pay scale
   B. arranging every job in the organization in descending order and then following this up with a job analysis of the key jobs
   C. preparing accurate job descriptions after a job analysis and then arranging all jobs either in ascending or descending order based on job requirements
   D. arbitrarily establishing a hierarchy of job classes and grades and then fitting each job into a specific class and grade based on the opinions of unit supervisors

6. The above passage states that the system of classifying jobs MOST used in an organization is to
   A. organize all jobs in the organization in accordance with their requirements and then create categories or clusters of jobs
   B. classify all jobs in the organization according to the titles and rank by which they are currently known in the organization
   C. establish a pre-arranged series of grades or zones and then fit all jobs into one of the grades or zones
   D. determine the salary currently being paid for each job and then rank the jobs in order according to salary

7. According to the above passage, experience has shown that when a group of raters is assigned to the job evaluation task and each individual rates independently of the others, the raters GENERALLY
   A. *agree* with respect to all aspects of their rankings
   B. *disagree* with respect to all or nearly all aspects of the rankings
   C. *disagree* on overall ratings, but agree on specific rating factors
   D. *agree* on overall rankings, but have some variance in some details

8. The above passage states that the use of a detailed job description is of special value when
   A. employees of an organization have participated in the preliminary step involved in actual preparation of the job description
   B. labor representatives are not participating in ranking of the jobs
   C. an individual rater who is unsure of himself is ranking the jobs
   D. a group of raters is having difficulty reaching unanimity with respect to ranking a certain job

9. A comparison of the various rating systems as described in the above passage shows that
   A. the ranking system is not as appropriate for general use as a properly validated point system
   B. the point system is the same as the Factor Comparison Plan except that it places greater emphasis on money

C. no system is capable of combining the point system and the Factor Comparison Plan
D. the point system will be discontinued last when used in combination with the Factor comparison System

10. The above passage implies that the PRINCIPAL reason for creating job evaluation and rating systems was to help
    A. overcome union opposition to existing salary plans
    B. base wage determination on a more objective and orderly foundation
    C. eliminate personal bias on the part of the trained scientific job evaluators
    D. management determine if it was overpricing the various jobs in the organizational hierarchy

10.____

Questions 11-13.

DIRECTIONS: Questions 11 through 13 are to be answered SOLELY on the basis of the following passage.

The common sense character of the merit system seems so natural to most Americans that many people wonder why it should ever have been inoperative. After all, the American economic system, the most phenomenal the world has ever known, is also founded on a rugged selective process which emphasizes the personal qualities of capacity, industriousness, and productivity. The criteria may not have always been appropriate and competition has not always been fair, but competition there was, and the responsibilities and the rewards—with exceptions, of course—have gone to those who could measure up in terms of intelligence, knowledge, or perseverance. This has been true not only in the economic area, in the money-making process, but also in achievement in the professions and other walks of life.

11. According to the above passage, economic rewards in the United State have
    A. always been based on appropriate, fair criteria
    B. only recently been based on a competitive system
    C. not going to people who compete too ruggedly
    D. usually gone to those people with intelligence, knowledge, and perseverance

11.____

12. According to the above passage, a merit system is
    A. an unfair criterion on which to base rewards
    B. unnatural to anyone who is not American
    C. based only on common sense
    D. based on the same principles as the American economic system

12.____

13. According to the above passage, it is MOST accurate to say that
    A. the United States has always had a civil service merit system
    B. civil service employees are very rugged
    C. the American economic system has always been based on a merit objective
    D. competition is unique to the American way of life

13.____

Questions 14-15.

DIRECTIONS: Questions 14 and 15 are to be answered SOLELY on the basis of the following passage.

In-basket tests are often used to assess managerial potential. The exercise consists of a set of papers that would be likely to be found in the in-basket of an administrator or manager at any given time, and requires the individuals participating in the examination to indicate how they would dispose of each item found in the in-basket. In order to handle the in-basket effectively, they must successfully manage their time, refer and assign some work to subordinates, juggle potentially conflicting appointments and meetings, and arrange for follow-up of problems generated by the items in the in-basket. In other words, the in-basket test is attempting to evaluate the participants' abilities to organize their work, set priorities, delegate, control, and make decisions.

14. According to the above passage, to succeed in an in-basket test, an administrator must
    A. be able to read very quickly
    B. have a great deal of technical knowledge
    C. know when to delegate work
    D. arrange a lot of appointments and meetings

    14.____

15. According to the above passage, all of the following abilities are indications of managerial potential EXCEPT the ability to
    A. organize and control
    B. manage time
    C. write effective reports
    D. make appropriate decisions

    15.____

Questions 16-19.

DIRECTIONS: Questions 16 through 19 are to be answered SOLELY on the basis of the following passage.

A personnel researcher has at his disposal various approaches for obtaining information, analyzing it, and arriving at conclusions that have value in predicting and affecting the behavior of people at work. The type of method to be used depends on such factors as the nature of the research problem, the available data, and the attitudes of those people being studied to the various kinds of approaches. While the experimental approach, with its use of control groups, is the most refined type of study, there are others that are often found useful in personnel research. Surveys, in which the researcher obtains facts on a problem from a variety of sources, are employed in research on wages, fringe benefits, and labor relations. Historical studies are used to trace the development of problems in order to understand them better and to isolate possible causative factors. Case studies are generally developed to explore all the details of a particular problem that is representative of other similar problems. A researcher chooses the most appropriate form of study for the problem he is investigating. He should recognize, however, that the experimental method, commonly referred to as the scientific method, if used validly and reliably, gives the most conclusive results.

16. The above passage discusses several approaches used to obtain information on particular problems.
Which of the following may be MOST reasonably concluded from the passage?
A(n)
   A. historical study cannot determine causative factors
   B. survey is often used in research on fringe benefits
   C. case study is usually used to explore a problem that is unique and unrelated to other problems
   D. experimental study is used when the scientific approach to a problem fails

16.____

17. According to the above passage, all of the following are factors that may determine the type of approach a researcher uses EXCEPT
   A. the attitudes of people toward being used in control groups
   B. the number of available sources
   C. his desire to isolate possible causative factors
   D. the degree of accuracy he requires

17.____

18. The words *scientific method*, as used in the last sentence of the above passage, refer to a type of study which, according to the above passage
   A. uses a variety of sources
   B. traces the development of problems
   C. uses control groups
   D. analyzes the details of a representative problem

18.____

19. Which of the following can be MOST reasonably concluded from the above passage?
In obtaining and analyzing information on a particular problem, a researcher employs the method which is the
   A. most accurate   B. most suitable
   C. least expensive   D. least time-consuming

19.____

Questions 20-25.

DIRECTIONS: Questions 20 through 25 are to be answered SOLELY on the basis of the following passage.

   The quality of the voice of a worker is an important factor in conveying to clients and co-workers his attitude and, to some degree, his character. The human voice, when not consciously disguised, may reflect a person's mood, temper, and personality. It has been shown in several experiments that certain character traits can be assessed with better than chance accuracy through listening to the voice of an unknown person who cannot be seen.
   Since one of the objectives of the worker is to put clients at ease and to present an encouraging and comfortable atmosphere, a harsh, shrill, or loud voice could have a negative effect. A client who displays emotions of anger or resentment would probably be provoked even further by a caustic tone. In a face-to-face situation, an unpleasant voice may be compensated for, to some degree, by a concerned and kind facial expression. However, when one speaks on the telephone, the expression on one's face cannot be seen by the listener. A supervising clerk who wishes to represent himself effectively to clients should try to eliminate as many faults as possible in striving to develop desirable voice qualities.

20. If a worker uses a sarcastic tone while interviewing a resentful client, the client, according to the above passage, would MOST likely
    A. avoid the face-to-face problem
    B. be ashamed of his behavior
    C. become more resentful
    D. be provoked to violence

20.____

21. According to the passage, experiments comparing voice and character traits have demonstrated that
    A. prospects for improving an unpleasant voice through training are better than chance
    B. the voice can be altered to project many different psychological characteristics
    C. the quality of the human voice reveals more about the speaker than his words do
    D. the speaker's voice tells the hearer something about the speaker's personality

21.____

22. Which of the following, according to the above passage, is a person's voice MOST likely to reveal?
    His
    A. prejudices
    B. intelligence
    C. social awareness
    D. temperament

22.____

23. It may be MOST reasonably concluded from the above passage that an interested and sympathetic expression on the face of a worker
    A. may induce a client to feel certain he will receive welfare benefits
    B. will eliminate the need for pleasant vocal qualities in the interviewer
    C. may help to make up for an unpleasant voice in the interviewer
    D. is desirable as the interviewer speaks on the telephone to a client

23.____

24. Of the following, the MOST reasonable implication of the above paragraph is that a worker should, when speaking to a client, control and use his voice to
    A. simulate a feeling of interest in the problems of the client
    B. express his emotions directly and adequately
    C. help produce in the client a sense of comfort and security
    D. reflect his own true personality

24.____

25. It may be concluded from the above passage that the PARTICULAR reason for a worker to pay special attention to modulating her voice when talking on the phone to a client is that, during a telephone conversation
    A. there is a necessity to compensate for the way in which a telephone distorts the voice
    B. the voice of the worker is a reflection of her mood and character
    C. the client can react only on the basis of the voice and words she hears
    D. the client may have difficulty getting a clear understanding over the telephone

25.____

KEY (CORRECT ANSWERS)

1.	D	11.	D
2.	B	12.	D
3.	B	13.	C
4.	B	14.	C
5.	C	15.	C
6.	A	16.	B
7.	D	17.	D
8.	D	18.	C
9.	A	19.	B
10.	B	20.	C

21.	D
22.	D
23.	C
24.	C
25.	C

TEST 2

DIRECTIONS: Each question or incomplete statement is followed by several suggested answers or completions. Select the one that BEST answers the question or completes the statement. *PRINT THE LETTER OF THE CORRECT ANSWER IN THE SPACE AT THE RIGHT.*

Questions 1-3.

DIRECTIONS: Questions 1 through 3 are to be answered SOLELY on the basis of the following paragraph.

Suppose you are given the job of printing, collating, and stapling 8,000 copies of a ten-page booklet as soon as possible. You have available one photo-offset machine, a collator with an automatic stapler, and the personnel to operate these machines. All will be available for however long the job takes to complete. The photo-offset machine prints 5,000 impressions an hour, and it takes about 15 minutes to set up a plate. The collator, including time for insertion of pages and stapling, can process about 2,000 booklets an hour. (Answers should be based on the assumption that there are no breakdowns or delays.)

1. Assuming that all the printing is finished before the collating is started, if the job is given to you late Monday and your section can begin work the next day and is able to devote seven hours a day, Monday through Friday, to the job until it is finished, what is the BEST estimate of when the job will be finished?
    A. Wednesday afternoon of the same week
    B. Thursday morning of the same week
    C. Friday morning of the same week
    D. Monday morning of the next week

1.____

2. An operator suggests to you that instead of completing all the printing and then beginning collating and stapling, you first print all the pages for 4,000 booklets, so that they can be collated and stapled while the last 4,000 pages are being printed.
   If you accepted this suggestion, the job would be completed
    A. sooner but would require more man-hours
    B at the same time using either method
    C. later and would require more man-hours
    D. sooner but there would be more wear and tear on the plates

2.____

3. Assume that you have the same assignment and equipment as described above, but 16,000 copies of the booklet are needed instead of 8,000.
   If you decided to print 8,000 complete booklets, then collate and staple them while you started printing the next 8,000 booklets, which of the following statements would MOST accurately describe the relationship between this new method and your original method of printing all the booklets at one time, and then collating and stapling them? The
    A. job would be completed at the same time regardless of the method used
    B. new method would result in the job's being completed 3½ hours earlier
    C. original method would result in the job's being completed an hour later
    D. new method would result in the job's being completed 1½ hours earlier

3.____

Questions 4-6.

DIRECTIONS: Questions 4 through 6 are to be answered SOLELY on the basis of the following passage.

When using words like company, association, council, committee, and board in place of the full official name, the writer should not capitalize these short forms unless he intends them to invoke the full force of the institution's authority. In legal contracts, in minutes, or in formal correspondence where one is speaking formally and officially on behalf of the company, the term Company is usually capitalized, but in ordinary usage, where it is not essential to load the short form with this significance, capitalization would be excessive. (Example: The company will have many good openings for graduates this June.)

The treatment recommended for short forms of place names is essentially the same as that recommended for short forms of organizational names. In general, we capitalize the full form but not the short form. If Park Avenue is referred to in one sentence, then the *avenue* is sufficient in subsequent references. The same is true with words like building, hotel, station, and airport, which are capitalized when part of a proper name changed (Pan Am Building, Hotel Plaza, Union Station, O'Hare Airport), but are simply lower-cased when replacing these specific names.

4. The above passage states that USUALLY the short forms of names of organizations
    A. and places should not be capitalized
    B. and places should be capitalized
    C. should not be capitalized, but the short forms of names of places should be capitalized
    D. should be capitalized, but the short forms of names of places should not be capitalized

5. The above passage states that in legal contracts, in minutes, and in formal correspondence, the short forms of names of organizations should
    A. usually not be capitalized   B. usually be capitalized
    C. usually not be used   D. never be used

6. It can be inferred from the above passage that decisions regarding when to capitalize certain words
    A. should be left to the discretion of the writer
    B. should be based on generally accepted rules
    C. depend on the total number of words capitalized
    D. are of minor importance

Questions 7-10.

DIRECTIONS: Questions 7 through 10 are to be answered SOLELY on the basis of the following passage.

Use of the systems and procedures approach to office management is revolutionizing the supervision of office work. This approach views an enterprise as an entity which seeks to fulfill definite objectives. Systems and procedures help to organize repetitive work into a routine, thus reducing the amount of decision making required for its accomplishment. As a result, employees are guided in their efforts and perform only necessary work. Supervisors are relieved of any details of execution and are free to attend to more important work. Establishing work guides which require that identical tasks be performed the same way each time permits standardization of forms, machine operations, work methods, and controls. This approach also reduces the probability of errors. Any error committed is usually discovered quickly because the incorrect work does not meet the requirement of the work guides. Errors are also reduced through work specialization, which allows each employee to become thoroughly proficient in a particular type of work. Such proficiency also tends to improve the morale of the employees.

7. The above passage states that the accuracy of an employee's work is INCREASED by
   A. using the work specialization approach
   B. employing a probability sample
   C. requiring him to shift at one time into different types of tasks
   D. having his supervisor check each detail of work execution

8. Of the following, which one BEST expresses the main theme of the above passage? The
   A. advantages and disadvantages of the systems and procedures approach to office management
   B. effectiveness of the systems and procedures approach to office management in developing skills
   C. systems and procedures approach to office management as it relates to office costs
   D. advantages of the systems and procedures approach to office management for supervisors and office workers

9. Work guides are LEAST likely to be used when
   A. standardized forms are used
   B. a particular office task is distinct and different from all others
   C. identical tasks are to be performed in identical ways
   D. similar work methods are expected from each employee

10. According to the above passage, when an employee makes a work error, it USUALLY
    A. is quickly corrected by the supervisor
    B. necessitates a change in the work guides
    C. can be detected quickly if work guides are in use
    D. increases the probability of further errors by that employee

Questions 11-12.

DIRECTIONS: Questions 11 and 12 are to be answered SOLELY on the basis of the following passage.

The coordination of the many activities of a large public agency is absolutely essential. Coordination, as an administrative principle, must be distinguished from and is independent of cooperation. Coordination can be of either the horizontal or the vertical type. In large organizations, the objectives of vertical coordination are achieved by the transmission of orders and statements of policy down through the various levels of authority. It is an accepted generalization that the more authoritarian the organization, the more easily may vertical coordination be accomplished. Horizontal coordination is arrived through staff work, administrative management, and conferences of administrators of equal rank. It is obvious that of the two types of coordination, the vertical kind is more important, for at best horizontal coordination only supplements the coordination effected up and down the line,

11. According to the above passage, the ease with which vertical coordination is achieved in a large agency depends upon
    A. the extent to which control is firmly exercised from above
    B. the objectives that have been established for the agency
    C. the importance attached by employees to the orders and statements of policy transmitted through the agency
    D. the cooperation obtained at the various levels of authority

11.____

12. According to the above passage,
    A. vertical coordination is dependent for its success upon horizontal coordination
    B. one type of coordination may work in opposition to the other
    C. similar methods may be used to achieve both types of coordination
    D. horizontal coordination is at most an addition to vertical coordination

12.____

Questions 13-17.

DIRECTIONS: Questions 13 through 17 are to be answered SOLELY on the basis of the following situation.

Assume that you are a newly appointed supervisor in the same unit in which you have been acting as a provisional for some time. You have in your unit the following workers:

WORKER I: He has always been an efficient worker. In a number of his cases, the clients have recently begun to complain that they cannot manage on the departmental budget.

WORKER II: He has been under selective supervision for some time as an experienced, competent worker. He now begins to be late for his supervisory conferences and to stress how much work he has to do.

WORKER III: He has been making considerable improvement in his ability to handle the details of his job. He now tells you, during an individual conference, that he does not need such close supervision and that he wants to operate more independently. He says that Worker II is always available when he needs a little information or help but, in general, he can manage very well by himself.

5 (#2)

WORKER IV: He brings you a complex case for decision as to eligibility. Discussion of the case brings out the fact that he has failed to consider all the available resources adequately but has stressed the family's needs to include every extra item in the budget. This is the third case of a similar nature that his worker has brought to you recently. This worker and Worker I work in adjacent territory and are rather friendly.

In the following questions, select the option that describes the method of dealing with these workers that illustrate BEST supervisory practice.

13. With respect to supervision of Worker I, the assistant supervisor should   13._____
    A. discuss with the worker, in an individual conference, any problems that he may be having due to the increase in the cost of living
    B. plan a group conference for the unit around budgeting, as both Workers I and IV seem to be having budgetary difficulties
    C. discuss with Workers I and IV together the meaning of money as acceptance or rejection to the clients
    D. discuss with Worker I the budgetary data in each case in relation to each client's situation

14. With respect to supervision of Worker II, the supervisory should   14._____
    A. move slowly with this worker and give him time to learn that the supervisor's official appointment has not changed his attitudes or methods of supervision
    B. discuss the worker's change of attitude and asks him to analyze the reasons for his change in behavior
    C. take time to show the worker how he is avoiding his responsibility in the supervisor-worker relationship and that he is resisting supervision
    D. hold an evaluatory conference with the worker and show him how he is taking over responsibilities that are not his by providing supervision for Worker III

15. With respect to supervision of Worker III, the supervisor should discuss with   15._____
    this worker
    A. why he would rather have supervision from Worker II than from the supervisor
    B. the necessity for further improvement before he can go on selective supervision
    C. an analysis of the improvement that has been made and the extent to which the worker is able to handle the total job for which he is responsible
    D. the responsibility of the supervisor to see that clients receive adequate service

16. With respect to supervision of Worker IV, the supervisor should   16._____
    A. show the worker that resources figures are incomplete but that even if they were complete, the family would probably be eligible for assistance
    B. ask the worker why he is so protective of these families since there are three cases so similar

C. discuss with the worker all three cases at the same time so that the worker may see his own role in the three situations
D. discuss with the worker the reasons for departmental policies and procedures around budgeting

17. With respect to supervision of Workers I and IV, since these two workers are friends and would seem to be influencing each other, the supervisor should

    A. hold a joint conference with them both, pointing out how they should clear with the supervisor and not make their own rules together
    B. handle the problems of each separately in individual conferences
    C. separate them by transferring one to another territory or another unit
    D. take up the problem of workers asking help of each other rather than from the supervisor in a group meeting

17.____

Questions 18-20.

DIRECTIONS: Questions 18 through 20 are to be answered SOLELY on the basis of the following passage.

One of the key supervisory problems in a large municipal recreation department is that many leaders are assigned to isolated playgrounds or small centers, where it is difficult to observe their work regularly. Often their facilities are extremely limited. In such settings, as well as in larger recreation centers, where many recreation leaders tend to have other jobs as well, there tends to be a low level of morale and incentive. Still, it is the supervisor's task to help recreation personnel to develop pride in their work and to maintain a high level of performance. With isolated leaders, the supervisor may give advice or assistance. Leaders may be assigned to different tasks or settings during the year to maximize their productivity and provide new challenges. When it is clear that leaders are no willing to make a real effort to contribute to the department, the possibility of penalties must be considered, within the scope of departmental policy and the union contract. However, the supervisor should be constructive, encourage and assist workers to take a greater interest in their work, be innovative, and try to raise morale and to improve performance in positive ways.

18. The one of the following that would the MOST appropriate title for the above passage is

    A. Small Community Centers – Pro and Con
    B. Planning Better Recreation Programs
    C. The Supervisor's Task in Upgrading Personnel Performance
    D. The Supervisor and the Municipal Union – Rights and Obligations

18.____

19. The above passage makes clear that recreation leadership performance in all recreation playgrounds and centers throughout a large city is

    A. generally above average, with good morale on the part of most recreation leaders
    B. beyond description since no one has ever observed or evaluated recreation leaders

19.____

C. a key test of the personnel department's effort to develop more effective hiring standards
D. of mixed quality, with many recreation leaders having poor morale and a low level of achievement

20. According to the above passage, the supervisor's role is to 20.____
    A. use disciplinary action as his major tool in upgrading performance
    B. tolerate the lack of effort of individual employees since they are assigned to isolated playgrounds or small centers
    C. employ encouragement, advice, and, when appropriate, disciplinary action to improve performance
    D. inform the county supervisor whenever malfeasance or idleness is detected

Questions 21-25.

DIRECTIONS: Questions 21 through 25 are to be answered SOLELY on the basis of the following passage.

EMPLOYEE LEAVE REGULATIONS

Peter Smith, as a full-time permanent city employee under the Career and Salary Plan, earns an *annual leave allowance*. This consists of a certain number of days off a year with pay and may be used for vacation, personal business, and for observing religious holidays. As a newly appointed employee, during his first 8 years of city service, he will earn an annual leave allowance of 20 days off a year (an average of $1^2/_3$ days off a month). After he has finished 8 full years of working for the city, he will begin earning an additional 5 days off a year. His annual leave allowance, therefore, will then be 25 days a year and will remain at this amount for seven full years. He will begin earning an additional two days off a year at this amount for seven full years. He will begin earning an additional two days off a year after he has completed a total of 15 years of city employment. Therefore, in his sixteenth year of working for the city, Mr. Smith will be earning 27 days off a year as his annual leave allowance (an average of $2^1/_4$ days off a month).

A *sick leave allowance* of one day a month is also given to Mr. Smith, but it can be used only in cases of actual illness. When Mr. Smith returns to work after using sick leave allowance, he must have a doctor's note if the absence is for a total of more than 3 days, but he may also be required to show a doctor's note for absences of 1, 2, or 3 days.

21. According to the above passage, Mr. Smith's annual leave allowance consists 21.____
    of a certain number of days off a year which he
    A. does not get paid for
    B. gets paid for at time and a half
    C. may use for personal business
    D. may not use for observing religious holidays

22. According to the above passage, after Mr. Smith has been working for the city 22.____
    for 9 years, his annual leave allowance will be _____ days a year.
    A. 20   B. 25   C. 27   D. 37

23. According to the above passage, Mr. Smith will begin earning an average of 2 days off a month as his annual leave allowance after he has worked for the city for _____ full years.
    A. 7   B. 8   C. 15   D. 17

24. According to the above passage, Mr. Smith is given a sick leave allowance of
    A. 1 day every 2 months
    B. 1 day per month
    C. $1^{2}/_{3}$ days per month
    D. 2¼ days a month

25. According to the above passage, when he uses sick leave allowance, Mr. Smith may be required to show a doctor's note
    A. even if his absence is for only 1 day
    B. only if his absence is for more than 2 days
    C. only if his absence is for more than 3 days
    D. only if his absence is for 3 days or more

KEY (CORRECT ANSWERS)

1. C
2. C
3. D
4. A
5. B

6. B
7. A
8. D
9. B
10. C

11. A
12. D
13. D
14. A
15. C

16. C
17. B
18. C
19. D
20. C

21. C
22. B
23. C
24. B
25. A

TEST 3

DIRECTIONS: Each question or incomplete statement is followed by several suggested answers or completions. Select the one that BEST answers the question or completes the statement. *PRINT THE LETTER OF THE CORRECT ANSWER IN THE SPACE AT THE RIGHT.*

Questions 1-6.

DIRECTIONS: Questions 1 through 6 are to be answered SOLELY on the basis of the following passage.

    A folder is made of a sheet of heavy paper (manila, kraft, pressboard, or red rope stock) that has been folded once so that the back is about one-half inch higher than the front. Folders are larger than the papers they contain in order to protect them. Two standard folder sizes are *letter size* for papers that are 8½" x 11" and *legal cap* for papers that are 8½" x 13".
    Folders are cut across the top in two ways: so that the back is straight (straight-cut) or so that the back has a tab that projects above the top of the folder. Such tabs bear captions that identify the contents of each folder. Tabs vary in width and position. The tabs of a set of folders that are *one-half cut* are half the width of the folder and have only two positions.
    One-third cut folders have three positions, each tab occupying a third of the width of the folder. Another standard tabbing is *one-fifth cut*, which has five positions. There are also folders with *two-fifths cut*, with the tabs in the third and fourth or fourth and fifth positions.

1. Of the following, the BEST title for the above passage is   1.____
   A. Filing Folders   B. Standard Folder Sizes
   C. The Uses of the Folder   D. The Use of Tabs

2. According to the above passage, one of the standard folder sizes is called   2.____
   A. Kraft cut   B. legal cap
   C. one-half cut   D. straight-cut

3. According to the above passage, tabs are GENERALLY placed along the ____ of the folder.   3.____
   A. back   B. front   C. left side   D. right side

4. According to the above passage, a tab is GENERALLY used to   4.____
   A. distinguish between standard folder sizes
   B. identify the contents of a folder
   C. increase the size of the folder
   D. protect the papers within the folder

5. According to the above passage, a folder that is two-fifths cut has ____ tabs.   5.____
   A. no   B. two   C. three   D. five

6. According to the above passage, one reason for making folders larger than the papers they contain is that
    A. only a certain size folder can be made from heavy paper
    B. they will protect the papers
    C. they will aid in setting up a tab system
    D. the back of the folder must be higher than the front

Questions 7-15.

DIRECTIONS: Questions 7 through 15 are to be answered SOLELY on the basis of the following passage.

The City University of New York traces its origins to 1847, when the Free Academy, which later became City College, was founded as the first tuition-free municipal college. City and Hunter Colleges were placed under the direction of the Board of Higher Education in 1926, and Brooklyn and Queens Colleges were subsequently added to the system of municipal colleges. In 1955, Staten Island Community College, the first of the two-year colleges sponsored by the Board of Higher Education under the program of the State University of New York, joined the system.

In 1961, the four senior colleges and three community colleges then under the jurisdiction of the Board of Higher Education became the City University of New York, and a University Graduate Division was organized to offer programs leading to the Ph.D. Since then, the university has undergone even more rapid growth. Today, it consists of nine senior colleges, an upper division college which admits students at the junior level, eight community colleges, a graduate division, and an affiliated medical center.

In the summer of 1969, the Board of Higher Education resolved that the time had come to commit the resources of the university to meeting an urgent social need—unrestricted access to higher education for all youths of the City. Determined to prevent the waste of human potential represented by the thousands of high school graduates whose limited educational opportunities left them unable to meet existing admission standards, the Board moved to adopt a policy of Open Admissions. It was their judgment that the best way of determining whether a potential student can benefit from college work is to admit him to college, provide him with the learning assistance he needs, and then evaluate his performance.

Beginning with the class of June 1970, every New York City resident who received a high school diploma from a public or private high school was guaranteed a place in one of the colleges of City University.

7. Of the following, the BEST title for the above passage is
    A. A Brief History of the City University
    B. High Schools and the City University
    C. The Components of the University
    D. Tuition-free Colleges

8. According to the above passage, which one of the following colleges of the City University was ORIGINALLY called the Free Academy?
    A. Brooklyn College   B. City College
    C. Hunter College   D. Queens College

9. According to the above passage, the system of municipal colleges became the City University of New York in
   A. 1926   B. 1955   C. 1961   D. 1969

9.____

10. According to the above passage, Staten Island Community College came under the jurisdiction of the Board of Higher Education
    A. 6 years after a Graduate Division was organized
    B. 8 years before the adoption of the Open Admissions Policy
    C. 29 years after Brooklyn and Queens Colleges
    D. 29 years after City and Hunter Colleges

10.____

11. According to the above passage, the Staten Island Community College is
    A. a graduate division center   B. a senior college
    C. a two-year college   D. an upper division college

11.____

12. According to the above passage, the TOTAL number of colleges, divisions, and affiliated branches of the City University is
    A. 18   B. 19   C. 20   D. 21

12.____

13. According to the above passage, the Open Admissions Policy is designed to determine whether a potential student will benefit from college by PRIMARILY
    A. discouraging competition for placement in the City University among high school students
    B. evaluating his performance after entry into college
    C. lowering admission standards
    D. providing learning assistance before entry into college

13.____

14. According to the above passage, the FIRST class to be affected by the Open Admissions Policy was the
    A. high school class which graduated in January 1970
    B. City University class which graduated in June 1970
    C. high school class when graduated in June 1970
    D. City University class when graduated in June 1970

14.____

15. According to the above passage, one of the reasons that the Board of Higher Education initiated the policy of Open Admission was to
    A. enable high school graduates with a background of limited educational opportunities to enter college
    B. expand the growth of the City University so as to increase the number and variety of degrees offered
    C. provide a social resource to the qualified youth of the City
    D. revise admission standards to meet the needs of the City

15.____

Questions 16-18.

DIRECTIONS: Questions 16 through 18 are to be answered SOLELY on the basis of the following passage.

Hereafter, all probationary students interested in transferring to community college career programs (associate degrees) from liberal arts programs in senior colleges (bachelor degrees) will be eligible for such transfers if they have completed no more than three semesters.
For students with averages 1.5 or above, transfer will be automatic. Those with 1.0 to 1.5 averages can transfer provisionally and will be required to make substantial progress during the first semester in the career program. Once transfer has taken place, only those courses in which passing grades were received will be computed in the community college grade-point average.
No request for transfer will be accepted from probationary students wishing to enter the liberal arts programs at the community college.

16. According to the above passage, the one of the following which is the BEST statement concerning the transfer of probationary students is that a probationary student
    A. may transfer to a career program at the end of one semester
    B. must complete three semester hours before he is eligible for transfer
    C. is not eligible to transfer to a career program
    D. is eligible to transfer to a liberal arts program

17. Which of the following is the BEST statement of academic evaluation for transfer purposes in the case of probationary students?
    A. No probationary student with an average under 1.5 may transfer.
    B. A probationary student with an average of 1.3 may not transfer.
    C. A probationary student with an average of 1.6 may transfer.
    D. A probationary student with an average of .8 may transfer on a provisional basis.

18. It is MOST likely that, of the following, the next degree sought by one who already holds the Associate in Science degree would be a(n) _____ degree.
    A. Assistantship in Science
    B. Associate in Applied Science
    C. Bachelor of Science
    D. Doctor of Philosophy

Questions 19-20.

DIRECTIONS: Questions 19 and 20 are to be answered SOLELY on the basis of the following passage.

Auto: Auto travel requires prior approval by the President and/or appropriate Dean and must be indicated in the *Request for Travel Authorization* form. Employees authorized to use personal autos on official College business will be reimbursed at the rate of 28¢ per mile for the first 500 miles driven and 18¢ per mile for mileage driven in excess of 500 mile. The Comptroller's Office may limit the amount of reimbursement to the expenditure that would have been made if a less expensive mode of transportation (railroad, airplane, bus, etc.) had been utilized. If this occurs, the traveler will have to pick up the excess expenditure as a personal expense.

Tolls, Parking Fees, and Parking Meter Fees are not reimbursable and many not be claimed.

19. Suppose that Professor T gives the office assistant the following memorandum: Used car for official trip to Albany, New York, and return. Distance from New York to Albany is 148 miles. Tolls were $3.50 each way. Parking garage cost $3.00. When preparing the Travel Expense Voucher for Professor T, the figure which should be claimed for transportation is
    A. $120.88   B. $113.88   C. $82.88   D. $51.44

    19.____

20. Suppose that Professor V gives the office assistant the following memorandum: Used car for official trip to Pittsburgh, Pennsylvania, and return. Distance from New York to Pittsburgh is 350 miles. Tolls were $3.30, $11.40 going, and $3.30, $2.00 returning.
    When preparing the Travel Expense Voucher for Professor V, the figure which should be claimed for transportation is
    A. $225.40   B. $176.00   C. $127.40   D. $98.00

    20.____

Questions 21-25.

DIRECTIONS: Questions 21 through 25 are to be answered SOLELY on the basis of the following passage.

For a period of nearly fifteen years, beginning in the mid-1950's, higher education sustained a phenomenal rate of growth. The factor principally responsible were continuing improvement in the rate of college entrance by high school graduates, a 50 percent increase in the size of the college-age (eighteen to twenty-one) group and—until about 1967—a rapid expansion of university research activity supported by the Federal government.

Today, as one looks ahead to the year 2010, it is apparent that each of these favorable stimuli will either be abated or turn into a negative factor. The rate of growth of the college-age group has already diminished; and from 2000 to 2005, the size of the college-age group has shrunk annually almost as fast as it grew from 1965 to 1970. From 2005 to 2010, this annual decrease will slow down so that by 2010 the age group will be about the same size as it was in 2009. This substantial net decrease in the size of the college-age group (from 1995 to 2010) will dramatically affect college enrollments since, currently, 83 percent of undergraduates are twenty-one and under, and another 11 percent are twenty-to to twenty-four.

21. Which one of the following factors is NOT mentioned in the above passage as contributing to the high rate of growth of higher education?
    A. A large increase in the size of the eighteen to twenty-one age group
    B. The equalization of educational opportunities among socio-economic groups
    C. The Federal budget impact on research and development spending in the higher education sector
    D. The increasing rate at which high school graduates enter college

    21.____

22. Based on the information in the above passage, the size of the college-age group in 2010 will be
    A. larger than it was in 2009
    B. larger than it was in 1995
    C. smaller than it was in 2005
    D. about the same as it was in 2000

23. According to the above passage, the tremendous rate of growth of higher education started around
    A. 1950
    B. 1955
    C. 1960
    D. 1965

24. The percentage of undergraduates who are over age 24 is MOST NEARLY
    A. 6%
    B. 8%
    C. 11%
    D. 17%

25. Which one of the following conclusions can be substantiated by the information given in the above passage?
    A. The college-age group was about the same size in 2000 as it was in 1965.
    B. The annual decrease in the size of the college-age group from 2000 to 2005 is about the same as the annual increase from 1965 to 1970.
    C. The overall decrease in the size of the college-age group from 2000 to 2005 will be followed by an overall increase in its size from 2005 to 2010.
    D. The size of the college-age group is decreasing at a fairly constant rate from 1995 to 2010.

KEY (CORRECT ANSWERS)

1.	A	11.	C
2.	B	12.	C
3.	A	13.	B
4.	B	14.	C
5.	B	15.	A
6.	B	16.	A
7.	A	17.	C
8.	B	18.	C
9.	C	19.	C
10.	D	20.	B

21.	B
22.	C
23.	B
24.	A
25.	B

READING COMPREHENSION
UNDERSTANDING AND INTERPRETING WRITTEN MATERIAL

EXAMINATION SECTION

TEST 1

DIRECTIONS: Each question or incomplete statement is followed by several suggested answers or completions. Select the one that BEST answers the question or completes the statement. *PRINT THE LETTER OF THE CORRECT ANSWER IN THE SPACE AT THE RIGHT.*

Questions 1-5.

DIRECTIONS: Questions 1 through 5 are to be answered SOLELY on the basis of the following passage.

The most effective control mechanism to prevent gross incompetence on the part of public employees is a good personnel program. The personnel officer in the line departments and the central personnel agency should exert positive leadership to raise levels of performance. Although the key factor is the quality of the personnel recruited, staff members other than personnel officers can make important contributions to efficiency. Administrative analysts, now employed in many agencies, make detailed studies of organization and procedures, with the purpose of eliminating delays, waste, and other inefficiencies. Efficiency is, however, more than a question of good organization and procedures; it is also the product of the attitudes and value of the public employees. Personal motivation can provide the will to be efficient. The best management studies will not result in substantial improvement of the performance of those employees who feel no great urge to wok up to their abilities.

1. The above passage indicates that the KEY factor in preventing gross incompetence of public employees is the
   A. hiring of administrative analysts to assist personnel people
   B. utilization of effective management studies
   C. overlapping of responsibility
   D. quality of the employees hired

1.____

2. According to the above passage, the central personnel agency staff SHOULD
   A. work more closely with administrative analysts in the line departments than with personnel officers
   B. make a serious effort to avoid jurisdictional conflicts with personnel officers in line departments
   C. contribute to improving the quality of work of public employees
   D. engage in a comprehensive program to change the public's negative image of public employees

2.____

3. The above passage indicates that efficiency in an organization can BEST be brought about by
   A. eliminating ineffective control mechanisms
   B. instituting sound organizational procedures
   C. promoting competent personnel
   D. recruiting people with desire to do good work

3.____

4. According to the above passage, the purpose of administrative analysts in a public agency is to
   A. prevent injustice to the public employee
   B. promote the efficiency of the agency
   C. protect the interests of the public
   D. ensure the observance of procedural due process

4.____

5. The above passage implies that a considerable rise in the quality of work of public employees can be brought about by
   A. encouraging positive employee attitudes toward work
   B. controlling personnel officers who exceed their powers
   C. creating warm personal associations among public employees in an agency
   D. closing loopholes in personnel organization and procedures

5.____

Questions 6-8.

DIRECTIONS: Questions 6 through 8 are to be answered SOLELY on the basis of the following passage.

EMPLOYEE NEEDS

The greatest waste in industry and in government may be that of human resources. This waste usually derives not from employees' unwillingness or inability, but from management's ineptness to meet the maintenance and motivational needs of employees. Maintenance needs refer to such needs as providing employees with safe places to work, written work rules, job security, adequate salary, employer-sponsored social activities, and with knowledge of their role in the overall framework of the organization. However, of greatest significance to employees are the motivational needs of job growth, achievement, responsibility, and recognition.

Although employee dissatisfaction may stem from either poor maintenance or poor motivation factors, the outward manifestation of the dissatisfaction may be very much like, i.e., negativism, complaints, deterioration of performance, and so forth. The improvement in the lighting of an employee's work area or raising his level of ay won't do much good if the source of the dissatisfaction is the absence of a meaningful assignment. By the same token, if an employee is dissatisfied with what he considers inequitable pay, the introduction of additional challenge in his work may simply make matters worse.

It is relatively easy for an employee to express frustration by complaining about pay, washroom conditions, fringe benefits, and so forth; but most people cannot easily express resentment in terms of the more abstract concepts concerning job growth, responsibility, and achievement.

It would be wrong to assume that there is no interaction between maintenance and motivational needs of employee. For example, conditions of high motivation often overshadow poor maintenance conditions. If an organization is in a period of strong growth and expansion, opportunities for job growth, responsibility, recognition, and achievement are usually abundant, but the rapid growth may have outrun the upkeep of maintenance factors. In this situation, motivation may be high, but only if employees recognize the poor maintenance conditions as unavoidable and temporary. The subordination of maintenance factors cannot go on indefinitely, even with the highest motivation.

Both maintenance and motivation factors influence the behavior of all employees, but employees are not identical and, furthermore, the needs of any individual do not remain orientation toward maintenance factors and those with greater sensitivity toward motivation factors.

A highly maintenance-oriented individual, preoccupied with the factors peripheral to his job rather than the job itself, is more concerned with comfort than challenge. He does not get deeply involved with his work but does with the condition of his work area, toilet facilities, and his time for going to lunch. By contrast, a strongly motivation-oriented employee is usually relatively indifferent to his surroundings and is caught up in the pursuit of work goals.

Fortunately, there are few people who are either exclusively maintenance-oriented or purely motivation-oriented. The former would be deadwood in an organization, while the latter might trample on those around him in his pursuit to achieve his goals.

6. With respect to employee motivational and maintenance needs, the management policies of an organization which is growing rapidly will probably result
   A. more in meeting motivational needs rather than maintenance needs
   B. more in meeting maintenance needs rather than motivational needs
   C. in meeting both of these needs equally
   D. in increased effort to define the motivational and maintenance needs of its employees

6.____

7. In accordance with the above passage, which of the following CANNOT be considered as an example of an employee maintenance need for railroad clerks?
   A. Providing more relief periods
   B. Providing fair salary increases at periodic intervals
   C. Increasing job responsibilities
   D. Increasing health insurance benefits

7.____

8. Most employees in an organization may be categorized as being interested in
   A. maintenance needs only
   B. motivational needs only
   C. both motivational and maintenance needs
   D. money only, to the exclusion of all other needs

8.____

Questions 9-11.

DIRECTIONS: Questions 9 through 11 are to be answered SOLELY on the basis of the following passage.

GOOD EMPLOYEE PRACTICES

As a city employee, you will be expected to take an interest in you work and perform the duties of your job to the best of your ability and in a spirit of cooperation. Nothing shows an interest in your work more than coming to work on time, not only at the start of the day but also when returning from lunch. If it is necessary for you to keep a personal appointment at lunch hour which might cause a delay in getting back to work on time, you should explain the situation to your supervisor and get his approval to come back a little late before you leave for lunch.

You should do everything that is asked of you willingly and consider important even the small jobs that your supervisor gives you. Although these jobs may seem unimportant, if you forget to do them or if you don't do them right, trouble may develop later.

Getting along well with your fellow workers will add much to the enjoyment of your work. You should respect your fellow workers and try to see their side when a disagreement arises. The better you get along with your fellow workers and your supervisor, the better you will like your job and the better you will be able to do it.

9. According to the above passage, in your job as a city employee, you are expected to
   A. show a willingness to cooperate on the job
   B. get your supervisor's approval before keeping any personal appointments at lunch hour
   C. avoid doing small jobs that seem unimportant
   D. do the easier jobs at the start of the day and the more difficult ones later on

9._____

10. According to the above passage, getting to work on time shows that you
    A. need the job
    B. have an interest in your work
    C. get along well with your fellow workers
    D. like your supervisor

10._____

11. According to the above passage, the one of the following statements that is NOT true is:
    A. If you do a small job wrong, trouble may develop
    B. You should respect your fellow workers
    C. If you disagree with a fellow worker, you should try to see his side of the story
    D. The less you get along with your supervisor, the better you will be able to do your job

11._____

Questions 12-15.

DIRECTIONS: Questions 12 through 15 are to be answered SOLELY on the basis of the following passage.

EMPLOYEE SUGGESTIONS

To increase the effectiveness of the city government, the city asks its employees to offer suggestions when they feel an improvement could be made in some government operation. The Employees' Suggestions Program was started to encourage city employees to do this. Through this Program, which is only for city employees, cash awards may be given to those whose suggestions are submitted and approved. Suggestions are looked for not only from supervisors but from all city employees as any city employee may get an idea which might be approved and contribute greatly to the solution of some problem of city government.

Therefore, all suggestions for improvement are welcome, whether they be suggestions on how to improve working conditions, or on how to increase the speed with which work is done, or on how to reduce or eliminate such things as waste, time losses, accidents or fire hazards. There are, however, a few types of suggestions for which cash awards cannot be given. An example of this type would be a suggestion to increase salaries or a suggestion to change the regulations about annual leave or about sick leave. The number of suggestions sent in has increased sharply during the past few years. It is hoped that it will keep increasing in the future in order to meet the city's needs for more ideas for improved ways of doing things.

12. According to the above passage, the MAIN reason why the city asks its employees for suggestions about government operations is to
    A. increase the effectiveness of the city government
    B. show that the Employees' Suggestion Program is working well
    C. show that everybody helps run the city government
    D. have the employee win a prize

13. According to the above passage, the Employees' Suggestion Program can approve awards ONLY for those suggestions that come from
    A. city employees
    B. city employees who are supervisors
    C. city employees who are not supervisors
    D. experienced employee of the city

14. According to the above passage, a cash award cannot be given through the Employees' Suggestion Program for a suggestion about
    A. getting work done faster
    B. helping prevent accidents on the job
    C. increasing the amount of annual leave for city employees
    D. reducing the chance of fire where city employees work

15. According to the above passage, the suggestions sent in during the past few years have
    A. all been approved
    B. generally been well written
    C. been mostly about reducing or eliminating waste
    D. been greater in number than before

Questions 16-18.

DIRECTIONS: Questions 16 through 18 are to be answered SOLELY on the basis of the following passage.

The supervisor will gain the respect of the members of his staff and increase his influence over them by controlling his temper and avoiding criticizing anyone publicly. When a mistake is made, the good supervisor will take it over with the employee quietly and privately. The supervisor will listen to the employee's story, suggest the better way of doing the job, and offer help so the mistake won't happen again. Before closing the discussion, the supervisor should try to find something good to say about other parts of the employee's work. Some praise and appreciation, along with instruction, is more likely to encourage an employee to improve in those areas where he is weakest.

16. A good title that would show the meaning of the above passage would be
    A. How to Correct Employee Errors
    B. How to Praise Employees
    C. Mistakes are Preventable
    D. The Weak Employee

17. According to the above passage, the work of an employee who has made a mistake is more likely to improve if the supervisor
    A. avoids criticizing him
    B. gives him a chance to suggest a better way of doing the work
    C. listens to the employee's excuses to see if he is right
    D. praises good work at the same time he corrects the mistake

18. According to the above passage, when a supervisor needs to correct an employee's mistake, it is important that he
    A. allow some time to go by after the mistake is made
    B. do so when other employee are not present
    C. show his influence with his tone of voice
    D. tell other employee to avoid the same mistake

Questions 19-23.

DIRECTIONS: Questions 19 through 23 are to be answered SOLELY on the basis of the following passage.

In studying the relationships of people to the organizational structure, it is absolutely necessary to identify and recognize the informal organizational structure. These relationships are necessary when coordination of a plan is attempted. They may be with *the boss*, line supervisors, staff personnel, or other representatives of the formal organization's hierarchy, and they may include the *liaison men* who serve as the leaders of the informal organization. An acquaintanceship with the people serving in these roles in the organization, and its formal counterpart, permits a supervisor to recognize sensitive areas in which it is simple to get conflict reaction. Avoidance of such areas, plus conscious efforts to inform other people of his own objectives for various plans, will usually enlist their aid and support. Planning *without* people can lead to disaster because the individuals who must act together to make any plan a success are more important than the plans themselves.

19. Of the following titles, the one that MOST clearly describes the above passage is
    A. Coordination of a Function
    B. Avoidance of Conflict
    C. Planning With People
    D. Planning Objectives

20. According to the above passage, attempts at coordinating plans may fail unless
    A. the plan's objectives are clearly set forth
    B. conflict between groups is resolved
    C. the plans themselves are worthwhile
    D. informal relationships are recognized

21. According to the above passage, conflict
    A. may, in some cases, be desirable to secure results
    B. produces more heat than light
    C. should be avoided at all costs
    D. possibilities can be predicted by a sensitive supervisor

22. The above passage implies that
    A. informal relationships are more important than formal structure
    B. the weakness of a formal structure depends upon informal relationships
    C. liaison men are the key people to consult when taking formal and informal structures into account
    D. individuals in a group are at least as important as the plans for the group

23. The above passage suggests that
    A. some planning can be disastrous
    B. certain people in sensitive areas should be avoided
    C. the supervisor should discourage acquaintanceships in the organization
    D. organizational relationships should be consciously limited

Questions 24-25.

DIRECTIONS: Questions 24 and 25 are to be answered SOLELY on the basis of the following passage.

Good personnel relations of an organization depend upon mutual confidence, trust, and good will. The basis of confidence is understanding. Most troubles start with people who do not understand each other. When the organization's intentions or motives are misunderstood, or when reasons for actions, practices, or policies are misconstrued, complete cooperation from individuals is not forthcoming. If management expects full cooperation from employees, it has a responsibility of sharing with them the information which is the foundation of proper understanding, confidence, and trust. Personnel management has long since outgrown the days when it was the vogue to *treat them rough and tell them nothing*. Up-to-date personnel management provides all possible information about the activities, aims, and purposes of the organization. It seems altogether creditable that a desire should exist among employees for such information which the best-intentioned executive might think would not interest them and which the worst-intentioned would think was none of their business.

24. The above passage implies that one of the causes of the difficulty which an organization might have with its personnel relations is that its employees
    A. have not expressed interest in the activities, aims, and purposes of the organization
    B. do not believe in the good faith of the organization
    C. have not been able to give full cooperation to the organization
    D. do not recommend improvements in the practices and policies of the organization

25. According to the above passage, in order for an organization to have good personnel relations, it is NOT essential that
    A. employees have confidence in the organization
    B. the purposes of the organization be understood by the employees
    C. employees have a desire for information about the organization
    D. information about the organization be communicated to employees

KEY (CORRECT ANSWERS)

1.	D	11.	D
2.	C	12.	A
3.	D	13.	A
4.	B	14.	C
5.	A	15.	D
6.	A	16.	A
7.	C	17.	D
8.	C	18.	B
9.	A	19.	C
10.	B	20.	D

21. D
22. D
23. A
24. B
25. C

TEST 2

DIRECTIONS: Each question or incomplete statement is followed by several suggested answers or completions. Select the one that BEST answers the question or completes the statement. *PRINT THE LETTER OF THE CORRECT ANSWER IN THE SPACE AT THE RIGHT.*

Questions 1-8.

DIRECTIONS: Questions 1 through 8 are to be answered SOLELY on the basis of the following passage.

Important figures in education and in public affairs have recommended development of a private organization sponsored in part by various private foundations which would offer installment payment plans to full-time matriculated students in accredited colleges and universities in the United States and Canada. Contracts would be drawn to cover either tuition and fees, or tuition, fees, room and board in college facilities, from one year up to and including six years. A special charge, which would vary with the length of the contract, would be added to the gross repayable amount. This would be in addition to interest at a rate which would vary with the income of the parents. There would be a 3% annual interest charge for families with total income, before income taxes, of $50,000 or less. The rate would increase by 1/10 of 1% for every $1,000 of additional net income in excess of $50,000 up to a maximum of 10% interest. Contracts would carry an insurance provision on the life of the parent or guardian who signs the contract; all contracts must have the signature of a parent or guardian. Payment would be scheduled in equal monthly installments.

1. Which of the following students would be eligible for the payment plan described in the above passage? A
    A. matriculated student taking six semester hours toward a graduate degree
    B. matriculated student taking seventeen semester hours toward an undergraduate degree
    C. graduate matriculated at the University of Mexico taking eighteen semester hours toward a graduate degree
    D. student taking eighteen semester hours in a special pre-matriculation program

1.____

2. According to the above passage, the organization described would be sponsored in part by
    A. private foundations   B. colleges and universities
    C. persons in the field of education   D. persons in public life

2.____

3. Which of the following expenses could NOT be covered by a contract with the organization described in the above passage?
    A. Tuition amounting to $20,000 per year
    B. Registration and laboratory fees
    C. Meals at restaurants near the college
    D. Rent for an apartment in a college dormitory

3.____

4. The total amount to be paid would include ONLY the   4.____
   A. principal
   B. principal and interest
   C. principal, interest, and special charge
   D. principal, interest, special charge, and fee

5. The contract would carry insurance on the   5.____
   A. life of the student
   B. life of the student's parents
   C. income of the parents of the student
   D. life of the parent who signed the contract

6. The interest rate for an annual loan of $25,000 from the organization described   6.____
   in the above passage for a student whose family's net income was $55,000
   should be
   A. 3%   B. 3.5%   C. 4%   D. 4.5%

7. The interest rate for an annual loan of $35,000 from the organization described   7.____
   in the above passage for a student whose family's net income was $100,000
   should be
   A. 5%   B. 8%   C. 9%   D. 10%

8. John Lee has submitted an application for the installment payment plan   8.____
   described in the above passage. John's mother and father have a store which
   grossed $500,000 last year, but the income which the family received from the
   store was $90,000 before taxes. They also had $5,000 income from stock
   dividends. They paid $10,000 in income taxes.
   The amount of income upon which the interest should be based is
   A. $85,000   B. $90,000   C. $95,000   D. $105,000

Questions 9-13.

DIRECTIONS: Questions 9 through 13 are to be answered SOLELY on the basis of the following passage.

   Since the organization chart is pictorial in nature, there is a tendency for it to be drawn in an artistically balanced and appealing fashion, regardless of the realities of actual organizational structure. In addition to being subject to this distortion, there is the difficulty of communicating in any organization chart the relative importance or the relative size of various component parts of an organizational structure. Furthermore, because of the need for simplicity of design, an organization chart can never indicate the full extent of the interrelationships among the component parts of an organization.

   These interrelationships are often just as vital as the specifications which an organization chart endeavors to indicate. Yet, if an organization chart were to be drawn with all the wide variety of criss-crossing communication and cooperation networks existent within a typical organization, the chart would probably be much more confusing than informative. It is also obvious that no organization chart as such can prove or disprove that the organizational structure it represents is effective in realizing the objectives of the organization. At best, an organization chart can only illustrate some of the various factors to be taken into consideration in understanding, devising, or altering organizational arrangements.

9. According to the above passage, an organization chart can be expected to portray the
    A. structure of the organization along somewhat ideal lines
    B. relative size of the organizational units quite accurately
    C. channels of information distribution within the organization graphically
    D. extent of the obligation of each unit to meet the organizational objectives

10. According to the above passage, those aspects of internal functioning which are NOT shown on an organization chart
    A. can be considered to have little practical application in the operations of the organization
    B. might well be considered to be as important as the structural relationships which a chart does present
    C. could be the cause of considerable confusion in the operations of an organization which is quite large
    D. would be most likely to provide the information needed to determine the overall effectiveness of an organization

11. In the above passage, the one of the following conditions which is NOT implied as being a defect of an organization chart is that an organization chart may
    A. present a picture of the organizational structure which is different from the structure that actually exists
    B. fail to indicate the comparative size of various organizational units
    C. be limited in its ability to convey some of the meaningful aspects of organizational relationships
    D. become less useful over a period of time during which the organizational facts which it illustrated have changed

12. The one of the following which is the MOST suitable title for the above passage is
    A. The Design and Construction of an Organization Chart
    B. The Informal Aspects of an Organization Chart
    C. The Inherent Deficiencies of an Organization Chart
    D. The Utilization of a Typical Organization Chart

13. It can be inferred from the above passage that the function of an organization chart is to
    A. contribute to the comprehension of the organization form and arrangements
    B. establish the capabilities of the organization to operate effectively
    C. provide a balanced picture of the operations of the organization
    D. eliminate the need for complexity in the organization's structure

Questions 14-16.

DIRECTIONS: Questions 14 through 16 are to be answered SOLELY on the basis of the following passage.

In dealing with visitors to the school office, the school secretary must use initiative, tact, and good judgment. All visitors should be greeted promptly and courteously. The nature of their business should be determined quickly and handled expeditiously. Frequently, the secretary should be able to handle requests, deliveries, or passes herself. Her judgment should determine when a visitor should see members of the staff or the principal. Serious problems or doubtful cases should be referred to a supervisor.

14. In general, visitors should be handled by the 14.____
 A. school secretary B. principal
 C. appropriate supervisor D. person who is free

15. It is wise to obtain the following information from visitors: 15.____
 A. Name B. Nature of business
 C. Address D. Problems they have

16. All visitors who wish to see members of the staff should 16.____
 A. be permitted to do so B. produce identification
 C. do so for valid reasons only D. be processed by a supervisor

Questions 17-19.

DIRECTIONS: Questions 17 through 19 are to be answered SOLELY on the basis of the following passage.

Information regarding payroll status, salary differentials, promotional salary increments, deductions, and pension payments should be given to all members of the staff who have questions regarding these items. On occasion, if the secretary is uncertain regarding the information, the staff member should be referred to the principal or the appropriate agency. No question by a staff member regarding payroll status should be brushed aside as immaterial or irrelevant. The school secretary must always try to handle the question or pass it on to the person who can handle it.

17. If a teacher is dissatisfied with information regarding her salary status, as given 17.____
 by the school secretary, the matter should be
 A. dropped
 B. passed on to the principal
 C. passed on by the secretary to proper agency or the principal
 D. made a basis for grievance procedures

18. The following is an adequate summary of the above passage: 18.____
 A. The secretary must handle all payroll matters
 B. The secretary must handle all payroll matter or know who can handle them
 C. The secretary or the principal must handle all payroll matters
 D. Payroll matter too difficult to handle must be followed up until they are solved

19. The above passage implies that
    A. many teachers ask immaterial questions regarding payroll status
    B. few teachers ask irrelevant pension questions
    C. no teachers ask immaterial salary questions
    D. no question regarding salary should be considered irrelevant

19.____

Questions 20-22.

DIRECTIONS: Questions 20 through 22 are to be answered SOLELY on the basis of the following passage.

The necessity for good speech on the part of the school secretary cannot be overstated. The school secretary must deal with the general public, the pupils, the members of the staff, and the school supervisors. In every situation which involves the general public, the secretary serves as a representative of the school. In dealing with pupils, the secretary's speech must serve as a model from which students may guide themselves. Slang, colloquialisms, malapropisms, and local dialects must be avoided.

20. The above passage implies that the speech pattern of the secretary must be
    A. perfect   B. very good
    C. average   D. on a level with that of the pupils

20.____

21. The last sentence indicates that slang
    A. is acceptable   B. occurs in all speech
    C. might be used occasionally D. should be shunned

21.____

22. The above passage implies that the speech of pupils
    A. may be influenced   B. does not change readily
    C. is generally good   D. is generally poor

22.____

Questions 23-25.

DIRECTIONS: Questions 23 through 25 are to be answered SOLELY on the basis of the following passage.

The school secretary who is engaged in the task of filing records and correspondence should follow a general set of rules. Items which are filed should be available to other secretaries or to supervisors quickly and easily by means of the application of a modicum of common sense and good judgment. Items which, by their nature, may be difficult to find should be cross-indexed. Folders and drawers should be neatly and accurately labeled. There should never be a large accumulation of papers which have not been filed.

23. A good general rule to follow in filing is that materials should be
    A. placed in folders quickly   B. neatly stored
    C. readily available   D. cross-indexed

23.____

24. Items that are filed should be available to
    A. the secretary charged with the task of filing
    B. secretaries and supervisors
    C. school personnel
    D. the principal

    24._____

25. A modicum of common sense means _____ common sense.
    A. an average amount of   B. a great deal of
    C. a little   D. no

    25._____

KEY (CORRECT ANSWERS)

1. B
2. A
3. C
4. C
5. D

6. B
7. B
8. C
9. A
10. B

11. D
12. C
13. A
14. A
15. B

16. C
17. C
18. B
19. D
20. B

21. D
22. A
23. C
24. B
25. C

TEST 3

DIRECTIONS: Each question or incomplete statement is followed by several suggested answers or completions. Select the one that BEST answers the question or completes the statement. *PRINT THE LETTER OF THE CORRECT ANSWER IN THE SPACE AT THE RIGHT.*

Questions 1-4.

DIRECTIONS: Questions 1 through 4 are to be answered SOLELY on the basis of the following passage.

The proposition that administrative activity is essentially the same in all organizations appears to underlie some of the practices in the administration of private higher education. Although the practice is unusual in public education, there are numerous instances of industrial, governmental, or military administrators being assigned to private institutions of higher education and, to a lesser extent, of college and university presidents assuming administrative positions in other types of organizations. To test this theory that administrators are interchangeable, there is a need for systematic observation and classification. The myth that an educational administrator must first have experience in the teaching profession is firmly rooted in a long tradition that has historical prestige. The myth is bound up in the expectations of the public and personnel surrounding the administrator. Since administrative success depends significantly on how well an administrator meets the expectations others have of him, the myth may be more powerful than the special experience in helping the administrator attain organizational and educational objectives. Educational administrators who have risen through the teaching profession have often expressed nostalgia for the life of a teacher or scholar, but there is no evidence that this nostalgia contributes to administrative success.

1. Which of the following statements as completed is MOST consistent with the above passage?
   The greatest number of administrators has moved from
   A. industry and the military to government and universities
   B. government and universities to industry and the military
   C. government, the armed forces, and industry to colleges and universities
   D. colleges and universities to government, the armed forces, and industry

1.____

2. Of the following, the MOST reasonable inference from the above passage is that a specific area requiring further research is the
   A. place of myth in the tradition and history of the educational profession
   B. relative effectiveness of educational administrators from inside and outside the teaching profession
   C. performance of administrators in the administration of public colleges
   D. degree of reality behind the nostalgia for scholarly pursuits often expressed by educational administrators

2.____

3. According to the above passage, the value to an educational administrator of experience in the teaching profession
   A. lies in the first-hand knowledge he has acquired of immediate educational problems
   B. may lie in the belief of his colleagues, subordinates, and the public that such experience is necessary
   C. has been supported by evidence that the experience contributes to administrative success in educational fields
   D. would be greater if the administrator were able to free himself from nostalgia for his former duties

3.____

4. Of the following, the MOST suitable title for the above passage is
   A. Educational Administration, Its Problems
   B. The Experience Needed For Educational Administration
   C. Administration in Higher Education
   D. Evaluating Administrative Experience

4.____

Questions 5-6.

DIRECTIONS: Questions 5 and 6 are to be answered SOLELY on the basis of the following passage.

Management by objectives (MBO) may be defined as the process by which the superior and the subordinate managers of an organization jointly define its common goals, define each individual's major areas of responsibility in terms of the results expected of him and use these measure as guides for operating the unit and assessing the contribution of each of its members.

The MBO approach requires that after organizational goals are established and communicated, targets must be set for each individual position which are congruent with organizational goals. Periodic performance reviews and a final review using the objectives set as criteria are also basic to this approach.

Recent studies have shown that MBO programs are influenced by attitudes and perceptions of the boss, the company, the reward-punishment system, and the program itself. In addition, the manner in which the MBO program is carried out can influence the success of the program. A study done in the late sixties indicates that the best results are obtained when the manager sets goals which deal with significant problem areas in the organizational unit, or with the subordinate's personal deficiencies. These goals must be clear with regard to what is expected of the subordinate. The frequency of feedback is also important in the success of a management-by-objectives program. Generally, the greater the amount of feedback, the more successful the MBO program.

5. According to the above passage, the expected output for individual employees should be determined
   A. after a number of reviews of work performance
   B. after common organizational goals are defined
   C. before common organizational goals are defined
   D. on the basis of an employee's personal qualities

5.____

6. According to the above passage, the management-by-objectives approach requires
   A. less feedback than other types of management programs
   B. little review of on-the-job performance after the initial setting of goals
   C. general conformance between individual goals and organizational goals
   D. the setting of goals which deal with minor problem areas in the organization

Questions 7-10.

DIRECTIONS: Questions 7 through 10 are to be answered SOLELY on the basis of the following passage.

Management, which is the function of executive leadership, has as its principal phases the planning, organizing, and controlling of the activities of subordinate groups in the accomplishment of organizational objectives. Planning specifies the kind and extent of the factors, forces, and effects, and the relationships among them, that will be required for satisfactory accomplishment. The nature of the objectives and their requirements must be known before determinations can be made as to what must be done, how it must be done and why, where actions should take place, who should be responsible, and similar programs pertaining to the formulation of a plan. Organizing, which creates the conditions that must be present before the execution of the plan can be undertaken successfully, cannot be done intelligently without knowledge of the organizational objectives. Control, which has to do with the constraint and regulation of activities entering into the execution of the plan, must be exercised in accordance with the characteristics and requirements of the activities demanded by the plan.

7. The one of the following which is the MOST suitable title for the above passage is
   A. The Nature of Successful Organization
   B. The Planning of Management Functions
   C. The Importance of Organizational Functions
   D. The Principle Aspects of Management

8. It can be inferred from the above passage that the one of the following functions whose existence is essential to the existence of the other three is the
   A. regulation of the work needed to carry out a plan
   B. understanding of what the organization intends to accomplish
   C. securing of information of the factors necessary for accomplishment of objectives
   D. establishment of the conditions required for successful action

9. The one of the following which would NOT be included within any of the principal phases of the function of executive leadership as defined in the above passage is
   A. determination of manpower requirements
   B. procurement of required material
   C. establishment of organizational objectives
   D. scheduling of production

10. The conclusion which can MOST reasonably be drawn from the above passage is that the control phase of managing is most directly concerned with the
    A. influencing of policy determinations
    B. administering of suggestion systems
    C. acquisition of staff for the organization
    D. implementation of performance standards

Questions 11-12.

DIRECTIONS: Questions 11 and 12 are to be answered SOLELY on the basis of the following passage.

Under an open-and-above-board policy, it is to be expected that some supervisors will gloss over known shortcomings of subordinates rather than face the task of discussing team face-to-face. It is also to be expected that at least some employees whose job performance is below par will reject the supervisor's appraisal as biased and unfair. Be that as it may, these are inescapable aspects of any performance appraisal system in which human beings are involved. The supervisor who shies away from calling a spade a spade, as well as the employee with a chip on his shoulder, will each in his own way eventually be revealed in his true light—to the benefit of the organization as a whole.

11. The BEST of the following interpretations of the above passage is that
    A. the method of rating employee performance requires immediate revision to improve employee acceptance
    B. substandard performance ratings should be discussed with employees even if satisfactory ratings are not
    C. supervisors run the risk of being called unfair by the subordinates even though their appraisals are accurate
    D. any system of employee performance rating is satisfactory if used properly

12. The BEST of the following interpretations of the above passage is that
    A. supervisors generally are not open-and-above-board with their subordinates
    B. it is necessary for supervisors to tell employees objectively how they are performing
    C. employees complain when their supervisor does not keep them informed
    D. supervisors are afraid to tell subordinates their weaknesses

Questions 13-15.

DIRECTIONS: Questions 13 through 15 are to be answered SOLELY on the basis of the following passage.

During the last decade, a great deal of interest has been generated around the phenomenon of *organizational development,* or the process of developing human resources through conscious organization effort. Organizational development (OD) stresses improving interpersonal relationships and organizational skills, such as communication, to a much greater degree than individual training ever did. The kind of training that an organization should emphasize depends upon the present and future structure of the organization. If future organizations are to be unstable, shifting coalitions, then individual skills and abilities, particularly those emphasizing innovativeness, creativity, flexibility, and the latest technological knowledge, are crucial and individual training is most appropriate.

But if there is to be little change in organizational structure, then the main thrust of training should be group-oriented or organizational development. This approach seems better designed for overcoming hierarchical barriers, for developing a degree of interpersonal relationships which make communication along the chain of command possible, and for retaining a modicum of innovation and/or flexibility.

13. According to the above passage, group-oriented training is MOST useful in in
    A. developing a communications system that will facilitate understanding through the chain of command
    B. highly flexible and mobile organizations
    C. preventing the crossing of hierarchical barriers within an organization
    D. saving energy otherwise wasted on developing methods of dealing with rigid hierarchies

14. The one of the following conclusions which can be drawn MOST appropriately from the above passage is that
    A. behavioral research supports the use of organizational development training methods rather than individualized training
    B. it is easier to provide individualized training in specific skills than to set up sensitivity training programs
    C. organizational development eliminates innovative or flexible activity
    D. the nature of an organization greatly influences which training methods will be most effective

15. According to the above passage, the one of the following which is LEAST important for large-scale organizations geared to rapid and abrupt change is
    A. current technological information
    B. development of a high degree of interpersonal relationships
    C. development of individual skills and abilities
    D. emphasis on creativity

Questions 16-18.

DIRECTIONS: Questions 16 through 18 are to be answered SOLELY on the basis of the following passage.

The increase in the extent to which each individual is personally responsible to others is most noticeable in a large bureaucracy. No one person *decides* anything; each decision of any importance, is the product of an intricate process of brokerage involving individuals inside and outside the organization who feel some reason to be affected by the decision, or two have special knowledge to contribute to it. The more varied the organization's constituency, the more inside *veto-groups* will need to be taken into account. But even if no outside consultations were involved, sheer size would produce a complex process of decision. For a large organization is a deliberately created system of tensions into which each individual is expected to bring work-ways, viewpoints, and outside relationships markedly different from those of his colleagues. It is the administrator's task to draw from these disparate forces the elements of wise action from day to day, consistent with the purposes of the organization as a whole.

16. The above passage is essentially a description of decision-making as 16.____
    A. an organization process
    B. the key responsibility of the administrator
    C. the one best position among many
    D. a complex of individual decisions

17. Which one of the following statements BEST describes the responsibilities of 17.____
    an administrator?
    A. He modifies decisions and goals in accordance with pressures from within and outside the organization.
    B. He creates problem-solving mechanisms that rely on the varied interests of his staff and *veto-groups*.
    C. He makes determinations that will lead to attainment of his agency's objectives.
    D. He obtains agreement among varying viewpoints and interests

18. In the context of the operations of a central public personnel agency, a 18.____
    veto-group would LEAST likely consist of
    A. employee organizations
    B. professional personnel societies
    C. using agencies
    D. civil service newspapers

Questions 19-25.

DIRECTIONS: Questions 19 through 25 are to be answered SOLELY on the basis of the following passage, which is an extract from a report prepared for Department X, which outlines the procedure to be followed in the case of transfers of employees.

Every transfer, regardless of the reason therefore, requires completion of the record of transfer, Form DT411. To denote consent to the transfer, DT411 should contain the signatures of the transferee and the personnel officer(s) concerned, except that, in the case of an involuntary transfer, the signatures of the transferee's present and prospective supervisors shall be entered in Boxes 8A and 8B, respectively, since the transferee does not consent. Only a permanent employee may request a transfer; in such cases, the employee's attendance record shall be duly considered with regard to absences, latenesses, and accrued overtime balances. In the case of an inter-district transfer, the employee's attendance record must be included in Section 8A of the transfer request, Form DT410, by the personnel officer of the district from which the transfer is requested. The personnel officer of the district to which the employee requested transfer may refuse to accept accrued overtime balances in excess of ten days.

An employee on probation shall be eligible for transfer. If such employee is involuntarily transferred, he shall be credited for the period of time already served on probation. However, if such transfer is voluntary, the employee shall be required to serve the entire period of his probation in the new position. An employee who has occurred a disability which prevents him from performing his normal duties may be transferred during the period of such disability to other appropriate duties. A disability transfer requires the completion of either DT414 if the disability is job-connected, or Form DT415 if it is not a job-connected disability. In either case, the personnel officer of the district from which the transfer is made signs in Box 6A of the first two copies and the personnel officer of the district to which the transfer is made signs in Box 6B of the last two copies, or, in the case of an intra-district disability transfer, the personnel officer must sign in Box 6A of the first two copies and Box 6B of the last two copies.

19. When a personnel officer consents to an employee's request for transfer from his district, this procedure requires that the personnel officer sign Forms
    A. DT411
    B. DT410 and DT411
    C. DT411 and either Form DT414 or DT415
    D. DT410 and DT411, and either Form DT414 or DT415

20. With respect to the time record of an employee transferred against his wishes during his probationary period, this procedure requires that
    A. he serve the entire period of his probation in his present office
    B. he lose his accrued overtime balance
    C. his attendance record be considered with regard to absences and latenesses
    D. he be given credit for the period of time he has already served on probation

21. Assume you are a supervisor and an employee must be transferred into your office against his wishes.
    According to this procedure, the box you must sign on the record of transfer is
    A. 6A   B. 8A   C. 6B   D. 8B

22. Under this procedure, in the case of a disability transfer, when must Box 6A on Forms DT414 and DT415 be signed by the personnel officer of the district to which the transfer is being made?
    A. In all cases when either Form DT414 or Form DT415 is used
    B. In all cases when Form DT414 is used and only under certain circumstances when Form DT415 is used
    C. In all cases when Form DT415 is used and only under certain circumstances when Form DT414 is used
    D. Only under certain circumstances when either Form DT414 or Form DT415 is used

23. From the above passage, it may be inferred MOST correctly that the number of copies of Form DT414 is
    A. no more than 2
    B. at least 3
    C. at least 5
    D. more than the number of copies of Form DT415

23.____

24. A change in punctuation and capitalization only which would change one sentence into two and possibly contribute to somewhat greater ease of reading this report extract would be MOST appropriate in the
    A. 2nd sentence, 1st paragraph
    B. 3rd sentence, 1st paragraph
    C. next to the last sentence, 2nd paragraph
    D. 2nd sentence, 2nd paragraph

24.____

25. In the second paragraph, a word that is INCORRECTLY used is
    A. *shall* in the 1st sentence
    B. *voluntary* in the 3rd sentence
    C. *occurred* in the 4th sentence
    D. *intra-district* in the last sentence

25.____

KEY (CORRECT ANSWERS)

1.	C		11.	C
2.	B		12.	B
3.	B		13.	A
4.	B		14.	D
5.	B		15.	B
6.	C		16.	A
7.	D		17.	C
8.	B		18.	B
9.	C		19.	A
10.	D		20.	D

21.	D
22.	D
23.	B
24.	B
25.	C

EXAMINATION SECTION
TEST 1

DIRECTIONS: Each question or incomplete statement is followed by several suggested answers or completions. Select the one that BEST answers the question or completes the statement. *PRINT THE LETTER OF THE CORRECT ANSWER IN THE SPACE AT THE RIGHT.*

Questions 1-4.

DIRECTIONS: Questions 1 through 4 are to be answered on the basis of the following passage.

    A State department which is interested in finding acceptable solutions to the operational problems of specific types of community self-help organizations recently sent two of its staff members to meet with one such organization. At that meeting, the leaders of the community organization voiced the need for increased activity planning input of a more detailed nature from the citizens regularly served by that organization. There followed a discussion of a number of information-gathering methods, including surveys by telephone, questionnaires mailed to the citizens' residences, in-person interviews with the citizens, and the placing of suggestion boxes in the organization's headquarters building. Concern was expressed by one of the leaders that the organization's funds be spent judiciously. The State department representatives present promised to investigate the possibility of a matching fund grant of money to the organization.

    Later, the proposed survey was conducted using questionnaires completed by those citizens who visited the organization's headquarters. The results of the survey included the information that twice as many citizens wanted more educational activities scheduled than wanted more social activities scheduled, whereas one-half of those who wanted more educational activities scheduled were interested mainly in special job training.

1. A similar survey conducted by a State department employee involved special job training. That survey uncovered the information below. The following four sentences are to be rearranged to form the most effective and logical paragraph.
Select the letter representing the BEST sequence for these sentences.
   I. The majority of those who are still in this group are ethnic minorities.
   II. The number of economically disadvantaged people who enjoyed their special job training is larger than the number of economically disadvantaged people who did not enjoy it.
   III. Thirty-five percent of all those who are economically disadvantaged are not ethnic minorities.
   IV. Eighty percent of those who have completed special job training in the past ten years are economically disadvantaged.
   The CORRECT answer is:
   A. IV, I, III, II   B. I, III, II, IV   C. IV, II, I, III   D. I, II, III, IV

2. In the above reading passage, the word *judiciously* means MOST NEARLY
   A. legally   B. immediately   C. prudently   D. uniformly

3. Based only on the information in the reading passage, which one of the following statements is MOST fully supported?
   A. The leaders of the community organization in question wanted to increase the quantity and quality of feedback about that organization's suggestion boxes.
   B. The number of citizens surveyed who wanted more educational activities scheduled and were mainly interested in special job training was the same as the number of citizens surveyed who wanted more social activities to be scheduled.
   C. At the meeting concerned, matching funds were promised to the community organization in question by the two State department representatives present.
   D. Telephone surveys generally yield more accurate information than do surveys conducted through the use of mailed questionnaires.

4. The following four sentences are to be rearranged to form the most effective and logical paragraph.
   Select the letter representing the BEST sequence for these sentences.
   I. Formal surveys of citizens within a community also convey to those citizens the interest of the community leadership in hearing the citizens' ideas about community improvement.
   II. Such surveys can provide needed input into the process of establishing specific community program goals.
   III. Formally conducted surveys of community residents often yield valuable information to the local area leaders responsible for community-based programs.
   IV. No community should formulate these goals without attempting to obtain the views of its citizenry.
   The CORRECT answer is:
   A. III, I, IV, II   B. I, III, II, IV   C. III, II, IV, I   D. IV, III, II, I

Questions 5-8.

DIRECTIONS: Questions 5 through 8 are to be answered on the basis of the following passage.

The Smith Paint Company, which currently employs 2,000 persons, has been in existence for 20 years. A new chemical plant, Futuron, was recently developed by an employee of that company. This paint was released for public use a month ago on a trial basis. The sales were phenomenal, and there is a great demand for more Futuron to be manufactured. The profits to be made by increased manufacturing and sale of Futuron could place the Smith Paint Company in a leading role in the paint industry.

The Smith Paint Company currently produces 2 million gallons of the more traditional paint per year. The Smith Paint Company's Board of Directors wishes to reduce its production of this traditional paint by 50%, and to produce 1 million gallons of Futuron per year.

The employees are quite concerned about this potential production change. A public nonprofit research group has been investigating the chemical make-up of Futuron. Initial research indicates that negative physical reactions may result from working closely with the chemicals necessary to manufacture Futuron. For this reason, most of the company employees do not want the proposed change in production to occur. The members of the Board of Directors, however, argue that the research results are too inconclusive to cause great concern. They say that the company would lose 25% to 50% of its potential profit if the large-scale manufacturing of Futuron is not initiated immediately.

5. Seventy-five percent of the Smith Paint Company's current employees were hired during its first 10 years of operation. Fifteen percent were hired in the past five years. During the five-year interval between the first ten years and the most recent five years, 40 persons were hired per year.
   What percentage of its total employees were hired during the Smith Paint Company's first 13 years of operation?
   A. 75%   B. 81%   C. 85%   D. 90%

6. Assume that the total possible profit the Smith Paint Company could make during its first year of manufacturing the proposed amount of Futuron would be $1.00 per gallon. The purchase of new machinery would reduce this first-year profit by 50%. The anticipated delay, during the first production year, in establishing large-scale manufacturing facilities would reduce the total possible profit by an additional 25%.
   Given this information, what would be the actual profit made from the first year of manufacturing Futuron?
   A. $250,000   B. $375,000   C. $500,000   D. $750,000

7. In the reading passage, the word *inconclusive* means MOST NEARLY
   A. ineluctable   B. incorrect
   C. unreasonable   D. indeterminate

8. Based on the information in the reading passage, which of the following statements represents the MOST accurate conclusion?
   A. The proposed reduction in the production of its traditional paint would not financially injure the Smith Paint Company.
   B. A greater proportion of the Smith Paint Company's employees are in favor of the proposed increase in Futuron production than are opposed to it.
   C. The increased Futuron production proposed by the Smith Paint Company's Board of Directors would cause that company's employees considerable health damage.
   D. Positive public response to the sale of Futuron suggests that considerable profit can be made by increasing the manufacturing and sale of Futuron.

KEY (CORRECT ANSWERS)

1. A   5. B
2. C   6. A
3. B   7. D
4. C   8. D

5 (#1)

SOLUTIONS TO PROBLEMS

1. For the following reasons, Choice A is correct and the other three choices are incorrect.

    a. Both Choice B and Choice D begin with Sentence I, which states, *The majority of those who are still in this group are ethnic minorities.* The paragraph cannot logically begin with a statement such as Sentence I, because no one reading the paragraph would know what *this group* refers to. Therefore, Choice B and Choice D are not correct and may be eliminated from consideration.

    b. Both Choice A and Choice B begin with Sentence IV, which states, *Eighty percent of those who have completed special job training in the past ten years are economically disadvantaged.* The problem then becomes selecting the best sequence of the other three sentences so that they most logically follow the initial Sentence IV.

    c. If you select Choice C, then you are choosing Sentence II as the correct second sentence. Sentence II states, *The number of economically disadvantaged people who enjoyed their special job training is larger than the number of economically disadvantaged people who did not enjoy it.* Then Sentence I would be the third sentence. However, that would not be logical, because you could not tell whether *this group* in Sentence I refers to *economically disadvantaged people who enjoyed their special job training* or whether *this group* refers to *economically people who did not enjoy it.* Therefore, Choice C is not correct.

    d. By the process of elimination, only Choice A remains. Choice A specifies Sentence I as the second sentence, which is logically correct in that *this group* in Sentence I will then refer to those who are *economically disadvantaged* in Sentence IV. The two remaining sentences also refer back to *economically disadvantaged*, thus creating a paragraph that reads logically from start to finish. Therefore, Choice A is the correct answer.

2. Choices B and D should be eliminated from further consideration due to the context in which the word *judiciously* was used in the reading passage. Specifically, concern was expressed that funds be spent judiciously. Nothing in the paragraph suggests a need for concern if the funds were not spent immediately or uniformly. Choice A must be considered, because public funds should be spent legally. However, the word *judiciously* is related to the word *judgment* rather than to the word *judiciary*. It is the latter word that has to do with courts of law and is related to legality, so Choice A is incorrect. On the other hand, *judiciously* and *prudently* both mean *wisely* and *with direction*. Therefore, Choice C is correct.

3. Choice B is the correct choice. No matter what numbers you apply, Choice B still will be correct. This is because when you multiply any number by two and then divide the result in half, you end up with the same number that you begin with. For example, suppose that 20 citizens wanted more social activities. Twice that number (40 citizens) wanted more educational activities. But of those 40 citizens, one-half (20 citizens) wanted mainly special job training.

Choice A is incorrect because, first of all, the organization did not have any suggestion boxes; although suggestion boxes were discussed, questionnaires ultimately were used instead. In addition, Choice A is incorrect because it was input about the planning of activities that the leaders of the community organization wanted rather than feedback concerning suggestion boxes.

Choice C also is not correct. Instead of promising the matching funds, the State department representatives promised to investigate (or look into) the possibility of obtaining the matching funds.

Choice D is incorrect because the reading passage does not tell whether telephone surveys or mailed questionnaires provide more accurate information. Remember, the instructions for this question state that the question is to be answered ONLY on the information in the applicable reading passage.

4. The correct answer is Choice C. Choice A and Choice C both begin with Sentence III, which certainly could be the logical first sentence of a paragraph. However, the next sentence (Sentence I) in Choice A leaves the initial topic of obtaining information from citizens. The third sentence in Choice A would be Sentence IV, *No community should formulate these goals without attempting to obtain the views of its citizenry*. The words *these goals* do not logically refer to anything in the previous two sentences, so Choice A is incorrect.

Choice B also is incorrect because the word *also* in its first sentence (Sentence I) has nothing to logically refer to. *Also* would have to be used in a sentence that comes later in the paragraph.

Choice D has the same problem as Choice A. Choice D begins with Sentence IV, which starts off, *No community should formulate these goals....* Again, the words *these goals* need to refer to something in a previous sentence about goals in order to be logically correct.

5. Choice B is correct. Here are the mathematical computations you might use to arrive at the correct answer of 81%.

   a. The reading passage states that the Smith Paint Company currently employs 2,000 persons. The first part of this question states that 75% of those current employees were hired during the first ten years that the company was in operation. By multiplying 75% by 2,000, you would find that 1,500 of the current employees were hired during the company's first ten years.

   b. The question asks about the first 13 years of the company's operation rather than just the first ten years. Therefore, you need the arithmetical information for the three years that immediately followed the first ten years. You know from the reading passage that the company has been operating for 20 years. You have the information for the first ten years. Twenty minus ten leaves the most recent ten years.

c. You know from the question that 40 persons were hired each year during the five-year period of time between the first ten years and the most recent five years. However, you need the information about only the first three years. By multiplying 40 persons per year by three years, you would find that 120 people were hired during the first three years that came immediately after the first ten years of the company's operation.

d. Next, you would need to add 1,500 people (for the first ten years) and 120 people (for the next three years). That would give you a total of 1,620 people hired during the first 13 years.

e. The question asks for the percentage of the Smith Paint Company's total employees hired during its first 13 years. You know that the total number of employees is 2,000. The question then is: 1,620 people is what percentage of 2,000 people? By dividing 2,000 into 1,620, you would find that the correct answer is 81%.

Choice A is incorrect because it deals with only the first ten years that the company was in operation, rather than the first 13 years. If you took 1,500 people (from Step a in the explanatory material for the correct answer) and divided that number by 2,000 people, you would arrive at 75%, which is not correct.

Choice C is incorrect. If you correctly arrived at 1,500 people for the first ten years but then incorrectly dealt with the next five years instead of the next three years, you would end up with the wrong answer of 85%. First, you would multiply 40 people by five years and end up with 200 people. Next, you would add 200 to 1,500 and end up with 1,700 people. Finally, you would divide 1,700 by 2,000 and get 85%.

Choice D also is incorrect. If you correctly arrived at 1,500 people for the first ten years but then used the information for the most recent five years instead of the information for the five years that came just before the most recent five years, you would end up with the incorrect answer of 90%. First, you would find from the question that 15% of the total employees were hired in the past five years. Next, you would multiply 15% by 2,000 total employees and end up with 300. Next, you would add 1,500 employees and 300 employees, ending up with a total of 1,800 employees. By dividing 1,800 by 2,000, you would arrive at 90%.

6. Choice A is correct. Here are the mathematical computations you would need to make to arrive at the correct answer of $250,000.

    a. The reading passage states that the amount of Futuron proposed for manufacture each year is 1 million gallons. The question states that the possible profit per gallon would be $1.00. By multiplying $1.00 by 1,000,000, you would find that $1,000,000 would be the total possible profit to be made during the first year.

    b. The question states that the $1,000,000 possible profit would have to be reduced by 50% because of the purchase of new machinery, plus by an additional 25% due to the delay in establishing manufacturing facilities. The possible profit must, therefore, be reduced by 50% plus 25%, or by a total of 75%, leaving only 25% of the $1,000,000 as possible profit.

c. By multiplying 25% by $1,000,000, you would arrive at $250,000 as the actual profit which would be made.

Choice B is incorrect. If the two profit reductions were incorrectly multiplied by one another (50% times 25%) and the product (12½%) added to 50%, there would have been a net reduction of 62 ½%, yielding $375,000. However, the two profit reductions are independent of each other and should be added together.

Choice C also is incorrect. It would occur if you only took into account the 50% profit reduction. However, as the paragraph states, you must also deduct an additional 25% of the total profit.

Choice D ($75,000) would be made if you incorrectly multiplied the total profit reduction (75%) by $1,000,000. However, the question asks for the profit, not the profit reduction.

7. Both *indeterminate* and *inconclusive* mean *vague* and *indefinite*, so Choice D is correct. Choice A is incorrect, because the word *ineluctable* means *inescapable* or *inevitable*. The reading passage does not support the conclusion that the research results are incorrect or unreasonable, so Choice B and Choice C can be eliminated from consideration.

8. Choice D is correct. The reading passage states, *The sales were phenomenal, and there is a great demand for more Futuron to be manufactured. The profits to be made by increasing the manufacturing and sale of Futuron could place the Smith Paint Company in a leading role in the paint industry.* Since the sales of Futuron were phenomenal (remarkable; extraordinary) and there still is a great demand for it, the suggestion of considerable future profit is reasonable.

Choice A is not the most accurate conclusion based on the reading passage. The financial impact of decreasing the production of the traditional paint cannot be ascertained. Therefore, it is not certain that the proposed 50% reduction in the manufacturing of the Smith Paint Company's traditional paint would not financially injure that company. Certainly, Choice D is a more accurate conclusion.

Choice B is incorrect. A greater proportion of the employees being in favor of the proposed increase in Futuron production than not being in favor of it implies that over 50% of the employees are in favor of it. However, the reading passage states that most of the employees (which, logically, means over 50% of the employees) do not want the proposed change to occur.

Choice C also is not the most accurate conclusion. It states that the proposed increase in Futuron production would cause employees considerable health damage. The reading passage is not definite on this issue of health damage. It states, *Initial research indicates that negative physical reactions may result from working closely with the chemicals necessary....* How serious the health damage might be is not stated in the reading passage.

PREPARING WRITTEN MATERIAL

PARAGRAPH REARRANGEMENT
COMMENTARY

The sentences that follow are in scrambled order. You are to rearrange them in proper order and indicate the letter choice containing the correct answer at the space at the right.

Each group of sentences in this section is actually a paragraph presented in scrambled order. Each sentence in the group has a place in that paragraph; no sentence is to be left out. You are to read each group of sentences and decide upon the best order in which to put the sentences so as to form a well-organized paragraph.

The questions in this section measure the ability to solve a problem when all the facts relevant to its solution are not given.

More specifically, certain positions of responsibility and authority require the employee to discover connection between events sometimes, apparently, unrelated. In order to do this, the employee will find it necessary to correctly infer that unspecified events have probably occurred or are likely to occur. This ability becomes especially important when action must be taken on incomplete information.

Accordingly, these questions require competitors to choose among several suggested alternatives, each of which presents a different sequential arrangement of the events. Competitors must choose the MOST logical of the suggested sequences.

In order to do so, they may be required to draw on general knowledge to infer missing concepts or events that are essential to sequencing the given events. Competitors should be careful to infer only what is essential to the sequence. The plausibility of the wrong alternatives will always require the inclusion of unlikely events or of additional chains of events which are NOT essential to sequencing the given events.

It's very important to remember that you are looking for the best of the four possible choices, and that the best choice of all may not even be one of the answers you're given to choose from.

There is no one right way to solve these problems. Many people have found it helpful to first write out the order of the sentences, as they would have arranged them, on their scrap paper before looking at the possible answers. If their optimum answer is there, this can save them some time. If it isn't, this method can still give insight into solving the problem. Others find it most helpful to just go through each of the possible choices, contrasting each as they go along. You should use whatever method feels comfortable and works for you.

While most of these types of questions are not that difficult, we've added a higher percentage of the difficult type, just to give you more practice. Usually there are only one or two questions on this section that contain such subtle distinctions that you're unable to answer confidently. And you then may find yourself stuck deciding between two possible choices, neither of which you're sure about.

PREPARING WRITTEN MATERIAL
EXAMINATION SECTION
TEST 1

DIRECTIONS: The following groups of sentences need to be arranged in an order that makes sense. Select the letter preceding the sequence that represents the BEST sentence order. *PRINT THE LETTER OF THE CORRECT ANSWER IN THE SPACE AT THE RIGHT.*

1. I. A large Naval station on Alameda Island, near Oakland, held many warships in port, and the War Department was worried that if the bridge were to be blown up by the enemy, passage to and from the bay would be hopelessly blocked.
    II. Though many skeptics were opposed to the idea of building such an enormous bridge, the most vocal opposition came from a surprising source: the United States War Department.
    III. The War Department's concerns led to a showdown at San Francisco City Hall between Strauss and the Secretary of War, who demanded to know what would happen if a military enemy blew up the bridge.
    IV. In 1933, by submitting a construction cost estimate of $17 million, an engineer named Joseph Strauss won the contract to build the Golden Gate Bridge of San Francisco, which would then become one of the world's largest bridges.
    V. Strauss quickly ended the debate by explaining that the Golden Gate Bridge was to be a suspension bridge, whose roadway would hang in the air from cables strung between two huge towers, and would immediately sink into three hundred feet of water if it were destroyed.
    The BEST order is:
    A. II, III, I, IV, V   B. I, II, III, V, IV   C. IV, II, I, III, V   D. IV, I, III, V, II

    1.____

2. I. Plastic surgeons have already begun to use virtual reality to map out the complex nerve and tissue structures of a particular patient's face, in order to prepare for delicate surgery.
    II. A virtual reality program responds to these movements by adjusting the images that a person sees on a screen or through goggles, thereby creating an "interactive" world in which a person can see and touch three-dimensional graphic objects.
    III. No more than a computer program that is designed to build and display graphic images, the virtual reality program takes graphic programs a step further by sensing a person's head and body movements.
    IV. The computer technology known as virtual reality, now in its very first stages of development, is already revolutionizing some aspects of contemporary life.
    V. Virtual reality computers are also being used by the space program, most recently to simulate conditions for the astronauts who were launched on a repair mission to the Hubble telescope.

    2.____

The BEST order is:
A. IV, II, I, V, III   B. III, I, V, II, IV   C. IV, III, II, I, V   D. III, I, II, IV, V

3. I. Before you plant anything, the soil in your plant bed should be carefully raked level, a small section at a time, and any clods or rocks that can't be broken up should be removed.
    II. Your plant should be placed in a hole that will position it at the same level it was at the nursery, and a small indentation should be pressed into the soil around the plant in order to hold water near its roots.
    III. Before placing the plant in the soil, lightly separate any roots that may have been matted together in the container, cutting away any thick masses that can't be separated, so that the remaining roots will be able to grow outward.
    IV. After the bed is ready, remove your plant from its container by turning it upside down and tapping or pushing on the bottom —never remove it by pulling on the plant.
    V. When you bring home a small plant in an individual container from the nursery, there are several things to remember while preparing to plant it in your own garden.
    The BEST order is:
    A. V, IV, III, II, I   B. V, II, IV, III, II   C. I, IV, II, III, V   D. I, IV, V, II, III

4. I. The motte and its tower were usually built first, so that sentries could use it as a lookout to warn the castle workers of any danger that might approach the castle.
    II. Though the moat and palisade offered the bailey a good deal of protection, it was linked to the motte by a set of stairs that led to a retractable drawbridge at the motte's gate, to enable people to evacuate onto the motte in case of an attack.
    III. The motte of these early castles was a fortified hill, sometimes as high as one hundred feet, on which stood a palisade and tower.
    IV. The bailey was a clear, level spot below the motte, also enclosed by a palisade, which in turn was surrounded by a large trench or moat.
    V. The earliest castles built in Europe were not the magnificent stone giants that still tower over much of the European landscape, but simpler wooden constructions called motte-and-bailey castles.
    The BEST order is:
    A. V, III, I, IV, II   B. V, IV, I, II, III   C. I, IV, III, II, V   D. I, III, II, IV, V

5. I. If an infant is left alone or abandoned for a short while, its immediate response is to cry loudly, accompanying its screams with aggressive flailing of its legs and limbs.
    II. If a child has been abandoned for a longer period of time, it becomes completely still and quiet, as if realizing that now its only chance for survival is to shut its mouth and remain motionless.
    III. Along with their intense fear of the dark, the crying behavior of human infants offers insights into how prehistoric newborn children might have evolved instincts that would prevent them from becoming victims of predators.

IV. This behavior often surprises people who enter a hospital's maternity ward for the first time and encounter total silence from a roomful of infants.
V. This violent screaming response is quite different from an infant's cries of discomfort or hunger, and seems to serve as either the child's first line of defense against an unwanted intruder, or a desperate attempt to communicate its position to the mother.
The BEST order is:
A. III, II, IV, I, V   B. III, I, V, II, IV   C. I, V, IV, II, III   D. II, IV, I, V, III

6. I. When two cats meet who are strangers, their first actions and gestures determine who the "dominant" cat will be, at least for the time being.
II. Unlike dogs, cats are typically a solitary animal species who avoid social interaction, but they do display specific social responses to each other upon meeting.
III. This is unlikely, however; before such a point of open hostility is reached, one of the cats will usually take the "submissive" position of crouching down while looking away from the other dat.
IV. If a cat desires dominance or sees the other cat as a threat to its territory, it will stare directly at the intruder with a lowered tail.
V. If the other cat responds with a similar gesture, or with the strong defensive posture of an arched back, laid-back ears and raised tail, a fight or chase is likely if neither cat gives in.
The BEST order is:
A. IV, II, I, V, III   B. I, II, IV, V, III   C. I, IV, V, III, II   D. II, I, IV, V, III

6.____

7. I. A star or planet's gravitational force can best be explained in this way: anything passing through this "dent" in space will veer toward the star or planet as if it were rolling into a hole.
II. Objects that are massive or heavy, such as stars or planets, "sink" into this surface, creating a sort of dent or concavity in the surrounding space.
III. Black holes, the most massive objects known to exist in space, create dents so large and deep that the space surrounding them actually folds in on itself, preventing anything that falls in —even light —from ever escaping again.
IV. The sort of dent a star or planet makes depends on how massive it is; planets generally have weak gravitational pulls, but stars, which are larger and heavier, make a bigger "dent" that will attract more matter.
V. In outer space, the force of gravity works as if the surrounding space is a soft, flat surface.
The BEST order is:
A. III, V, II, I, IV   B. III, IV, I, V, II   C. V, II, I, IV, III   D. I, V, II, IV, III

7.____

8. I. Eventually, the society of Kyoto gave the world one of its first and greatest novels when Japan's most promising writer, Lady Murasaki Shikibu, wrote her chronicle of Kyoto's society, *The Tale of Genji*, which preceded the first European novels by more than 500 years.
II. The society of Kyoto was dedicated to the pleasures of art; the courtiers experimented with new and colorful methods of sculpture, painting, writing, decorative gardening, and even making clothes.

8.____

III. Japanese culture began under the powerful authority of Chinese Buddhism, which influenced every aspect of Japanese life from religion to politics and art.
IV. This new, vibrant culture was so sophisticated that all the people in Kyoto's imperial court considered themselves poets, and the line between life and art hardly existed —lovers corresponded entirely through written verses, and even government officials communicated by writing poems to each other.
V. In the eighth century, when the emperor established the town of Kyoto as the capital of the Japanese empire, Japanese society began to develop its own distinctive style.

The BEST order is:
  A. V, II, IV, I, III   B. II, I, V, IV, III   C. V, III, IV, I, II   D. III, V, II, IV, I

9. I. Instead of wheels, the HSST uses two sets of magnets, one which sits on the track, and another that is carried by the train; these magnets generate an identical magnetic field which forces the two sets apart.
II. In the last few decades, railway travel has become less popular throughout the world, because it is much slower than travel by airplane, and not much less expensive.
III. The HSST's designers say that the train can take passengers from one town to another as quickly as a jet plane —while consuming less than half the energy.
IV. This repellent effect is strong enough to lift the entire train above the trackway, and the train, literally traveling on air, rockets along at speeds of up to 300 miles per hour.
V. The revolutionary technology of magnetic levitation, currently being tested by Japan's experimental HSST (High Speed Surface Transport), may yet bring passenger trains back from the dead.

The BEST order is:
  A. II, V, I, IV, III   B. II, I, IV, III, V   C. V, II, III, I, IV   D. V, I, III, IV, II

9.____

10. I. When European countries first began to colonize the African continent, their impression of the African people was of a vast group of loosely organized tribal societies, without any great centralized source of power or wealth.
II. The legend of Timbuktu persisted until the nineteenth century, when a French adventurer visited Timbuktu and found that raids by neighboring tribesmen had made the city a shadow of its former self.
III. In the fifteenth century, when the stories of travelers who had traveled Africa's Sudan region began circulating around Europe, this impression began to change.
IV. In 1470, an Italian merchant named Benedetto Dei traveled to Timbuktu and confirmed these rumors, describing a thriving metropolis where rich and poor people worshipped together in the city's many ornate mosques — there was even a university in Timbuktu, much like its European counterparts, where African scholars pursued their studies in the arts and sciences.

10.____

V. The travelers' legends told of an enormous city in the western Sudan, Timbuktu, where the streets were crowded with goods brought by faraway caravans, and where there was a stone palace as large as any in Europe.

The BEST order is:

A. III, V, I, IV, II   B. I, II, IV, III, V   C. I, III, V, IV, II   D. II, I, III, IV, V

11.
I. Also, our reference points in sighting the moon make us believe that its size is changing; when the moon is rising through the trees, it seems huge, because our brains unconsciously compare the size of the moon with the size of the trees in the foreground.
II. To most people, the sky itself appears more distant at the horizon than directly overhead, and if the moon's size—which remains constant—is projected from the horizon, the apparent distance of the horizon makes the moon look bigger.
III. Up higher in the sky, the moon is set against tiny stars in the background, which will make the moon seem smaller.
IV. People often wonder why the moon becomes bigger when it approaches the horizon, but most scientists agree that this is a complicated optical illusion, produced by at least three factors.
V. The moon illusion may also be partially explained by a phenomenon that has nothing to do with errors in our perception—light that enters the earth's atmosphere is sometimes refracted, and so the atmosphere may act as a kind of magnifying glass for the moon's image.

The BEST order is:

A. IV, III, V, II, I   B. IV, II, I, III, V   C. V, II, I, III, IV   D. II, I, III, IV, V

11.____

12.
I. When the Native Americans were introduced to the horses used by white explorers, they were amazed at their new alternative—here was an animal that was strong and swift, would patiently carry a person or other loads on its back, and they later discovered, was right at home on the plains.
II. Before the arrival of European explorers to North America, the natives of the American plains used large dogs to carry their travois-long lodgepoles loaded with clothing, gear, and food.
III. These horses, it is now known, were not really strangers to North America; the very first horses originated here, on this continent, tens of thousands of years ago, and migrated into Asia across the Bering Land Bridge, a strip of land that used to link our continent with the Eastern world.
IV. At first, the natives knew so little about horses that at least one tribe tried to feed their new animals pieces of dried meat and animal fat, and were surprised when the horses turned their heads away and began to eat the grass of the prairie.
V. The American horse eventually became extinct, but its Asian cousins were reintroduced to the New World when the European explorers brought them to live among the Native Americans.

The BEST order is:

A. II, I, IV, III, V   B. II, IV, I, III, V   C. I, II, IV, III, V   D. I, III, V, II, IV

12.____

13.
I. The dress worn by the dancer is believed to have been adorned in the past by shells which would strike each other as the dancer performed, creating a lovely sound.
II. Today's jingle-dress is decorated with the tin lids of snuff cans, which are rolled into cones and sewn onto the dress,
III. During the jingle-dress dance, the dancer must blend complicated footwork with a series of gentle hos that cause the cones to jingle in rhythm to a drumbeat.
IV. When contemporary Native American tribes meet for a pow-wow, one of the most popular ceremonies to take place is the women's jingle-dress dance.
V. Besides being more readily available than shells, the lids are thought by many dancers to create a softer, more subtle sound.
The BEST order is:
A. II, IV, V, I, III   B. IV, II, I, III, V   C. II, I, III, V, IV   D. IV, I, II, V, III

14.
I. If a homeowner lives where seasonal climates are extreme, deciduous shade trees—which will drop their leaves in the winter and allow sunlight to pass through the windows—should be planted near the southern exposure in order to keep the house cool during the summer.
II. This trajectory is shorter and lower in the sky than at any other time of year during the winter, when a house most requires heating; the northern-facing parts of a house do not receive any direct sunlight at all.
III. In designing an energy-efficient house, especially in colder climates, it is important to remember that most of the house's windows should face south.
IV. Though the sun always rises in the east and sets in the west, the sun of the northern hemisphere is permanently situated in the southern portion of the sky.
V. The explanation for why so many architects and builders want this "southern exposure" is related to the path of the sun in the sky.
The BEST order is:
A. III, I, V, IV, II   B. III, V, IV, II, I   C. I, III, IV, II, V   D. I, II, V, IV, III

15.
I. His journeying lasted twenty-four years and took him over an estimated 75,000 miles, a distance that would not be surpassed by anyone other than Magellan—who sailed around the world—for another six hundred years.
II. Perhaps the most far-flung of these lesser-known travelers was Ibn Batuta, an African Moslem who left his birthplace of Tangier in the summer of 1325.
III. Ibn Batuta traveled all over Africa and Asia, from Niger to Peking, and to the islands of Maldive and Indonesia.
IV. However, a few explorers of the Eastern world logged enough miles and adventures to make Marco Polo's voyage look like an evening stroll.
V. In America, the most well-known of the Old World's explorers are usually Europeans such as Marco Polo, the Italian who brought many elements of Chinese culture to the Western world.
The BEST order is:
A. V, IV, II, III, I   B. V, IV, III, II, I   C. III, II, I, IV, V   D. II, III, I, IV, V

16.
I. In the rainforests of South America, a rare species of frog practices a reproductive method that is entirely different from this standard process.
II. She will eventually carry each of the tadpoles up into the canopy and drop each into its own little pool, where it will be easy to locate and safe from most predators.
III. After fertilization, the female of the species, who lives almost entirely on the forest floor, lays between 2 and 16 eggs among the leaf litter at the base of a tree, and stands watch over these eggs until they hatch.
IV. Most frogs are pond-dwellers who are able to deposit hundreds of eggs in the water and then leave them alone, knowing that enough eggs have been laid to insure the survival of some of their offspring.
V. Once the tadpoles emerge, the female backs in among them, and a tadpole will wriggle onto her back to be carried high into the forest canopy, where the female will deposit it in a little pool of water cupped in the leaf of a plant.
The BEST order is:
A. I, IV, III, II, V B. I, III, V, II, IV C. IV, III, II, V, I D. IV, I, III, V, II

16.____

17.
I. Eratosthenes had heard from travelers that at exactly noon on June 21, in the ancient city of Aswan, Egypt, the sun cast no shadow in a well, which meant that the sun must be directly overhead.
II. He knew the sun always cast a shadow in Alexandria, and so he figured that if he could measure the length of an Alexandria shadow at the time when there was no shadow in Aswan, he could calculate the angle of the sun, and therefore the circumference of the earth.
III. The evidence for a round earth was not new in 1492; in fact, Eratosthenes, an Alexandrian geographer who lived nearly sixteen centuries before Columbus's voyage (275-195 B.C.), actually developed a method for calculating the circumference of the earth that is still in use today.
IV. Eratosthenes's method was correct, but his result—28,700 miles—was about 15 percent too high, probably because of the inaccurate ancient methods of keeping time, and because Aswan was not due south of Alexandria, as Eratosthenes had believed.
V. When Christopher Columbus sailed across the Atlantic Ocean for the first time in 1492, there were still some people in the world who ignored scientific evidence and believed that the earth was flat, rather than round.
The BEST order is:
A. I, II, V, III, IV B. V, III, IV, I, II C. V, III, I, II, IV D. III, V, I, II, IV

17.____

18.
I. The first name for the child is considered a trial naming, often impersonal and neutral, such as the Ngoni name *Chabwera*, meaning "it has arrived."
II. This sort of name is not due to any parental indifference to the child, but is a kind of silent recognition of Africa's sometimes high infant death rate; most parents ease the pain of losing a child with the belief that it is not really a person until it has been given a final name.
III. In many tribal African societies, families often give two different names to their children, at different periods in time.
IV. After the trial naming period has subsided and it is clear that the child will survive, the parents choose a final name for the child, an act that symbolically completes the act of birth.

18.____

V. In fact, some African first-given names are explicitly uncomplimentary, translating as "I am dead" or "I am ugly," in order to avoid the jealousy of ancestral spirits who might wish to take a child that is especially healthy or attractive.

The BEST order is:
   A. III, I, II, V, IV   B. III, IV, II, I, V   C. IV, III, I, II, V   D. IV, V, III, I, II

19. I. Though uncertain of the definite reasons for this behavior, scientists believe the birds digest the clay in order to counteract toxins contained in the seeds of certain fruits that are eaten by macaws.
   II. For example, all macaws flock to riverbanks at certain times of the year to eat the clay that is found in river mud.
   III. The macaws of South America are not only among the largest and most beautifully colored of the world's flying birds, but they are also one of the smartest.
   IV. It is believed that macaws are forced to resort to these toxic fruits during the dry season, when foods are more scarce.
   V. The macaw's intelligence has led to intense study by scientists, who have discovered some macaw behaviors that have not yet been explained.

The BEST order is:
   A. III, IV, I, II, V   B. III, V, II, I, IV   C. V, II, I, IV, III   D. IV, I, II, III, V

20. I. Although Maggie Kuhn has since passed away, the Gray Panthers are still waging a campaign to reinstate the historical view of the elderly as people whose experience allows them to make their greatest contribution in their later years.
   II. In 1972, an elderly woman named Maggie Kuhn responded to this sort of treatment by forming a group called the Gray Panthers, an organization of both old and young adults with the common goal of creating change.
   III. This attitude is reflected strongly in the way elderly people are treated by our society; many are forced into early retirement, or are placed in rest homes in which they are isolated from their communities.
   IV. Unlike most other cultures around the world, Americans tend to look upon old age with a sense of dread and sadness.
   V. Kuhn believed that when the elderly are forced to withdraw into lives that lack purpose, society loses one of its greatest resources: people who have a lifetime of experience and wisdom to offer their communities.

The BEST order is:
   A. IV, III, II, V, I   B. IV, II, I, III, V   C. II, IV, III, V, I   D. II, I, IV, III, V

21. I. The current theory among most anthropologists is that humans evolved from apes who lived in trees near the grasslands of Africa.
   II. Still, some anthropologists insist that such an invention was necessary for the survival of early humans, and point to the Kung Bushmen of central Africa as a society in which the sling is still used in this way.
   III. Two of these inventions—fire, and weapons such as spears and clubs—were obvious defenses against predators, and there is archaeological evidence to support the theory of their use.

IV. Once people had evolved enough to leave the safety of trees and walk upright, they needed the protection of several inventions in order to survive.

V. But another invention, a feather or fiber sling that allowed mothers to carry children while leaving their hands free to gather roots or berries, would certainly have decomposed and left behind no trace of itself.

The BEST order is:
A. I, II, III, V, IV B. IV, I, II, III, V C. I, IV, III, V, II D. IV, III, V, II, I

22. I. The person holding the bird should keep it in hot water up to its neck, and the person cleaning should work a mild solution of dishwashing liquid into the bird's plumage, paying close attention to the head and neck.

II. When rinsing the bird, after all the oil has been removed, the running water should be directed against the lay of its feathers, until water begins to bead off the surface of the feathers—a sign that all the detergent has been rinsed out.

III. If you have rescued a sea bird from an oil spill and want to restore it to clean and normal living, you need a large sink, a constant supply of running hot water (a little over 100°F), and regular dishwashing liquid.

IV. This cleaning with detergent solution should be repeated as many times as it takes to remove all traces of oil from the bird's feathers, sometime over a period of several days.

V. But before you begin to clean the bird, you must find a partner because cleaning an oiled bird is a two-person job.

The BEST order is:
A. III, I, II, IV, V B. III, V, I, IV, II C. III, I, IV, V, II D. III, IV, V, I, II

22.____

23. I. The most difficult time of year for the Tsaatang is the spring calving, when the reindeer leave their wintering ground and rush to their accustomed calving place, without stopping by night or by day.

II. Reindeer travel in herds, and though some animals are tamed by the Tsaatang for riding or milking, the herds are allowed to roam free.

III. This journey is hard for the Tsaatang, who carry all their possessions with them, but once it's over it proves worthwhile; the Tsaatang can immediately begin to gather milk from reindeer cows who have given birth.

IV. The Tsaatang, a small tribe who live in the far northwest corner of Mongolia, practice a lifestyle that is completely dependent on the reindeer, their main resource for food, clothing, and transport.

V. The people must follow their yearly migrations, living in portable shelters that resemble Native American tepees.

The BEST order is:
A. I, III, II, V, IV B. I, IV, II, V, III C. IV, I, III, V, II D. IV II, V, I, III

23.____

24. I. The Romans later improved this system by installing these heated pipe networks throughout walls and ceilings, supplying heat to even the uppermost floors of a building—a system that, to this day, hasn't been much improved.

II. Air-conditioning, the method by which humans control indoor temperatures, was practiced much earlier than most people think.

24.____

III. The earliest heating devices other than open fires were used in 350 B.C. by the ancient Greeks, who directed air that had been heated by underground fires into baked clay pipes that ran under the floor.
IV. Ironically, the first successful cooling system, patented in England in 1831, used fire as its main energy source—fires were lit in the attic of a building, creating an updraft of air that drew cool air into the building through ducts that had underground openings near the river Thames.
V. Cooling buildings was more of a challenge, and wasn't attempted until 1500: a water-based system, designed by Leonardo da Vinci, does not appear to have been successful, since it was never used again.
The BEST order is:
A. III, V, IV, I, II   B. III, I, II, V, IV   C. II, III, I, V, IV   D. IV, II, III, I, V

25. I. Cold, dry air from Canada passes over the Rocky Mountains and sweeps down onto the plains, where it collides with warm, moist air from the waters of the Gulf of Mexico, and when the two air masses meet, the resulting disturbance sometimes forms a violent funnel cloud that strikes the earth and destroys virtually everything in its path.
II. Hurricanes, storms which are generally not this violent and last much longer, are usually given names by meteorologists, but this tradition cannot be applied to tornados, which have a life span measured in minutes and disappear in the same way as they are born—unnamed.
III. A tornado funnel forms rotating columns of air whose speed reaches three hundred miles an hour—a speed that can only be estimated, because no wind-measuring devices in the direct path of a storm have ever survived.
IV. The natural phenomena known as tornados occur primarily over the Midwestern grasslands of the United States.
V. It is here, meteorologists tell us, that conditions for the formation of tornados are sometimes perfect during the spring months.
The BEST order is:
A. II IV, V, I, III   B. II, III, I, V, IV   C. IV, V, I, III, II   D. IV, III, I, V, II

25.____

KEY (CORRECT ANSWERS)

1.	C		11.	B
2.	C		12.	A
3.	B		13.	D
4.	A		14.	B
5.	B		15.	A
6.	D		16.	D
7.	C		17.	C
8.	D		18.	A
9.	A		19.	B
10.	C		20.	A

21. C
22. B
23. D
24. C
25. C

EXAMINATION SECTION
TEST 1

DIRECTIONS: The following groups of sentences need to be arranged in an order that makes sense. Select the letter preceding the sequence that represents the BEST sentence order. *PRINT THE LETTER OF THE CORRECT ANSWER IN THE SPACE AT THE RIGHT.*

1. I. The keyboard was purposely designed to be a little awkward to slow typists down.
    II. The arrangement of letters on the keyboard of a typewriter was not designed for the convenience of the typist.
    III. Fortunately, no one is suggesting that a new keyboard be designed right away.
    IV. If one were, we would have to learn to type all over again.
    V. The reason was that the early machines were slower than the typists and would jam easily.
    The CORRECT answer is:
    A. I, III, IV, II, V
    B. II, V, I, IV, III
    C. V, I, II, III, IV
    D. II, I, V, III, IV

1.____

2. I. The majority of the new service jobs are part-time or low-paying.
    II. According to the U.S. Bureau of Labor Statistics, jobs in the service sector constitute 72% of all jobs in this country.
    III. If more and more workers receive less and less money, who will buy the goods and services needed to keep the economy going?
    IV. The service sector is by far the fastest growing part of the United States economy.
    V. Some economists look upon this trend with great concern.
    The CORRECT answer is:
    A. II, IV, I, V, III
    B. II, III, IV, I, V
    C. V, IV, II, III, I
    D. III, I, II, IV, V

2.____

3. I. They can also affect one's endurance.
    II. This can stabilize blood sugar levels, and ensure that the brain is receiving a steady, constant, supply of glucose, so that one is *hitting on all cylinders* while taking the test.
    III. By food, we mean real food, not junk food or unhealthy snacks.
    IV. For this reason, it is important not to skip a meal, and to bring food with you to the exam.
    V. One's blood sugar levels can affect how clearly one is able to think and concentrate during an exam.
    The CORRECT answer is:
    A. V, IV, II, III, I
    B. V, II, I, IV, III
    C. V, I, IV, III, II
    D. V, IV, I, III, II

3.____

4. I. Those who are the embodiment of desire are absorbed in material quests, and those who are the embodiment of feeling are warriors who value power more than possession.
    II. These qualities are in everyone, but in different degrees.
    III. But those who value understanding yearn not for goods or victory, but for knowledge.
    IV. According to Plato, human behavior flows from three main sources: desire, emotion, and knowledge.
    V. In the perfect state, the industrial forces would produce but not rule, the military would protect but not rule, and the forces of knowledge, the philosopher kings, would reign.
    The CORRECT answer is:
    A. IV, V, I, II, III
    B. V, I, II, III, IV
    C. IV, III, II, I, V
    D. IV, II, I, III, V

5. I. Of the more than 26,000 tons of garbage produced daily in New York City, 12,000 tons arrive daily at Fresh Kills.
    II. In a month, enough garbage accumulates there to fill the Empire State Building.
    III. In 1937, the Supreme Court halted the practice of dumping the trash of New York City into the sea.
    IV. Although the garbage is compacted, in a few years the mounds of garbage at Fresh Kills will be the highest points south of Maine's Mount Desert Island on the Eastern Seaboard.
    V. Instead, tugboats now pull barges of much of the trash to Staten Island and the largest landfill in the world, Fresh Kills.
    The CORRECT answer is:
    A. III, V, IV, I, II
    B. III, V, II, IV, I
    C. III, V, I, II, IV
    D. III, II, V, IV, I

6. I. Communists rank equality very high, but freedom very low.
    II. Unlike communists, conservatives place a high value on freedom and a very low value on equality.
    III. A recent study demonstrated that one way to classify people's political beliefs is to look at the importance placed on two words: freedom and equality.
    IV. Thus, by demonstrating how members of these groups feel about the two words, the study has proved to be useful for political analysts in several European countries.
    V. According to the study, socialists and liberals rank both freedom and equality very high, while fascists rate both very low.
    The CORRECT answer is:
    A. III, V, I, II, IV
    B. V, IV, III, I, II
    C. III, V, IV, II, I
    D. III, I, II, IV, V

7.
   I. "Can there be anything more amazing than this?"
   II. If the riddle is successfully answered, his dead brothers will be brought back to life.
   III. "Even though man sees those around him dying every day," says Dharmaraj, "he still believes and acts as if he were immortal."
   IV. "What is the cause of ceaseless wonder?" asks the Lord of the Lake.
   V. In the ancient epic, The Mahabharata, a riddle is asked of one of the Pandava brothers.
   The CORRECT answer is:
   A. V, II, I, IV, III
   B. V, IV, III, I, II
   C. V, II, IV, III, I
   D. V, II, IV, I, III

8.
   I. On the contrary, the two main theories—the cooperative (neoclassical) theory and the radical (labor theory)—clearly rest on very different assumptions, which have very different ethical overtones.
   II. The distribution of income is the primary factor in determining the relative levels of material well-being that different groups or individuals attain.
   III. Of all issues in economics, the distribution of income is one of the most controversial.
   IV. The neoclassical theory tends to support the existing income distribution (or minor changes), while the labor theory ends to support substantial changes in the way income is distributed.
   V. The intensity of the controversy reflects the fact that different economic theories are not purely neutral, *detached* theories with no ethical or moral implications.
   The CORRECT answer is:
   A. II, I, V, IV, III
   B. III, II, V, I, IV
   C. III, V, II, I, IV
   D. III, V, IV, I, II

9.
   I. The pool acts as a broker and ensures that the cheapest power gets used first.
   II. Every six seconds, the pool's computer monitors all of the generating stations in the state and decides which to ask for more power and which to cut back.
   III. The buying and selling of electrical power is handled by the New York Power Pool in Guilderland, New York.
   IV. This is to the advantage of both the buying and selling utilities.
   V. The pool began operation in 1970, and consists of the state's eight electric utilities.
   The CORRECT answer is:
   A. V, I, II, III, IV
   B. IV, II, I, III, V
   C. III, V, I, IV, II
   D. V, III, IV, II, I

10. I. Modern English is much simpler grammatically than Old English.
    II. Finnish grammar is very complicated; there are some fifteen cases, for example.
    III. Chinese, a very old language, may seem to be the exception, but it is the great number of characters/words that must be mastered that makes it so difficult to learn, not its grammar.
    IV. The newest literary language—that is, written as well as spoken—is Finish, whose literary roots go back only to about the middle of the nineteenth century.
    V. Contrary to popular belief, the longer a language is been in use the simpler its grammar—not the reverse.
    The CORRECT answer is:
    A. IV, I, II, III, V
    B. V, I, IV, II, III
    C. I, II, IV, III, V
    D. IV, II, III, I, V

KEY (CORRECT ANSWERS)

1.	D	6.	A
2.	A	7.	C
3.	C	8.	B
4.	D	9.	C
5.	C	10.	B

TEST 2

DIRECTIONS: This type of question tests your ability to recognize accurate paraphrasing, well-constructed paragraphs, and appropriate style and tone. It is important that the answer you select contains only the facts or concepts given in the original sentences. It is also important that you be aware of incomplete sentences, inappropriate transitions, unsupported opinions, incorrect usage, and illogical sentence order. Paragraphs that do not include all the necessary facts and concepts, that distort them, or that add new ones are not considered correct.

The format for this section may vary. Sometimes, long paragraphs are given, and emphasis is placed on style and organization. Our first five questions are of this type. Other times, the paragraphs are shorter, and there is less emphasis on style and more emphasis on accurate representation of information. Our second group of five questions are of this nature.

For each of Questions 1 through 10, select the paragraph that BEST expresses the ideas contained in the sentences above it. *PRINT THE LETTER OF THE CORRECT ANSWER IN THE SPACE AT THE RIGHT.*

1.
   I. Listening skills are very important for managers.
   II. Listening skills are not usually emphasized.
   III. Whenever managers are depicted in books, manuals or the media, they are always talking, never listening.
   IV. We'd like you to read the enclosed handout on listening skills and to try to consciously apply them this week.
   V. We guarantee they will improve the quality of your interactions.

   A. Unfortunately, listening skills are not usually emphasized for managers. Managers are always depicted as talking, never listening. We'd like you to read the enclosed handout on listening skills. Please try to apply these principles this week. If you do, we guarantee they will improve the quality of your interactions.
   B. The enclosed handout on listening skills will be important improving the quality of your interactions. We guarantee it. All you have to do is take sometime this week to read and to consciously try to apply the principles. Listening skills are very important for manages, but they are not usually emphasized. Whenever managers are depicted in books, manuals or the media, they are always talking, never listening.
   C. Listening well is one of the most important skills a manager can have, yet it's not usually given much attention. Think about any representation of managers in books, manuals, or in the media that you may have seen. They're always talking, never listening. We'd like you to read the enclosed handout on listening skills and consciously try to apply them the rest of the week. We guarantee you will see a difference in the quality of your interactions.

1.____

D. Effective listening, one very important tool in the effective manager's arsenal, is usually not emphasized enough. The usual depiction of managers in books, manuals or the media is one in which they are always talking, never listening. We'd like you to read the enclosed handout and consciously try to apply the information contained therein throughout the rest of the week. We feel sure that you will see a marked difference in the quality of your interactions.

2.
I. Chekhov wrote three dramatic masterpieces which share certain themes and formats: Uncle Vanya, The Cherry Orchard, and The Three Sisters.
II. They are primarily concerned with the passage of time and how this erodes human aspirations.
III. The plays are haunted by the ghosts of the wasted life.
IV. The characters are concerned with life's lesser problems; however, such as the inability to make decisions, loyalty to the wrong cause, and the inability to be clear.
V. This results in sweet, almost aching, type of a sadness referred to as Chekhovian.

2.____

A. Chekhov wrote three dramatic masterpieces: Uncle Vanya, The Cherry Orchard, and The Three Sisters. These masterpieces share certain themes and formats: the passage of time, how time erodes human aspirations, and the ghosts of wasted life. Each masterpiece is characterized by a sweet, almost aching, type of sadness that has become known as Chekhovian. The sweetness of this sadness hinges on the fact that it is not the great tragedies of life which are destroying these characters, but their minor flaws: indecisiveness, misplaced loyalty, unclarity.
B. The Cherry Orchard, Uncle Vanya, and The Three Sisters are three dramatic masterpieces written by Chekhov that use similar formats to explore a common theme. Each is primarily concerned with the way that passing time wears down human aspirations, and each is haunted by the ghosts of the wasted life. The characters are shown struggling futilely with the lesser problems of life: indecisiveness, loyalty to the wrong cause, and the inability to be clear. These struggles create a mood of sweet, almost aching, sadness that has become known as Chekhovian.
C. Chekhov's dramatic masterpieces are, along with The Cherry Orchard, Uncle Vanya, and The Three Sisters. These plays share certain thematic and formal similarities. They are concerned most of all with the passage of time and the way in which time erodes human aspirations. Each play is haunted by the specter of the wasted life. Chekhov's characters are caught, however, by life's lesser snares: indecisiveness, loyalty to the wrong cause, and unclarity. The characteristic mood is a sweet, almost aching type of sadness that has come to be known as Chekhovian.
D. A Chekhovian mood is characterized by sweet, almost aching, sadness. The term comes from three dramatic tragedies by Chekhov which revolve around the sadness of a wasted life. The three masterpieces (Uncle Vanya, The Three Sisters, and The Cherry Orchard) share the same

theme and format. The plays are concerned with how the passage of time erodes human aspirations. They are peopled with characters who are struggling with life's lesser problems. These are people who are indecisive, loyal to the wrong causes, or are unable to make themselves clear.

3. I. Movie previews have often helped producers decide which parts of movies they should take out or leave in.
    II. The first 1933 preview of King Kong was very helpful to the producers because many people ran screaming from the theater and would not return when four men first attacked by Kong were eaten by giant spiders.
    III. The 1950 premiere of Sunset Boulevard resulted in the filming of an entirely new beginning, and a delay of six months in the film's release.
    IV. In the original opening scene, William Holden was in a morgue talking with thirty-six other "corpses" about the ways some of them had died.
    V. When he began to tell them of his life with Gloria Swanson, the audience found this hilarious, instead of taking the scene seriously.

3.____

   A. Movie previews have often helped producers decide what parts of movies they should leave in or take out. For example, the first preview of King Kong in 1933 was very helpful. In one scene, four men were first attacked by Kong and then eaten by giant spiders. Many members of the audience ran screaming from the theater and would not return. The premiere of the 1950 film Sunset Boulevard was also very helpful. In the original opening scene, William Holden was in a morgue with thirty-six other "corpses," discussing the ways some of them had died. When he began to tell them of his life with Gloria Swanson, the audience found this hilarious. They were supposed to take the scene seriously. The result was a delay of six months in the release of the film while a new beginning was added.
   B. Movie previews have often helped producers decide whether they should change various parts of a movie. After the 1933 preview of King Kong, a scene in which four men who had been attacked by Kong were eaten by giant spiders was taken out as many people ran screaming from the theater and would not return. The 1950 premiere of Sunset Boulevard also led to some changes. In the original opening scene, William Holden was in a morgue talking with thirty-six other "corpses" about the ways some of them had died. When he began to tell them of his life with Gloria Swanson, the audience found this hilarious, instead of taking the scene seriously.
   C. What do Sunset Boulevard and King Kong have in common? Both show the value of using movie previews to test audience reaction. The first 1933 preview of King Kong showed that a scene showing four men being eaten by giant spiders after having been attacked by Kong was too frightening for many people. They ran screaming from the theater and couldn't be coaxed back. The 1950 premiere of Sunset Boulevard was also a scream, but not the kind the producers intended. The movie opens

with William Holden lying in a morgue discussing the ways they had died with thirty-six other "corpses." When he began to tell them of his life with Gloria Swanson, the audience couldn't take him seriously. Their laughter caused a six-month delay while the beginning was rewritten.

D. Producers very often use movie previews to decide if changes are needed. The premiere of Sunset Boulevard in 1950 led to a new beginning and a six-month delay in film release. At the beginning, William Holden and thirty-six other "corpses" discuss the ways some of them died. Rather than taking this seriously, the audience thought it was hilarious when he began to tell them of his life with Gloria Swanson. The first 1933 preview of King Kong was very helpful for its producers because one scene so terrified the audience that many of them ran screaming from the theater and would not return. In this particular scene, four men who had first been attacked by Kong were eaten by giant spiders.

4.
I. It is common for supervisors to view employees as "things" to be manipulated.
II. This approach does not motivate employees, nor does the carrot-and-stick approach because employees often recognize these behaviors and resent them.
III. Supervisors can change these behaviors by using self-inquiry and persistence.
IV. The best managers genuinely respect those they work with, are supportive and helpful, and are interested in working as a team with those they supervise.
V. They disagree with the Golden Rule that says "he or she who has the gold makes the rules."

4.____

A. Some managers act as if they think the Golden Rule means "he or she who has the gold makes the rules." They show disrespect to employees by seeing them as "things" to be manipulated. Obviously, this approach does not motivate employees any more than the carrot-and-stick approach motivates them. The employees are smart enough to spot these behaviors and resent them. On the other hand, the managers genuinely respect those they work with, are supportive and helpful, and are interested in working as a team. Self-inquiry and persistence can change even the former type of supervisor into the latter.

B. Many supervisors all into the trap of viewing employees as "things" to be manipulated, or try to motivate them by using a carrot-and-stick approach. These methods do not motivate employees, who often recognize the behaviors and resent them. Supervisors can change these behaviors, however, by using self-inquiry and persistence. The best managers are supportive and helpful, and have genuine respect for those with whom they work. They are interested in working as a team with those they supervise. To them, the Golden Rule is not "he or she who has the gold makes the rules."

C. Some supervisors see employees as "things" to be used or manipulated using a carrot-and-stick technique. These methods don't work. Employees often see through them and resent them. A supervisor who wants to change may do so. The techniques of self-inquiry and persistence can be used to turn him or her into the type of supervisor who doesn't think the Golden Rule is "he or she who has the gold makes the rules." They may become like the best managers who treat those with whom they work with respect and give them help and support. These are the manager who know how to build a team.

D. Unfortunately, many supervisors act as if their employees are objects whose movements they can position at will. This mistaken belief has the same result as another popular motivational technique—the carrot-and-stick approach. Both attitudes can lead to the same result—resentment from those employees who recognize the behaviors for what they are. Supervisors who recognize these behaviors can change through the use of persistence and the use of self-inquiry. It's important to remember that the best managers respect their employees. They readily give necessary help and support and are interested in working as a team with those they supervise. To these managers, the Golden Rule is not "he or she who has the gold makes the rules."

5.
I. The first half of the nineteenth century produced a group of pessimistic poets—Byron, De Musset, Heine, Pushkin, and Leopardi.
II. It also produced a group of pessimistic composers—Schubert, Chopin, Schumann, and even the later Beethoven.
III. Above all, in philosophy, there was the profoundly pessimistic philosopher, Schopenhauer.
IV. The Revolution was dead, the Bourbons were restored, the feudal barons were reclaiming their land, and progress everywhere was being suppressed, as the great age was over.
V. "I thank God," said Goethe, "that I am not young in so thoroughly finished a world."

5.____

A. "I thank God," said Goethe, "that I am not young in so thoroughly finished a world." The Revolution was dead, the Bourbons were restored, the feudal barons were reclaiming their land, and progress everywhere was being suppressed. The first half of the nineteenth century produced a group of pessimistic poets: Byron, De Musset, Heine, Pushkin, and Leopardi. It also produced pessimistic composers: Schubert, Chopin, Schumann. Although Beethoven came later, he fits into this group, too. Finally and above all, it also produced a profoundly pessimistic philosopher, Schopenhauer. The great age was over.

B. The first half of the nineteenth century produced a group of pessimistic poets: Byron, De Musset, Heine, Pushkin, and Leopardi. It produced a group of pessimistic composers: Schubert, Chopin, Schumann, and even the later Beethoven. Above all, it produced a profoundly pessimistic philosopher, Schopenhauer. For each of these men, the great age was over. The Revolution was dead, and the Bourbons were restored. The feudal barons were reclaiming their land, and progress everywhere was being suppressed.

C. The great age was over. The Revolution was dead—the Bourbons were restored, and the feudal barons were reclaiming their land. Progress everywhere was being suppressed. Out of this climate came a profound pessimism. Poets, like Byron, De Musset, Heine, Pushkin, and Leopardi; composers, like Schubert, Chopin, Schumann, and even the later Beethoven; and above all, a profoundly pessimistic philosopher, Schopenauer. This pessimism which arose in the first half of the nineteenth century is illustrated by these words of Goethe, "I thank God that I am not young in so thoroughly finished a world."

D. The first half of the nineteenth century produced a group of pessimistic poets, Byron, De Musset, Heine, Pushkin, and Leopardi—and a group of pessimistic composers, Schubert, Chopin, Schumann, and the later Beethoven. Above it all, it produced a profoundly pessimistic philosopher, Schopenhauer. The great age was over. The Revolution was dead, the Bourbons were restored, the feudal barons were reclaiming their land, and progress everywhere was being suppressed. "I thank God," said Goethe, "that I am not young in so thoroughly finished a world."

6. I. A new manager sometimes may feel insecure about his or her competence in the new position.
    II. The new manager may then exhibit defensive or arrogant behavior towards those one supervises, or the new manager may direct overly flattering behavior toward one's new supervisor.

    A. Sometimes, a new manager may feel insecure about his or her ability to perform well in this new position. The insecurity may lead him or her to treat others differently. He or she may display arrogant or defensive behavior towards those he or she supervises, or be overly flattering to his or her new supervisor.
    B. A new manager may sometimes feel insecure about his or her ability to perform well in the new position. He or she may then become arrogant, defensive, or overly flattering towards those he or she works with.
    C. There are times when a new manager may be insecure about how well he or she can perform in the new job. The new manager may also behave defensive or act in an arrogant way towards those he or she supervises, or overly flatter his or her boss.
    D. Sometimes a new manager may feel insecure about his or her ability to perform well in the new position. He or she may then display arrogant or defensive behavior towards those they supervise, or become overly flattering towards their supervisors.

6.____

7. I. It is possible to eliminate unwanted behavior by bringing it under stimulus control—tying the behavior to a cue, and then never, or rarely, giving the cue.
    II. One trainer successfully used this method to keep an energetic young porpoise from coming out of her tank whenever she felt like it, which was potentially dangerous.
    III. Her trainer taught her to do it for a reward, in response to a hand signal, and then rarely gave the signal.

7.____

A. Unwanted behavior can be eliminated by tying the behavior to a cue, and then never, or rarely, giving the cue. This is called stimulus control. One trainer was able to use this method to keep an energetic young porpoise from coming out of her tank by teaching her to come out for a reward in response to a hand signal, and then rarely giving the signal.
B. Stimulus control can be used to eliminate unwanted behavior. In this method, behavior is tied to a cue, and then the cue is rarely, if ever, given. One trainer was able to successfully use stimulus control to keep an energetic young porpoise from coming out of her tank whenever she felt like it—a potentially dangerous practice. She taught the porpoise to come out for a reward when she gave a hand signal, and then rarely gave the signal.
C. It is possible to eliminate behavior that is undesirable by bringing it under stimulus control by tying behavior to a signal, and then rarely giving the signal. One trainer successfully used this method to keep an energetic porpoise from coming out of her tank, a potentially dangerous situation. Her trainer taught the porpoise to do it for a reward, in response to a hand signal, and then would rarely give the signal.
D. By using stimulus control, it is possible to eliminate unwanted behavior by tying the behavior to a cue, and then rarely or never give the cue. One trainer was able to use this method to successfully stop a young porpoise from coming out of her tank whenever she felt like it. To curb this potentially dangerous practice, the porpoise was taught by the trainer to come out of the tank for a reward, in response to a hand signal, and then rarely given the signal.

8. I. There is a great deal of concern over the safety of commercial trucks, caused by their greatly increased role in serious accidents since federal deregulation in 1981.
    II. Recently, 60 percent of trucks in New York and Connecticut and 70 percent of trucks in Maryland randomly stopped by state troopers failed safety inspections.
    III. Sixteen states in the United States require no training at all for truck drivers.

    A. Since federal deregulation in 1981, there has been a great deal of concern over the safety of commercial trucks, and their greatly increased role in serious accidents. Recently, 60 percent of trucks in New York and Connecticut, and 70 percent of trucks in Maryland failed safety inspections. Sixteen states in the United States require no training at all for truck drivers.
    B. There is a great deal of concern over the safety of commercial trucks since federal deregulation in 1981. Their role in serious accidents has greatly increased. Recently, 60 percent of trucks randomly stopped in Connecticut and New York and 70 percent in Maryland failed safety inspections conducted by state troopers. Sixteen states in the United States provide no training at all for truck drivers.
    C. Commercial trucks have a greatly increased role in serious accidents since federal deregulation in 1981. This has led to a great deal of concern.

8.____

Recently, 70 percent of trucks in Maryland and 60 percent of trucks in New York and Connecticut failed inspection of those that were randomly stopped by state troopers. Sixteen states in the United States require no training for all truck drivers.

D. Since federal deregulation in 1981, the role that commercial trucks have played in serious accidents has greatly increased, and this has led to a great deal of concern. Recently, 60 percent of trucks in New York and Connecticut, and 70 percent of trucks in Maryland randomly stopped by state troopers failed safety inspections. Sixteen states in the U.S. don't require any training for truck drivers.

9. I. No matter how much some people have, they still feel unsatisfied and want more, or want to keep what they have forever.
    II. One recent television documentary showed several people flying from New York to Paris for a one-day shopping spree to buy platinum earrings, because they were bored.
    III. In Brazil, some people were ordering coffins that cost a minimum of $45,000 and are equipping them with deluxe stereos, televisions, and other graveyard necessities.

    A. Some people, despite having a great deal, still feel unsatisfied and want more, or think they can keep what they have forever. One recent documentary on television showed several people enroute from Paris to New York for a one day shopping spree to buy platinum earrings, because they were bored. Some people in Brazil are even ordering coffins equipped with such graveyard necessities as deluxe stereos and televisions. The price of the coffins start at $45,000.
    B. No matter how much some people have, they may feel unsatisfied. This leads them to want more, or to want to keep what they have forever. Recently, a television documentary depicting several people flying from New York to Paris for a one day shopping spree to buy platinum earrings. They were bored. Some people in Brazil are ordering coffins that cost at least $45,000 and come equipped with deluxe televisions, stereos and other necessary graveyard items.
    C. Some people will be dissatisfied no matter how much they have. They may want more, or they may want to keep what they have forever. One recent television documentary showed several people, motivated by boredom, jetting from New York to Paris for a one-day shopping spree to buy platinum earrings. In Brazil, some people are ordering coffins equipped with deluxe stereos, televisions and other graveyard necessities. The minimum price for these coffins—$45,000.
    D. Some people are never satisfied. No matter how much they have they still want more, or think they can keep what they have forever. One television documentary recently showed several people flying from New York to Paris for the day to buy platinum earrings because they were bored. In Brazil, some people are ordering coffins that cost $45,000 and are equipped with deluxe stereos, televisions and other graveyard necessities.

9.____

10.
I. A television signal or video signal has three parts.
II. Its parts are the black-and-white portion, the color portion, and the synchronizing (sync) pulses, which keep the picture stable.
III. Each video source, whether it's a camera or a video-cassette recorder contains its own generator of these synchronizing pulses to accompany the picture that it's sending in order to keep it steady and straight.
IV. In order to produce a clean recording, a video-cassette recorder must "lock-up" to the sync pulses that are part of the video it is trying to record, and this effort may be very noticeable if the device does not have gunlock.

10.____

A. There are three parts to a television or video signal: the black-and-white part, the color part, and the synchronizing (sync) pulses, which keep the picture stable. Whether it's a video-cassette recorder or a camera, each video source contains its own pulse that synchronizes and generates the picture it's sending in order to keep it straight and steady. A video-cassette recorder must "lock up" to the sync pulses that are part of the video it's trying to record. If the device doesn't have gunlock, this effort must be very noticeable.

B. A video signal or television is comprised of three parts: the black-and-white portion, the color portion, and the sync (synchronizing) pulses, which keep the picture stable. Whether it's a camera or a video-cassette recorder, each video source contains its own generator of these synchronizing pulses. These accompany the picture that it's sending in order to keep it straight and steady. A video-cassette recorder must "lock up" to the sync pulses that are part of the video it is trying to record in order to produce a clean recording. This effort may be very noticeable if the device does not have gunlock.

C. There are three parts to a television or video signal: the color portion, the black-and-white portion, and the sync (synchronizing pulses). These keep the picture stable. Each video source, whether it's a video-cassette recorder or a camera, generates these synchronizing pulses accompanying the picture it's sending in order to keep it straight and steady. If a clean recording is to be produced, a video-cassette recorder must store the sync pulses that are part of the video it is trying to record. This effort may not be noticeable if the device does not have gunlock.

D. A television signal or video signal has three parts: the black-and-white portion, the color portion, and the synchronizing (sync) pulses. It's the sync pulses which keep the picture stable, which accompany it and keep it steady and straight. Whether it's a camera or a video-cassette recorder, each video source contains its own generator of these synchronizing pulses. To produce a clean recording, a video-cassette recorder must "lock up" to the sync pulses that are part of the video it is trying to record. If the device does not have gunlock, this effort may be very noticeable.

KEY (CORRECT ANSWERS)

1. C
2. B
3. A
4. B
5. D

6. A
7. B
8. D
9. C
10. D

INTERPRETING STATISTICAL DATA GRAPHS, CHARTS, AND TABLES

EXAMINATION SECTION

TEST 1

DIRECTIONS: Each question or incomplete statement is followed by several suggested answers or completions. Select the one that BEST answers the question or completes the statement. *PRINT THE LETTER OF THE CORRECT ANSWER IN THE SPACE AT THE RIGHT.*

Questions 1-5.

DIRECTIONS: Questions 1 through 5 are to be answered SOLELY on the basis of the following chart.

DUPLICATION JOBS							
JOB NO.	DATES			PROCESS	NO. OF ORIGINALS	NO. OF COPIES OF EACH ORIGINAL	REQUESTING UNIT
	SUBMITTED	REQUIRED	COMPLETED				
324	6/22	6/25	6/25	Xerox	14	25	Research
325	6/25	6/27	6/28	Kodak	10	125	Training
326	6/25	6/25	6/25	Xerox	12	11	Budget
327	6/25	6/27	6/26	Press	17	775	Admin. Div. H
328	6/28	ASAP*	6/25	Press	5	535	Personnel
329	6/26	6/26	6/27	Xerox	15	8	Admin. Div. G

*ASAP – As soon as possible

1. The unit whose job was to be Xeroxed but was NOT completed by the date required is 1.____
   A. Administrative Division H
   B. Administrative Division G
   C. Research
   D. Training

2. The job with the LARGEST number of original pages to be Xeroxed is job number 2.____
   A. 324   B. 326   C. 327   D. 329

3. Jobs were completed AFTER June 26 for 3.____
   A. Training and Administrative Division G
   B. Training and Administrative Division H
   C. Research and Budget
   D. Administrative Division G only

4. Which one of the following units submitted a job which was completed SOONER than required? 4.____
   A. Training
   B. Administrative Division H
   C. Personnel
   D. Administrative Division G

159

5. The jobs which were submitted on different days but were completed on the SAME day and used the SAME process had job numbers
   A. 324 and 326
   B. 327 and 328
   C. 324, 326, and 328
   D. 324, 326, and 329

5.____

KEY (CORRECT ANSWERS)

1. B
2. D
3. A
4. B
5. A

TEST 2

DIRECTIONS: Each question or incomplete statement is followed by several suggested answers or completions. Select the one that BEST answers the question or completes the statement. *PRINT THE LETTER OF THE CORRECT ANSWER IN THE SPACE AT THE RIGHT.*

Questions 1-10.

DIRECTIONS: Questions 1 through 10 are to be answered SOLELY on the basis of the Production Record table shown below for the Information Unit in Agency X for the work week ended Friday, December 6. The table shows, for each employee, the quantity of each type of work performed and the percentage of the work week spent in performing each type of work.

NOTE: Assume that each employee works 7 hours a day and 5 days a week, making a total of 35 hours for the work week.

PRODUCTION RECORD – INFORMATION UNIT IN AGENCY X
(For the Work Week ended Friday, December 6)

	NUMBER OF			
	Papers Filed	Sheets Proofread	Visitors Received	Envelopes Addressed
Miss Agar	3120	33	178	752
Mr. Brun	1565	59	252	724
Miss Case	2142	62	214	426
Mr. Dale	4259	29	144	1132
Miss Earl	2054	58	212	878
Mr. Farr	1610	69	245	621
Miss Glen	2390	57	230	790
Mr. Hope	3425	32	176	805
Miss Iver	3726	56	148	650
Mr. Joad	3212	55	181	495

	PERCENTAGE OF WORK WEEK SPENT ON				
	Filing Papers	Proofreading	Receiving Visitors	Addressing Envelopes	Performing Miscellaneous Work
Miss Agar	30%	9%	34%	11%	16%
Mr. Brun	13%	15%	52%	10%	10%
Miss Case	23%	18%	38%	6%	15%
Mr. Dale	50%	7%	17%	16%	10%
Miss Earl	24%	14%	37%	14%	11%
Mr. Farr	16%	19%	48%	8%	9%
Miss Glen	27%	12%	42%	12%	7%
Mr. Hope	38%	8%	32%	13%	9%
Miss Iver	43%	13%	24%	9%	11%
Mr. Joad	33%	11%	36%	7%	13%

2 (#2)

1. For the week, the average amount of time which the employees spent in proofreading was MOST NEARLY _____ hours.
   A. 3.1   B. 3.6   C. 4.4   D. 5.1

2. The average number of visitors received daily by an employee was MOST NEARLY
   A. 40   B. 57   C. 198   D. 395

3. Of the following employees, the one who addressed envelopes at the FASTEST rate was
   A. Miss Agar   B. Mr. Brun   C. Miss Case   D. Mr. Dale

4. Mr. Farr's rate of filing papers was MOST NEARLY _____ pages per minute.
   A. 2   B. 1.7   C. 5   D. 12

5. The average number of hours that Mr. Brun spent daily on receiving visitors exceeded the average number of hours that Miss Iver spent daily on the same type of work by MOST NEARLY _____ hours.
   A. 2   B. 3   C. 4   D. 5

6. Miss Earl worked at a FASTER rate than Miss Glen in
   A. filing papers
   B. proofreading sheets
   C. receiving visitors
   D. addressing envelopes

7. Mr. Joad's rate of filing papers _____ Miss Iver's rate of filing papers by APPROXIMATELY _____.
   A. was less than; 10%
   B. exceeded; 33%
   C. was less than; 16%
   D. exceeded; 12%

8. Assume that in the following week Miss Case is instructed to increase the percentage of her time spent on filing papers to 35%.
   If she continued to file papers at the same rate as she did for the week ended December 6, the number of additional papers that she filed the following week was MOST NEARLY
   A. 3260   B. 5400   C. 250   D. 1120

9. Assume that in the following week Mr. Hope increased his weekly total of envelopes addressed to 1092.
   If he continued to spend the same amount of time on this assignment as he did for the week ended December 6, the increase in his rate of addressing envelopes the following week was MOST NEARLY _____ envelopes her hour.
   A. 15   B. 65   C. 155   D. 240

10. Assume that in the following week Miss Agar and Mr. Dale spent 3 and 9 hours less, respectively, on filing papers than they had spent for the week ended December 6, without changing their rates of work.
    The total number of papers filed during the following week by both Miss Agar and Mr. Dale was MOST NEARLY
    A. 4235　　　B. 4295　　　C. 4315　　　D. 4370

KEY (CORRECT ANSWERS)

1. C   6. C
2. A   7. D
3. B   8. D
4. C   9. B
5. A   10. B

TEST 3

DIRECTIONS: Each question or incomplete statement is followed by several suggested answers or completions. Select the one that BEST answers the question or completes the statement. *PRINT THE LETTER OF THE CORRECT ANSWER IN THE SPACE AT THE RIGHT.*

Questions 1-6.

DIRECTIONS: Questions 1 through 6 are to be answered SOLELY on the basis of the following chart.

EMPLOYMENT RECORDS				
	Allan	Barry	Cary	David
July	5	4	1	7
August	8	3	9	8
September	7	8	7	5
October	3	6	5	3
November	2	4	4	6
December	5	2	8	4

1. The clerk with the HIGHEST number of errors for the 6-month period was
   A. Allan B. Barry C. Cary D. David

2. If the number of errors made by Allan in the six months shown represented one-eighth of the total errors made by the unit during the entire ear, what was the TOTAL number of errors made by the unit for the year?
   A. 124 B. 180 C. 240 D. 360

3. The number of errors made by David in November was what fraction of the total errors made in November?
   A. 1/3 B. 1/6 C. 378 D. 3/15

4. The average number of errors made per month per clerk was MOST NEARLY
   A. 4 B. 5 C. 6 D. 7

5. Of the total number of errors made during the six-month period, the percentage made in August was MOST NEARLY
   A. 2% B. 4% C. 23% D. 44%

6. If the number of errors in the unit were to decrease in the next six months by 30%, what would be MOST NEARLY the total number of errors for the unit for the next six months?
   A. 87 B. 94 C. 120 D. 137

KEY (CORRECT ANSWERS)

1. C
2. C
3. C
4. B
5. C
6. A

TEST 4

DIRECTIONS: Each question or incomplete statement is followed by several suggested answers or completions. Select the one that BEST answers the question or completes the statement. *PRINT THE LETTER OF THE CORRECT ANSWER IN THE SPACE AT THE RIGHT.*

Questions 1-5.

DIRECTIONS: Questions 1 through 5 are to be answered SOLELY on the basis of the following data. These data show the performance rates of the employees in a particular division for a period of six months.

Employee	Jan.	Feb.	March	April	May	June
A	96	53	64	48	76	72
B	84	58	69	56	67	79
C	73	68	71	54	59	62
D	98	74	79	66	86	74
E	89	78	67	74	75	77

1. According to the above data, the average monthly performance for a worker is MOST NEARLY
   A. 66　　B. 69　　C. 72　　D. 75

2. According to the above data, the mean monthly performance for the division is MOST NEARLY
   A. 350　　B. 358　　C. 387　　D. 429

3. According to the above data, the employee who shows the LEAST month-to-month variation in performance is
   A. A　　B. B　　C. C　　D. D

4. According to the above data, the employee who shows the GREATEST range in performance is
   A. A　　B. B　　C. C　　D. D

5. According to the above data, the median employee with respect to performance for the six-month period is
   A. A　　B. B　　C. C　　D. D

KEY (CORRECT ANSWERS)

1. C
2. B
3. C
4. A
5. B

TEST 5

DIRECTIONS: Each question or incomplete statement is followed by several suggested answers or completions. Select the one that BEST answers the question or completes the statement. *PRINT THE LETTER OF THE CORRECT ANSWER IN THE SPACE AT THE RIGHT.*

Questions 1-5.

DIRECTIONS: Questions 1 through 5 are to be answered SOLELY on the basis of the following chart, which shows the absences in Unit A for the period November 1 through November 15.

ABSENCE RECORD – UNIT A November 1-15															
Date:	1	2	3	4	5	6	7	8	9	10	11	12	13	14	15
Employee															
Ames	X	s	H					X			H			X	X
Bloom	X		H				X	X	S	s	H	S	S		X
Deegan	X	J	H	J	J	J	X	X			H				X
Howard	X		H					X			H			X	X
Jergens	X	M	H	M	M	M		X			X			X	X
Lange	X		H			S	X	X							X
Morton	X						X	X	V	V	H				X
O'Shea	X		H			O		X			H			X	X

CODE FOR TYPES OF ABSENCE
X - Saturday or Sunday
H - Legal Holiday
P - Leave Without Pay
M - Military Leave
J - Jury Duty
V - Vacation
S - Sick Leave
O - Other Leave of Absence

NOTE: If there is no entry against an employee's name under a date, the employee worked on that date.

1. According to the above chart, NO employee in Unit A was absent on 1.____
   A. leave without pay   B. military leave
   C. other leave of absence   D. vacation

2. According to the above chart, all but one of the employees in Unit A were present on the 2.____
   A. 3rd   B. 5th   C. 9th   D. 13th

3. According to the above chart, the ONLY employee who worked on a legal holiday when the other employees were absent are 3.____
   A. Deegan and Morton   B. Howard and O'Shea
   C. Lange and Morton   D. Morton and O'Shea

4. According to the above chart, the employee who was absent ONLY on a day that was a Saturday, Sunday, or legal holiday was
   A. Bloom   B. Howard   C. Morton   D. O'Shea

5. The employees who had more absences than anyone else are
   A. Bloom and Deegan
   B. Bloom, Deegan, and Jergens
   C. Deegan and Jergens
   D. Deegan, Jergens, and O'Shea

KEY (CORRECT ANSWERS)

1. A
2. D
3. C
4. B
5. B

TEST 6

DIRECTIONS: Each question or incomplete statement is followed by several suggested answers or completions. Select the one that BEST answers the question or completes the statement. *PRINT THE LETTER OF THE CORRECT ANSWER IN THE SPACE AT THE RIGHT.*

Questions 1-7.

DIRECTIONS: Questions 1 through 7 are to be answered SOLELY on the basis of the time sheet and instructions given below.

	MON.		TUES.		WED.		THURS.		FRI.	
	IN	OUT	IN	OUT	IN	OUT	IN	OUT	IN	OUT
Walker	8:45	5:02	9:20	5:00	9:00	5:02	Annual Lv.		9:04	5:05
Jones	9:01	5:00	9:03	5:02	9:08	5:01	8:55	5:04	9:00	5:00
Rubins	8:49	5:04	Sick Lv.		9:05	5:04	9:03	5:03	9:04	3:30 (PB)
Brown	9:00	5:01	8:55	5:03	9:00	5:05	9:04	5:07	9:05	5:03
Roberts	9:30	5:08	8:43	5:07	9:05	5:05	9:09	12:30	8:58	5:04
	PA						PB			

The above time sheet indicates the arrival and leaving times of five telephone operators who punched a time clock in a city agency for the week of April 14. The times they arrived at work in the mornings are indicated in the columns labeled *IN* and the times they left work are indicated in the columns labeled *OUT*. The letters (PA) mean prearranged lateness, and the letters (PB) mean personal business. Time lost for these purposes is charged to annual leave.

The operators are scheduled to arrive at 9:00. However, they are not considered late unless they arrive after 9:05. If they prearrange a lateness, they are not considered late. Time lost through lateness is charged to annual leave. A full day's work is eight hours, from 9:00 to 5:00.

1. Which operator worked the entire week WITHOUT using any annual leave or sick leave time?
   A. Jones
   B. Brown
   C. Roberts
   D. None of the above

2. On which days was NONE of the operators considered late?
   A. Monday and Wednesday
   B. Monday and Friday
   C. Wednesday and Thursday
   D. Wednesday and Friday

3. Which operator clocked out at a different time each day of the week?
   A. Roberts   B. Jones   C. Rubins   D. Brown

4. How many of the operators were considered late on Wednesday?
   A. 0   B. 1   C. 2   D. 3

169

5. What was the TOTAL number of charged latenesses for the week of April 14?
   A. 1   B. 3   C. 5   D. 7

   5._____

6. Which day shows the MOST time charged to all types of leave by all the operators?
   A. Monday   B. Tuesday   C. Wednesday   D. Thursday

   6._____

7. What operators were considered ON TIME all week?
   A. Jones and Rubins
   B. Rubins and Brown
   C. Brown and Roberts
   D. Walker and Brown

   7._____

KEY (CORRECT ANSWERS)

1. B
2. B
3. A
4. B
5. B
6. D
7. B

TEST 7

DIRECTIONS: Each question or incomplete statement is followed by several suggested answers or completions. Select the one that BEST answers the question or completes the statement. *PRINT THE LETTER OF THE CORRECT ANSWER IN THE SPACE AT THE RIGHT.*

Questions 1-10.

DIRECTIONS: Questions 1 through 10 are to be answered SOLELY on the basis of the information and code tables given below.

In accordance with these code tables, each employee in the department is assigned a code number consisting of ten digits arranged from left to right in the following order:
  I. Division in Which Employed
  II. Title of Position
  III. Annual Salary
  IV. Age
  V. Number of Years Employed in Department

EXAMPLE: A clerk is 21 years old, has been employed in the department for three years, and is working in the Supply Division at a yearly salary of $25,000. His code number is 90-115-13-02-2.

DEPARTMENTAL CODE

TABLE I		TABLE II		TABLE III		TABLE IV		TABLE V	
Code No.	Division in Which Employed	Code No.	Title of Position	Code No.	Annual Salary	Code No.	Age	Code No.	No. of Years Employed in Department
10	Accounting	115	Clerk	11	$18,000 or less	01	Under 20 yrs.	1	Less than 1 year
20	Construction	155	Typist	12	$18,001 to $24,000	02	20 to 20 yrs.	2	1 to 5 yrs.
30	Engineering	175	Stenographer					3	6 to 10 yrs.
40	Information	237	Bookkeeper			03	30 to 39 yrs.	4	11 to 15 yrs.
50	Maintenance	345	Statistician	13	$24,001 to $30,000			5	16 to 25 yrs.
60	Personnel	545	Storekeeper			04	40 to 49 yrs.	6	26 to 35 yrs.
70	Record	633	Draftsman					7	36 yrs. or over
80	Research	665	Civil Engineer						
90	Supply	865	Machinist	14	$30,001 to $36,000	05	50 to 59 yrs.		
		915	Porter			06	60 to 69 yrs.		
				15	$36,001 to $45,000	07	70 yrs. or over		
				16	$45,001 to $60,000				
				17	$60,001 to $70,000				
				18	$70,001 or over				

1. A draftsman employed in the Engineering Division at a yearly salary of $34,800 is 36 years old and has been employed in the department for 9 years.
   He should be coded
   A. 20-633-13-04-3
   B. 30-865-13-03-4
   C. 20-665-14-04-4
   D. 30-633-14-03-3

2. A porter employed in the Maintenance Division at a yearly salary of $28,800 is 52 years old and has been employed in the department for 6 years.
   He should be coded
   A. 50-915-12-03-3
   B. 90-545-12-05-3
   C. 50-915-13-05-3
   D. 90-545-13-03-3

3. Richard White, who has been employed in the department for 12 years, receives $50,000 a year as a civil engineer in the Construction Division. He is 38 years old.
   He should be coded
   A. 20-665-16-03-4
   B. 20-665-15-02-1
   C. 20-633-14-04-2
   D. 20-865-15-02-5

4. An 18-year-old clerk appointed to the department six months ago is assigned to the Record Division. His annual salary is $21,600.
   He should be coded
   A. 70-115-11-01-1
   B. 70-115-12-01-1
   C. 70-115-12-02-1
   D. 70-155-12-01-1

5. An employee has been coded 40-155-12-03-3.
   Of the following statements regarding this employee, the MOST accurate one is that he is
   A. a clerk who has been employed in the department for at least 6 years
   B. a typist who receives an annual salary which does not exceed $24,000
   C. under 30 years of age and has been employed in the department for at least 11 years
   D. employed in the Supply Division at a salary which exceeds $18,000 per annum

6. Of the following statements regarding an employee who is coded 60-175-13-01-2, the LEAST accurate statement is that this employee
   A. is a stenographer in the Personnel Division
   B. has been employed in the department for at least one year
   C. receives an annual salary which exceeds $24,000
   D. is more than 20 years of age

7. The following are the names of four employees of the department with their code numbers:
   James Black, 80-345-15-03-4
   William White, 30-633-14-03-4
   Sam Green, 80-115-12-02-3
   John Jones, 10-237-13-04-5

3 (#7)

If a salary increase is to be given to the employees who have been employed in the department for 11 years or more and who earn less than $36,001 a year, the two of the above employees who will receive a salary increase are
A. John Jones and William White B. James Black and Sam Green
C. James Black and William White D. John Jones and Sam Green

8. Code number 50-865-14-02-6, which has been assigned to a machinist, contains an obvious inconsistency.
This inconsistency involves the figures
A. 50-865 B. 865-14 C. 14-02 D. 02-6

9. Ten employees were awarded merit prizes for outstanding service during the year. Their code numbers were:
80-345-14-04-4   40-155-12-02-2
40-155-12-04-4   10-115-12-02-2
10-115-13-03-2   80-115-13-02-2
80-174-13-05-5   10-115-13-02-3
10-115-12-04-3   30-633-14-04-4
Of these outstanding employees, the number who were clerks employed in the Accounting Division at a salary ranging from $24,001 to $30,000 per annum is
A. 1 B. 2 C. 3 D. 4

10. The MOST accurate of the following statements regarding the ten outstanding employees listed in the previous question is that
A. fewer than half of the employees were under 40 years of age
B. there were fewer typists than stenographers
C. four of the employees were employed in the department 11 years or more
D. two of the employees in the Research Division receive annual salaries ranging from $30,001 to $36,000

KEY (CORRECT ANSWERS)

1.	D	6.	D
2.	C	7.	A
3.	A	8.	D
4.	B	9.	B
5.	B	10.	C

INTERPRETING STATISTICAL DATA GRAPHS, CHARTS, AND TABLES

EXAMINATION SECTION

TEST 1

DIRECTIONS: Each question or incomplete statement is followed by several suggested answers or completions. Select the one that BEST answers the question or completes the statement. *PRINT THE LETTER OF THE CORRECT ANSWER IN THE SPACE AT THE RIGHT.*

Questions 1-5.

DIRECTIONS: Questions 1 through 5 are to be answered SOLELY on the basis of the following table.

ANNUAL SALARIES PAID TO SELECTED CLERICAL TITLES IN FIVE MAJOR CITIES IN 2017 AND 2019

2019	Clerk	Typist	Steno	Legal Steno	Computer Operator
Newton	$33,900	$34,800	$36,300	$43,800	$35,400
Barton	$32,400	$34,200	$35,400	$43,500	$24,200
Phelton	$32,400	$32,400	$34,200	$42,000	$33,000
Washburn	$33,600	$34,800	$35,400	$43,800	$34,800
Biltmore	$33,000	$34,200	$35,100	$43,500	$34,500
2017					
Newton	$31,800	$33,600	$35,400	$41,400	$34,500
Barton	$30,000	$31,500	$33,000	$39,600	$31,500
Phelton	$29,400	$30,600	$31,800	$37,800	$31,200
Washburn	$30,600	$32,400	$33,600	$40,200	$32,400
Biltmore	$30,000	$31,800	$33,00	$39,600	$32,100

1. Assume that the value of the fringe benefits offered to clerical employees in 2019 amounted to 14% of their annual salaries in Newton, 17% in Barton, 18% in Phelton, 15% in Washburn, and 16% in Biltmore.
The total cost of employing a computer operator for 2019 was GREATEST in
   A. Newton   B. Barton   C. Phelton   D. Washburn

1.____

2. During negotiations for their 2020 contract, the stenographers of Biltmore are demanding that their rate of pay be fixed at 85% of the legal stenographer salary.
If this demand is granted and if the legal stenographer salary increases by 7% in 2020, the 2020 stenographer salary will be MOST NEARLY
   A. $36,972   B. $37,560   C. $39,564   D. $40,020

2.____

2 (#1)

3. Of the following, the GREATEST percentage increase in salary from 2017 to 2019 was gained by
   A. clerks in Newton
   B. stenographers in Barton
   C. legal stenographers in Washburn
   D. computer operators in Biltmore

4. The title which achieved the SMALLEST average percentage increase in salary from 2017 to 2019 was
   A. clerk
   B. typist
   C. stenographer
   D. legal stenographer

5. Assume that, in 2019, clerks accounted for 60% of the clerical work force in Barton. The clerical work force consists of 140 employees. In 2017, the clerks accounted for 65% of the clerical work force in Barton. The clerical work force then consisted of 120 employees.
   The difference between the 2017 and 2019 payroll for clerks in Barton is MOST NEARLY
   A. $120,000
   B. $240,000
   C. $360,000
   D. $480,000

3.____
4.____
5.____

KEY (CORRECT ANSWERS)

1. A
2. C
3. C
4. C
5. C

TEST 2

DIRECTIONS: Each question or incomplete statement is followed by several suggested answers or completions. Select the one that BEST answers the question or completes the statement. *PRINT THE LETTER OF THE CORRECT ANSWER IN THE SPACE AT THE RIGHT.*

Questions 1-9.

DIRECTIONS: Questions 1 through 9 are to be answered SOLELY on the basis of the facts given in the following table, which contains certain information about employees in a city bureau.

| \multicolumn{5}{c}{RECORD OF EMPLOYEES IN A CITY BUREAU} |
NAME	TITLE	AGE	ANNUAL SALARY	YEARS OF SERVICE	EXAMINATION RATING
Jones	Clerk	34	$40,800	10	82
Smith	Stenographer	25	$38,400	2	72
Black	Typist	19	$28,800	1	71
Brown	Stenographer	36	$50,400	12	88
Thomas	Accountant	49	$82,400	21	91
Gordon	Clerk	31	$60,000	8	81
Johnson	Stenographer	26	$52,800	5	75
White	Accountant	53	$72,000	30	90
Spencer	Clerk	42	$55,200	19	85
Taylor	Typist	24	$43,200	5	74
Simpson	Accountant	37	$100,000	1	87
Reid	Typist	20	$24,000	2	72
Fulton	Accountant	55	$110,000	31	100
Chambers	Clerk	22	$31,200	4	75
Calhoun	Stenographer	48	$57,600	16	80

1. The name of the employee whose salary would be the middle one if all the salaries were ranked in order of magnitude is
   A. White B. Johnson C. Brown D. Spencer

2. The combined monthly salary of all the stenographers EXCEEDS the combined monthly salary of all the clerks by
   A. $12,000 B. $1,000 C. $45,600 D. $1,200

3. The age of the employee who received the HIGHEST rating in the examination among those who have less than 10 years of service is _____ years.
   A. 22 B. 31 C. 55 D. 34

1.____

2.____

3.____

4. The average examination rating of those employees who had 15 years of service or more as compared with the average examination rating of those employees who had 5 years of service or less is MOST NEARLY _____ points _____.
   A. 16; greater   B. 7; greater   C. 10; less   D. 25; greater

5. The name of the youngest employee whose monthly salary is more than $2,000 per month and who has more than one year of service is
   A. Reid   B. Black   C. Chambers   D. Taylor

6. The name of the employee who received an examination rating of over 85%, who has more than 15 years of service, and who earns a yearly salary of more than $50,000 but less than $80,000 is
   A. Thomas   B. Spencer   C. Calhoun   D. White

7. The annual salary of the HIGHEST paid stenographer is
   A. more than twice as great as the salary of the youngest employee
   B. greater than the salary of the oldest typist but not as great as the salary of the oldest clerk
   C. greater than the salary of the highest paid typist but not as great as the salary of the lowest paid accountant
   D. less than the combined salaries of the two youngest typists

8. The number of employees whose annual salary is more than $31,200 but less than $57,600 and who have at least 5 years of service is
   A. 11   B. 8   C. 6   D. 5

9. Of the following, it would be MOST accurate to state that the
   A. youngest employee is lowest with respect to number of years of service, examination rating, and salary
   B. oldest employee is highest with respect to number of years of service, examination rating, but not with respect to salary
   C. annual salary of the youngest clerk is $2,400 more than the annual salary of the youngest typist and $4,800 less than the annual salary of the youngest stenographer
   D. difference in age between the youngest and oldest typist is less than one-fourth the difference in age between the youngest and oldest stenographer

KEY (CORRECT ANSWERS)

1. B 6. D
2. B 7. C
3. B 8. D
4. A 9. D
5. C

TEST 3

DIRECTIONS: Each question or incomplete statement is followed by several suggested answers or completions. Select the one that BEST answers the question or completes the statement. *PRINT THE LETTER OF THE CORRECT ANSWER IN THE SPACE AT THE RIGHT.*

Questions 1-10.

DIRECTIONS: Questions 1 through 10 are to be answered SOLELY on the basis of the Personnel Record of Division X shown below.

				No. of Days Absent		No. of Times Late
Employee	Bureau in Which Employed	Title	Annual Salary	On Vacation	On Sick Leave	
Abbot	Mail	Clerk	$31,200	18	0	1
Barnes	Mail	Clerk	$25,200	25	3	7
Davis	Mail	Typist	$24,000	21	9	2
Adams	Payroll	Accountant	$42,500	10	0	2
Bell	Payroll	Bookkeeper	$31,200	23	2	5
Duke	Payroll	Clerk	$27,600	24	4	3
Gross	Payroll	Clerk	$21,600	12	5	7
Lane	Payroll	Stenographer	$26,400	19	16	20
Reed	Payroll	Typist	$22,800	15	11	11
Arnold	Record	Clerk	$32,400	6	15	9
Cane	Record	Clerk	$24,500	14	3	4
Fay	Record	Clerk	$21,100	20	0	4
Hale	Record	Typist	$25,200	18	2	7
Baker	Supply	Clerk	$30,000	20	3	2
Clark	Supply	Clerk	$27,600	25	6	5
Ford	Supply	Typist	$22,800	25	4	22

1. The percentage of the total number of employees who are clerks is MOST NEARLY
   A. 25%   B. 33%   C. 38%   D. 56%

2. Of the following employees, the one who receives a monthly salary of $2,100 is
   A. Barnes   B. Gross   C. Reed   D. Clark

3. The difference between the annual salary of the highest paid clerk and that of the lowest paid clerk is
   A. $6,000   B. $8,400   C. $11,300   D. $20,900

1._____

2._____

3._____

4. The number of employees receiving more than $25,000 a year but less than $40,000 a year is
   A. 6   B. 9   C. 12   D. 15

   4.____

5. The TOTAL annual salary of the employees of the Mail Bureau is _____ the total annual salary of the employees of the _____.
   A. one-half of; Payroll Bureau
   B. less than; Record Bureau by $21,600
   C. equal to; Supply Bureau
   D. less than; Payroll Bureau by $71,600

   5.____

6. The average annual salary of the employees who are not clerks is MOST NEARLY
   A. $23,700   B. $25,450   C. $26,800   D. $27,850

   6.____

7. If all the employees were given a 10% increase in pay, the annual salary of Lane would then be
   A. *greater* than that of Barnes by $1,320
   B. *less* than that of Bell by $4,280
   C. *equal to* that of Clark
   D. *greater* than that of Ford by $3,600

   7.____

8. Of the clerks who earned less than $30,000 a year, the one who was late the FEWEST number of times was late _____ time(s).
   A. 1   B. 2   C. 3   D. 4

   8.____

9. The bureau in which the employees were late the FEWEST number of times on an average is the _____ Bureau.
   A. Mail   B. Payroll   C. Record   D. Supply

   9.____

10. The MOST accurate of the following statements is that
    A. Reed was late more often than any other typist
    B. Bell took more time off for vacation than any other employee earning $30,000 or more annually
    C. of the typists, Ford was the one who was absent the fewest number of times because of sickness
    D. three clerks took no time off because of sickness

    10.____

KEY (CORRECT ANSWERS)

1. D 6. D
2. A 7. A
3. C 8. C
4. B 9. A
5. C 10. B

TEST 4

DIRECTIONS: Each question or incomplete statement is followed by several suggested answers or completions. Select the one that BEST answers the question or completes the statement. *PRINT THE LETTER OF THE CORRECT ANSWER IN THE SPACE AT THE RIGHT.*

Questions 1-10.

DIRECTIONS: Questions 1 through 10 are to be answered SOLELY on the basis of the Weekly Payroll Record shown below of Bureau X in a public agency. In answering these questions, note that gross weekly salary is the salary before deductions have been made; take-home pay is the amount remaining after all indicated weekly deductions have been made from the gross weekly salary. In answering questions involving annual amounts, compute on the basis of 52 weeks per year.

BUREAU X
WEEKLY PAYROLL PERIOD

Unit in Which Employed	Employee	Title	Gross Weekly Salary (Before Deductions)	Weekly Deductions From Gross Salary		
				Medical Insurance	Income Tax	Pension System
Accounting	Allen	Accountant	$950	$14.50	$125.00	$53.20
Accounting	Barth	Bookkeeper	$720	$19.00	$62.00	$40.70
Accounting	Keller	Clerk	$580	$6.50	$82.00	$33.10
Accounting	Peters	Typist	$560	$6.50	$79.00	$35.30
Accounting	Simons	Stenographer	$610	$14.50	$64.00	$37.80
Information	Brown	Clerk	$560	$13.00	$56.00	$42.20
Information	Smith	Clerk	$590	$14.50	$61.00	$58.40
Information	Turner	Typist	$580	$13.00	$59.00	$62.60
Information	Williams	Stenographer	$620	$19.00	$44.00	$69.40
Mail	Conner	Clerk	$660	$13.00	$74.00	$55.40
Mail	Farrell	Typist	$540	$6.50	$75.00	$34.00
Mail	Johnson	Stenographer	$580	$19.00	$36.00	$37.10
Records	Dillon	Clerk	$640	$6.50	$94.00	$58.20
Records	Martin	Clerk	$540	$19.00	$29.00	$50.20
Records	Standish	Typist	$620	$14.50	$67.00	$60.10
Records	Wilson	Stenographer	$690	$6.50	$101.00	$75.60

1. Dillon's annual take-home pay is MOST NEARLY
   A. $25,000 B. $27,000 C. $31,000 D. $33,000

2. The difference between Turner's gross annual salary and his annual take-home pay is MOST NEARLY
   A. $3,000 B. $5,000 C. $7,000 D. $9,000

3. Of the following, the employee whose weekly take-home pay is CLOSEST to that of Keller's is
   A. Peters   B. Brown   C. Smith   D. Turner

4. The average gross annual salary of the typists is
   A. less than $27,500
   B. more than $27,500 but less than $30,000
   C. more than $30,000 but less than $32,500
   D. more than $32,500

5. The average gross weekly salary of the stenographers EXCEEDS the gross weekly salary of the clerk by
   A. $20   B. $30   C. $40   D. $50

6. Of the following employees in Accounting Unit, the one who pays the HIGHEST percentage of his gross weekly salary for the Pension System is
   A. Barth   B. Keller   C. Peters   D. Simons

7. For all of the Accounting Unit employees, the total annual deductions for Medical Insurance are less than the total annual deductions for the Pension System by MOST NEARLY
   A. $6,000   B. $7,000   C. $8,000   D. $9,000

8. Of the following, the employee whose total weekly deductions are MOST NEARLY 27% of his gross weekly salary is
   A. Barth   B. Brown   C. Martin   D. Wilson

9. The total amount of the gross weekly salaries of all the employees in the Records Unit is MOST NEARLY
   A. 95% of the total amount of the gross weekly salaries of all the employees in the Information Unit
   B. 10% greater than the total amount of the gross weekly salaries of all the employees in the Mail Unit
   C. 75% of the total amount of the gross weekly salaries of all the employees in the Accounting Unit
   D. four times as great as the total amount deducted weekly for tax for all the employees in the Records Unit

10. For the employees in the Information Unit, the AVERAGE weekly deductions for Income Tax _____ the average weekly deduction for _____.
    A. exceeds; Income Tax for the employees in the Records Unit
    B. is less than; the Pension System for the employees in the Mail Unit
    C. exceeds; Income Tax for the employees in the Accounting Unit
    D. is less than; the Pension System for the employees in the Records Unit

KEY (CORRECT ANSWERS)

1.	A	6.	C
2.	C	7.	B
3.	C	8.	D
4.	B	9.	C
5.	B	10.	D

TEST 5

DIRECTIONS: Each question or incomplete statement is followed by several suggested answers or completions. Select the one that BEST answers the question or completes the statement. *PRINT THE LETTER OF THE CORRECT ANSWER IN THE SPACE AT THE RIGHT.*

Questions 1-9.

DIRECTIONS: Questions 1 through 9 are to be answered SOLELY on the basis of the following information.

Assume that the following rules for computing service ratings are to be used experimentally in determining service ratings of seven permanent city employees. (Note that these rules are hypothetical and are NOT to be confused with the existing method of computing service ratings for city employees). The personnel record of each of these seven employees is given in Table II. You are to determine the answer to each of the questions on the basis of the rules given below for computing service ratings and the data contained in the personnel records of these seven employees.

All computations should be made as of the close of the rating period ending March 31, 2017.

Service Rating
The service rating of each permanent competitive class employee shall be computed by adding the following three scores: (1) a basic score, (2) the employee's seniority score, and (3) the employee's efficiency score.

Seniority Score
An employee's seniority score shall be computed by crediting him with ½% per year for each year of service starting with the date of the employee's entrance as a permanent employee into the competitive class, up to a maximum of 15 years (7½%).
A residual fractional period of eight months or more shall be considered as a full year and credited with ½%. A residual fraction of from four to, but not including, eight months shall be considered as half-year and credited with ¼%. A residual fraction of less than four months shall receive no credit in the seniority score.
For example, a person who entered the competitive class as a permanent employee on August 1, 2014 would, as of March 31, 2017, be credited with a seniority score of 1½% for his 2 years and 8 months of service.

Efficiency Score
An employee's efficiency score shall be computed by adding the annual efficiency ratings received by him during his service in his present position. (Where there are negative efficiency ratings, such ratings shall be subtracted from the sum of the positive efficiency ratings.) An employee's annual efficiency rating shall be based on the grade he receives from his supervisor for his work performance during the annual efficiency rating period.

Basic Score
A basic score of 70% shall be given to each employee upon permanent appointment to a competitive class position.

2 (#5)

An employee shall receive a grade of A for performing work of the highest quality and shall be credited with an efficiency rating of plus (+)3%. An employee shall receive a grade of F for performing work of the lowest quality and shall receive an efficiency rating of minus (-)2%. Table I, entitled BASS FOR DETERMINING ANNUAL EFFICIENCY RATINGS, lists the six grades of work performance with their equivalent annual efficiency ratings. Table I also lists the efficiency ratings to be assigned for service in a position for less than a year during the annual efficiency rating period.

The annual efficiency rating period shall run from April 1 to March 31, inclusive.

			Annual Efficiency Rating for Service in a Position For	
TABLE I – BASIS FOR DETERMINING ANNUAL EFFICIENCY RATINGS				
Quality of Work Performed	Grade Assigned	8 Months to a Full Year	At Least 4 Months But Less Than 8 Months	Less Than 4 Months
Highest	A	+3%	+1½%	0%
Good	B	+2%	+1%	0%
Standard	C	+1%	+½%	0%
Substandard	D	0%	0%	0%
Poor	E	-1%	-4%	0%
Lowest	F	-2%	-1%	0%

Appointment or Promotion During an Efficiency Rating Period

An employee who has been appointed or promoted during an efficiency rating period shall receive for that period an efficiency rating only for work performed by him during the portion of the period that he served in the position to which he was appointed or promoted. His efficiency rating for the period shall be determined in accordance with Table I.

Sample Computation of Service Rating

John Smith entered the competitive class as a permanent employee on December 1, 2012 and was promoted to his present position as a Clerk, Grade 3, on November 1, 2015. As a Clerk, Grade 3, he received a grade of B for work performed during the five-month period extending from November 1, 2015 to March 31, 2016 and a grade of C for work performed during the full annual period extending from April 1, 2016 to March 31, 2017.

On the basis of the RULES FOR COMPUTING SERVICE RATINGS, John Smith should be credited with:

70%   Basic Score
2¼%   Seniority Score – for 4 years and 4 months of service (from 12/1/12 to 3/31/17)
2%   Efficiency Score – for 5 months of B service and a full _____ year of C service
74¼%

TABLE II
PERSONNEL RECORD OF SEVEN PERMANENT COMPETITIVE CLASS EMPLOYEES

Employee	Present Position	Date of Appointment or Promotion to Present Position	Date of Entry as Permanent Employment in Competitive Class
Allen	Clerk, Gr. 5	6-1-13	7-1-00
Brown	Clerk, Gr. 4	1-1-15	7-1-17
Cole	Clerk, Gr. 3	9-1-13	11-1-10
Fox	Clerk, Gr. 3	10-1-13	9-1-08
Green	Clerk, Gr. 2	12-1-11	12-1-11
Hunt	Clerk, Gr. 2	7-1-12	7-1-12
Kane	Steno, Gr. 3	11-16-14	3-1-11

GRADES RECEIVED ANNUALLY FOR WORK PERFORMED IN PRESENT POSITION

Employee	4-1-11 to 3-31-12	4-1-12 to 3-31-13	4-1-13 to 3-31-14	4-1-14 to 3-31-15	4-1-15 to 3-31-16	4-1-16 to 3-31-17
Allen			C*	C	B	C
Brown				C*	C	B
Cole			A*	B	C	C
Fox			C*	C	D	C
Green	C*	D	C	D	C	C
Hunt		C*	C	E	C	C
Kane				B*	B	C

EXPLANATORY NOTES
* Served in present position for less than a full year during this rating period. (Note date of appointment, or promotion, to present position.)
 All seven employees have served continuously as permanent employees since their entry into the competitive class.

Questions 1 through 9 refer to the employees listed in Table II. You are to answer these questions SOLELY on the basis of the preceding RULES FOR COMPUTING SERVICE RATINGS and on the information concerning these seven employees given in Table II. You are reminded that all computations are to be made as of the close of the rating period ending March 31, 2017. Candidates may find it helpful to arrange their computations on their scratch paper in an orderly manner since the computations for one question may also be utilized in answering another question.

1. The seniority score of Allen is
 A. 7½%   B. 8½%   C. 8%   D. 8¼%

2. The seniority score of Fox EXCEEDS that of Cole by
 A. 1½%   B. 2%   C. 1%   D. ¾%

4 (#5)

3. The seniority score of Brown is
   A. *equal* to Hunt's
   B. *twice* Hunt's
   C. *more* than Hunt's by 1½%
   D. *less* than by Hunt's by ½%

   3._____

4. Green's efficiency score is
   A. *twice* that of Kane
   B. *equal* to that of Kane
   C. *less* than Kane's by ½%
   D. *less* than Kane's by 1%

   4._____

5. Of the following employees, the one who has the LOWEST efficiency score is
   A. Brown   B. Fox   C. Hunt   D. Kane

   5._____

6. A comparison of Hunt's efficiency score with his seniority score reveals that his efficiency score is
   A. *less* than his seniority score by ½%
   B. *less* than his seniority score by ¾%
   C. *equal* to his seniority score
   D. *greater* than his seniority score by ½%

   6._____

7. Fox's service rating is
   A. 72½%   B. 74%   C. 76½%   D. 76¾%

   7._____

8. Brown's service rating is
   A. less than 78%
   B. 78%
   C. 78¼%
   D. more than 78¼%

   8._____

9. Cole's service rating EXCEEDS Kane's by
   A. less than 2%
   B. 2%
   C. 2¼%
   D. more than 2¼%

   9._____

KEY (CORRECT ANSWERS)

1.	A	6.	D
2.	C	7.	D
3.	B	8.	B
4.	C	9.	A
5.	B		

ARITHMETICAL REASONING

EXAMINATION SECTION

TEST 1

DIRECTIONS: Each question or incomplete statement is followed by several suggested answers or completions. Select the one that BEST answers the question or completes the statement. *PRINT THE LETTER OF THE CORRECT ANSWER IN THE SPACE AT THE RIGHT.*

1. The ABC Corporation had a gross income of $125,500.00 in 2019. Of this, it paid 60% for overhead.
   If the gross income for 2020 increased by $6,500 and the cost of overhead increased to 61% of gross income, how much MORE did it pay for overhead in 2020 than in 2019?
   A. $1,320   B. $5,220   C. $7,530   D. $8,052

   1.____

2. After one year, Mr. Richards paid back a total of $16,950 as payment for a $15,000 loan. All the money paid over $15,000 was simple interest.
   The interest charge was MOST NEARLY
   A. 13%   B. 11%   C. 9%   D. 7%

   2.____

3. A checking account has a balance of $253.36.
   If deposits of $36.95, $210.23, and $7.34 and withdrawals of $117.35, $23.37, and $15.98 are made, what is the NEW balance of the account?
   A. $155.54   B. $351.18   C. $364.58   D. $664.58

   3.____

4. In 2020, the W Realty Company spent 27% of its income on rent.
   If it earned $97,254 in 2020, the amount it paid for rent was
   A. $26,258.58   B. 26,348.58   C. $27,248.58   D. $27,358.58

   4.____

5. Six percent simple annual interest on $2,436.18 is MOST NEARLY
   A. $145.08   B. $145.17   C. $146.08   D. $146.17

   5.____

6. H. Partridge receives a weekly gross salary (before deductions) of $397.50. Through weekly payroll deductions of $13.18, he is paying back a loan he took from his pension fund.
   If other fixed weekly deductions amount to $122.76, how much pay would Mr. Partridge take home over a period of 33 weeks?
   A. $7,631.28   B. $8,250.46   C. $8,631.48   D. $13,117.50

   6.____

7. Mr. Robertson is a city employee enrolled in a city retirement system. He has taken out a loan from the retirement fund and is paying it back at the rate of $14.90 every two weeks.
   In eighteen weeks, how much money will he have paid back on the loan?
   A. $268.20   B. $152.80   C. $134.10   D. $67.05

   7.____

8. In 2019, The Iridor Book Company had the following expenses: rent, $6,500; overhead, $52,585; inventory, $35,700; and miscellaneous, $1,275.
If all of these expenses went up 18% in 2020, what would they TOTAL in 2020?
A. $17,290.80 B. $78,769.20 C. $96,060.00 D. $113,350.80

9. Ms. Ranier had a gross salary of $710.72 paid once every two weeks.
If the deductions from each paycheck are $125.44, $50.26, $12.58, and $2.54, how much money would Ms. Ranier take home in eight weeks?
A. $2,079.60 B. $2,842.88 C. $4,159.20 D. $5,685.76

10. Mr. Martin had a net income of $95,500 in 2019.
If he spent 34% on rent and household expenses, 3% on house furnishings, 25% on clothes, and 36% on food, how much was left for savings and other expenses?
A. $980 B. $1,910 C. $3,247 D. $9,800

11. Mr. Elsberg can pay back a loan of $1,800 from the city employees' retirement system if he pays back $36.69 every two weeks for two full years.
At the end of the two years, how much more than the original $1,800 he borrowed will Mr. Elsberg have paid back?
A. $53.94 B. $107.88 C. $190.79 D. $214.76

12. Mr. Nusbaum is a city employee receiving a gross salary (salary before deductions) of $20,800. Every two weeks, the following deductions are taken out of his salary: Federal Income Tax, $162.84; FICA, $44.26; State Tax, $29.2; City Tax, $13.94; Health Insurance, $3.14.
If Mr. Nusbaum's salary and deductions remained the same for a full calendar year, what would his net salary (gross salary less deductions) be in that year?
A. $6,596.20 B. $14,198.60 C. $18,745.50 D. $20,546.30

13. Add: 8936, 7821, 8953, 4297, 9785, 6579.
A. 45,371 B. 45,381 C. 46,371 D. 46,381

14. Multiply: 987
867
A. 854,609 B. 854,729 C. 855,709 D. 855,729

15. Divide: 59)321439.0
A. 5438.1 B. 5447.1 C. 5448.1 D. 5457.1

16. Divide: .052)721
A. 12,648.0 B. 12,648.1 C. 12,649.0 D. 12,649.1

17. If the total number of employees in one city agency increased from 1,927 to 2,006 during a certain year, the percentage increase in the number of employees for that year is MOST NEARLY
A. 4% B. 5% C. 6% D. 7%

18. During a single fiscal year, which totaled 248 workdays, one account clerk verified 1,488 purchase vouchers.
Assuming a normal work week of five days, what is the AVERAGE number of vouchers verified by the account clerk in a one-week period during this fiscal year?
A. 25 B. 30 C. 35 D. 40

18.____

19. Multiplying a number by .75 is the same as
A. multiplying it by ²/₃
B. dividing it by ²/₃
C. multiplying it by ¾
D. dividing it by ¾

19.____

20. In City Agency A, ²/₃ of the employees are enrolled in a retirement system. City Agency B has the same number of employees as Agency A and 60% of these are enrolled in a retirement system.
If Agency A has a total of 660 employees, how many MORE employees does it have enrolled in a retirement system than does Agency B?
A. 36 B. 44 C. 56 D. 66

20.____

21. Net worth is equal to assets minus liabilities.
If, at the end of 2019, a textile company had assets of $98,695.83 and liabilities of $59,238.29, what was its net worth?
A. $38,478.54 B. $38,488.64 C. $39,457.54 D. $48,557.54

21.____

22. Mr. Martin's assets consist of the following: Cash on hand, $5,233.74, Automobile, $3,206.09; Furniture, $4,925.00; Government Bonds, $5,500.00; and House, $36,69.85.
What are his TOTAL assets?
A. $54,545.68 B. $54,455.68 C. $55,455.68 D. $55,555.68

22.____

23. If Mr. Mitchell has $627.04 in his checking account and then writes three checks for $241.75, $13.24, and $102.97, what will be his new balance?
A. $257.88 B. $269.08 C. $357.96 D. $369.96

23.____

24. An employee's net pay is equal to his total earnings less all deductions.
If an employee's total earnings in a pay period are $497.05, what is his net pay if he has the following deductions: Federal Income Tax, $18.79; City Tax, $7.25; Pension, $1.88?
A. $351.17 B. $351.07 C. $350.17 D. $350.07

24.____

25. A petty cash fund had an opening balance of $85.75 on December 1. Expenditures of $23.00, $15.65, $5.23, $14.75, and $26.38 were made out of this fund during the first 14 days of the month. Then, on December 17, another $38.50 was added to the fund.
If additional expenditures of $17.18, $3.29, and $11.64 were made during the remainder of the month, what was the FINAL balance of the petty cash fund at the end of December?
A. $6.93 B. $7.13 C. $46.51 D. $91.40

25.____

KEY (CORRECT ANSWERS)

1.	B	11.	B
2.	A	12.	B
3.	B	13.	C
4.	A	14.	D
5.	D	15.	C
6.	C	16.	D
7.	C	17.	A
8.	D	18.	B
9.	A	19.	C
10.	B	20.	B

21.	C
22.	D
23.	B
24.	D
25.	B

SOLUTIONS TO PROBLEMS

1. ($132,000)(.61) − ($125,500)(.60) = $5,220

2. Interest = $1,950. As a percent, $1950 ÷ 15,000 = 13%

3. New balance = $253.36 + $36.95 + $210.23 + $7.34 - $117.35 - $23.37 - $15.98 = $351.18

4. Rent = ($97,254)(.27) = $26,258.58

5. ($2,436.18)(.06) ≈ $146.17

6. ($397.50 - $13.18 - $122.76) = $8,631.48

7. ($14.90)$(\frac{18}{2})$ = $134.10

8. ($6,500 + $52,585 + $35,700 + $1,275)(1.18) = $113,350.80

9. ($710.72 - $125.44 - $50.26 - $12.58 - $2.54)$(\frac{8}{2})$ = $2,079.60

10. (1 - .34 - .03 - .25 - .36) - $1,800 = $107.88

11. (36.69)(52) - $1,800 = $107.88

12. $20,800 − (26)($162.84+$44.26+$29.72+$13.94+$3.14) = $14,198.60

13. 8,936 + 7,821 + 8,953 + 4,297 + 9,785 + 6,579 = 46,371

14. (987)(867) − 855,729

15. 321,439 ÷ 59 ≈ 5,448.1

16. 721 ÷ .057 ≈ 12,649.1

17. (2,006-1,927) ÷ 1,927 ≈ 4%

18. Let x = number of vouchers. Then, $\frac{x}{5} = \frac{1488}{248}$. Solving, x = 30

19. Multiplying by .75 is equivalent to multiplying by $\frac{3}{4}$

20. (660)$(\frac{2}{3})$ − (660)(.60) = 44

21. Net worth = $98,695.83 - $59,238.29 = $39,457.54

6 (#1)

22. Total Assets = $5,233.74 + $3,206.09 + $4,925.00 + $5,500.00) + $36,690.85 = $55,555.68.

23. New balance = $627.04 - $241.75 - $13.24 - $102.97 = $269.08

24. Net pay = $497.05 - $90.32 - $28.74 - $18.79 - $7.25 - $1.88 = $350.07

25. Final balance = $85.75 - $23.00 - $15.65 - $5.23 - $14.75 - $26.38 + $38.50 - $17.18 - $3.29 - $11.64 = $7.13

TEST 2

DIRECTIONS: Each question or incomplete statement is followed by several suggested answers or completions. Select the one that BEST answers the question or completes the statement. *PRINT THE LETTER OF THE CORRECT ANSWER IN THE SPACE AT THE RIGHT.*

1. The formula for computing base salary is: Earnings equals base gross plus additional gross.
   If an employee's earnings during a particular period are in the amounts of $597.45, $535.92, $639.91, and $552.83, and his base gross salary is $525.50 per paycheck, what is the TOTAL of the additional gross earned by the employee during that period?
   A. $224.11   B. $224.21   C. $224.51   D. $244.11

   1.____

2. If a lump sum death benefit is paid by the retirement system in an amount equal to 3/7 of an employee's last yearly salary of $13,486.50, the amount of the death benefit paid is MOST NEARLY
   A. $5,749.29   B. $5,759.92   C. $5,779.92   D. $5,977.29

   2.____

3. Suppose that a member has paid 15 installments on a 28-installment loan. The percentage of the number of installments paid to the retirement system is
   A. 53.57%   B. 53.97%   C. 54.57%   D. 55.37%

   3.____

4. If an employee takes a 1-month vacation during a calendar year, the percentage of the year during which he works is MOST NEARLY
   A. 90.9%   B. 91.3%   C. 91.6%   D. 92.1%

   4.____

5. Suppose that an employee took a leave of absence totaling 7 months during a calendar year.
   Assuming the employee did not take any vacation time during the remainder of that year, the percentage of the year in which he worked is MOST NEARLY
   A. 41.7%   B. 43.3%   C. 46.5%   D. 47.1%

   5.____

6. A member has borrowed $4,725 from her funds in the retirement system. If $3,213 has been repaid, the percentage of the loan which is still outstanding is MOST NEARLY
   A. 16%   B. 32%   C. 48%   D. 68%

   6.____

7. If an employee worked only 24 weeks during the year because of illness, the portion of the year he was out of work was MOST NEARLY
   A. 46%   B. 48%   C. 51%   D. 54%

   7.____

8. If an employee purchased credit for a 16-week period of service which he had prior to rejoining the retirement system, the percentage of a year he purchased credit for was MOST NEARLY
   A. 27.9%   B. 28.8%   C. 30.7%   D. 33.3%

   8.____

9. If an employee contributes 2/11 of his yearly salary to his pension fund account, the percentage of his yearly salary which he contributes is MOST NEARLY
   A. 17.9%   B. 18.2%   C. 18.4%   D. 19.0%

10. In 2018, the maximum amount of income from which social security tax could be withheld (base salary) was $70,500. In 2020, the base salary was $82,500. The 2020 base salary represents a percentage increase over the 2018 base salary of APPROXIMATELY
    A. 15%   B. 16%   C. 17%   D. 18%

11. If 17.5% of an employee's salary is withheld for taxes, the one of the following which is the fraction of the salary withheld is
    A. 3/20   B. 8/35   C. 7/40   D. 4/25

12. If a person withdraws 42% of the funds from his account with the retirement system, the remaining balance represents a fraction of MOST NEARLY
    A. 7/13   B. 5/9   C. 7/12   D. 4/7

13. A property decreases in value from $45,000 to $35,000. The percent of decrease is MOST NEARLY
    A. 20.5%   B. 22.2%   C. 25.0%   D. 28.6%

14. The fraction $\frac{487}{101326}$ expressed as a decimal is MOST NEARLY
    A. .0482   B. .00481   C. .0049   D. .00392

15. The reciprocal of the sum of 2/3 and 1/6 can be expressed as
    A. 0.83   B. 1.20   C. 1.25   D. 1.50

16. Total land and building costs for a new commercial property equal $50 per square foot.
    If the investors expect a 10 percent return on their costs, and if total operating expenses average 5 percent of total costs, annual gross rentals per square foot must be AT LEAST
    A. $7.50   B. $8.50   C. $10.00   D. $12.00

17. The formula for computing the amount of annual deposit in a compound interest bearing account to provide a lump sum at the end of a period of years is
    $X = \frac{r \cdot L}{(1+r)^{n-1}}$ (X is the amount of annual deposit, r is the rate of interest, and n is the number of years and L = lump sum).
    Using the formula, the annual amount of the deposit at the end of each year to accumulate $20,000 at the end of 3 years with interest at 2 percent on annual balances is
    A. $6,120.00   B. $6,203.33   C. $6,535.09   D. $6,666.66

3 (#2)

18. An investor sold two properties at $150,000 each. On one he made a 2.5 percent profit. On the other, he suffered a 25 percent loss.
The NET result of his sales was
    A. neither a gain nor a loss
    B. a $20,000 loss
    C. a $75,000 gain
    D. a $75,000 loss

18.____

19. A contractor decides to install a chain fence covering the perimeter of a parcel 75 feet wide and 112 feet in depth.
Which one of the following represents the number of feet to be covered?
    A. 187   B. 364   C. 374   D. 8,400

19.____

20. A builder estimates he can build an average of 4½ one-family homes to an acre. There are 640 acres to one square mile.
Which one of the following CORRECTLY represents the number of one-family homes the builder would estimate he can build on one square mile?
    A. 1,280   B. 1,920   C. 2,560   D. 2,880

20.____

21. $.01059 deposit at 7 percent interest will yield $1.00 in 30 years.
If a person deposited $1,059 at 7 percent interest on April 4, 1991, which one of the following amounts would represent the worth of this deposit on March 31, 2021?
    A. $100   B. $1,000   C. $10,000   D. $100,000

21.____

22. A building has an economic life of forty years.
Assuming the building depreciates at a constant annual rate, which one of the following CORRECTLY represents the yearly percentage of depreciation?
    A. 2.0%   B. 2.5%   C. 5.0%   D. 7.0%

22.____

23. A building produces a gross income of $200,000 with a net income of $20,000, before mortgage charges and capital recapture. The owner is able to increase the gross income 5 percent without a corresponding increase in operating costs.
The effect upon the net income will be an INCREASE of
    A. 5%   B. 10%   C. 12.5%   D. 50%

23.____

24. The present value of $1.00 not payable for 8 years, and at 10 percent interest, is $.4665.
Which of the following amounts represents the PRESENT value of $1,000 payable 8 years hence at 10 percent interest?
    A. $46.65   B. $466.50   C. $4,665.00   D. $46,650.00

24.____

25. The amount of real property taxes to be levied by a city is $100 million. The assessment roll subject to taxation shows an assessed valuation of $2 billion.
Which one of the following tax rates CORRECTLY represents the tax rate to be levied per $100 of assessed valuation?
    A. $.50   B. $5.00   C. $50.00   D. $500.00

25.____

KEY (CORRECT ANSWERS)

1.	A	11.	C
2.	C	12.	C
3.	A	13.	B
4.	C	14.	B
5.	A	15.	B
6.	B	16.	A
7.	D	17.	C
8.	C	18.	B
9.	B	19.	C
10.	C	20.	D

21. D
22. B
23. D
24. B
25. B

5 (#2)

SOLUTIONS TO PROBLEMS

1. $597.45 + $535.91 + $639.91 + $552.83 = $2,326.11. Then, $2,326.11 − (4)($525.50) = $224.11

2. Death benefit = ($13,486.50)($\frac{3}{7}$) ≈ $5,779.92

3. $\frac{15}{28}$ ≈ 53.57%

4. $\frac{11}{12}$ ≈ 91.6% (closer to 91.7%)

5. $\frac{5}{12}$ ≈ 41.7%

6. ($4,725-$3,213) ÷ $4,725 = 32%

7. $\frac{28}{52}$ ≈ 54%

8. $\frac{16}{52}$ ≈ 30.7% (closer to 30.8%)

9. $\frac{2}{11}$ ≈ 18.2%

10. ($82,500 - $70,500) ÷ $70,500 = 17%

11. 17.5% = $\frac{175}{1000}$ = $\frac{7}{40}$

12. 100% - 42% = 58% = $\frac{58}{100}$ = $\frac{29}{50}$, closest to $\frac{7}{12}$ in selections

13. $\frac{\$10,000}{\$45,000}$ ≈ 22.2%

14. 487/101,216 ≈ .00481

15. $\frac{2}{3} + \frac{1}{6} = \frac{5}{6}$ Then, 1 ÷ $\frac{5}{6} = \frac{6}{5}$ = 1.20

16. (.15)($50) = $7.50

17. x = (.02)($20,000)/[(1+.02)^3 − 1] = 400 ÷ .061208 ≈ $6,535.09

18. Sold 150,000, 25% loss = paid 200,000, loss of $50,000 Sold 150,000, 25% profit = paid 120,000, profit of 30,000 – 50,000 + 30,000 = 20,000 (loss)

19. Perimeter = (2)(75) + (2)(112) = 374 ft.

20. (640)(4½) = 2,880 homes

21. (1÷.01059)(1059) = $100,000

22. 1÷4 = .025 = 2.5%

23. New gross income = ($200,000)(X1.05) = $210,000
    Then, ($210,000-$200,000) ÷ $20,000 = 50%

24. Let x = present value of $1,000. Then, $\dfrac{\$1.00}{\$.4665} = \dfrac{\$1000}{x}$
    Solving, x = $466.50

25. Let x = tax rate. Then, $\dfrac{\$100,000,000}{\$2,000,000,000} = \dfrac{x}{\$100}$
    Solving, x = $5.00

TEST 3

DIRECTIONS: Each question or incomplete statement is followed by several suggested answers or completions. Select the one that BEST answers the question or completes the statement. *PRINT THE LETTER OF THE CORRECT ANSWER IN THE SPACE AT THE RIGHT.*

1. It is found that for the past three years the average weekly number of inspections per inspector ranged from 20 inspections to 40 inspections.
   On the basis of this information, it is MOST reasonable to conclude that
   A. on the average, 30 inspections per week were made
   B. the average weekly number of inspections never fell below 20
   C. the performance of inspectors deteriorated over the three-year period
   D. the range in average weekly inspections was 60

   1.____

Questions 2-4.

DIRECTIONS: Questions 2 through 4 are to be answered on the basis of the following information.

The number of students admitted to University X in 2019 from High School Y was 268 students. This represented 13.7 percent of University X's entering freshman classes. In 2020, it is expected that University X will admit 591 students from High School Y, which is expected to represent 19.4 percent of the 2020 entering freshman classes of University X.

2. Which of the following is CLOSEST estimate of the size of University's expected 2020 entering freshman classes?
   _____ students
   A. 2,000   B. 2,500   C. 3,000   D. 3,500

   2.____

3. Of the following, the expected percentage of increase from 2019 to 2020 in the number of students graduating from High School Y and entering University X as freshmen is MOST NEARLY
   A. 5.7%   B. 20%   C. 45%   D. 120%

   3.____

4. Assume that the cost of processing admission to University X from High School Y in 2019 was an average of $28. Also, that this was 1/3 more than the average cost of processing each of the other 2019 freshmen admissions to University X.
   Then, the one of the following that MOST closely shows the total processing cost of all 2019 freshman admissions to University X is
   A. $6,500   B. $20,000   C. $30,000   D. $40,000

   4.____

5. Assume that during the fiscal year 2019-2020, a bureau produced 20% more work units than it produced in the fiscal year 2018-2019. Also assume that during the fiscal year 2019-2020 that bureau's staff was 20% smaller than it was in the fiscal year 2018-2019.

   5.____

On the basis of this information, it would be MOST proper to conclude that the number of work units produced per staff member in that bureau in the fiscal year 2019-2020 exceeded the number of work units produced per staff member in that bureau in the fiscal year 2018-2019 by which one of the following percentages?
A. 20%   B. 25%   C. 40%   D. 50%

6. Assume that during the following fiscal years (FY), a bureau has received the following appropriations:
   FY 2015-2016 - $200,000
   FY 2016-2017 - $240,000
   FY 2017-2018 - $280,000
   FY 2018-2019 - $390,000
   FY 2019-2020 - $505,000

   The bureau's appropriation for which one of the following fiscal years showed the LARGEST percentage of increase over the bureau's appropriation for the immediately previous fiscal year?
   A. FY 2016-2017   B. FY 2017-2018
   C. FY 2018-2019   D. FY 2010-2020

7. Assume that the number of buses (U_t) required for a given line-haul system serving the Central Business District depends upon roundtrip time (t), capacity of bus (c), and the total number of people to be moved in a peak hour (P) in the major direction, i.e., in the morning and out in the evening.
   The formula for the number of buses required is $U_t =$
   A. Ptc   B. $\frac{tP}{c}$ C. $\frac{cP}{t}$ D. $\frac{ct}{P}$

8. The area, in blocks, that can be served by a single stop for any maximum walking distance is given by the following formula: $a = 2w^2$. In this formula, a = the area served by a stop and w = maximum walking distance.
   If people will tolerate a walk of up to three blocks, how many stops would be needed to service an area of 288 square blocks?
   A. 9   B. 16   C. 18   D. 27

Questions 9-11.

DIRECTIONS: Questions 9 through 11 are to be answered on the basis of the following information.

In 2019, a police precinct records 456 cases of car thefts, which is 22.6 percent of all grand larcenies. In 2020, there were 560 such cases, which constituted 35% of the broader category.

9. The number of crimes in the broader category in 2020 was MOST NEARLY
   A. 1,600   B. 1,700   C. 1,960   D. 2,800

3 (#3)

10. The change from 2019 to 2020 in the number of crimes in the broader category represented MOST NEARLY a
    A. 2.5% decrease
    B. 10.1% increase
    C. 12.5% increase
    D. 20% decrease

11. In 2020, one out of every 6 of these crimes was solved.
    This represents MOST NEARLY what percentage of the total number of crimes in the broader category that year?
    A. 5.8
    B. 6
    C. 9.3
    D. 12

12. Assume that a maintenance shop does 5 brake jobs to every 3 front-end jobs. It does 8,000 jobs altogether in a 240-day year. In one day, one worker can do 3 front-end jobs or 4 brake jobs.
    About how many workers will be needed in the shop?
    A. 3
    B. 5
    C. 10
    D. 18

13. Assume that the price of a certain item declines by 6% one year, and then increases by 5 and 10 percent, respectively, during the next two years.
    What is the OVERALL increase in price over the three-year period?
    A. 4.2
    B. 6
    C. 8.6
    D. 10.1

14. After finding the total percent change in a price (TO) over a three-year period, as in the preceding question, one could compute the average annual percent change in the price by using the formula
    A. $(1+TC)^{1/3}$
    B. $\frac{(1+TC)}{3}$
    C. $(1+TC)^{1/3-1}$
    D. $\frac{1}{(1+TC)^{1/3}-1}$

15. 357 is 6% of
    A. 2,142
    B. 5,950
    C. 4,140
    D. 5,900

16. In 2019, a department bought n pieces of a certain supply item for a total of $x. In 2020, the department bought k percent fewer of the item but had to pay a total of g percent more for it.
    Which of the following formulas is CORRECT for determining the average price per item in 2020?
    A. $100\frac{xg}{nk}$
    B. $\frac{x(100+g)}{n(100-k)}$
    C. $\frac{x(100-g)}{n(100+k)}$
    D. $\frac{x}{n} - 100\frac{g}{k}$

17. A sample of 18 income tax returns, each with 4 personal exemptions, is taken for 2019 and 2020. The breakdown is as follows in terms of income:

Average Gross Income (in thousands)	Number of Returns	
	2019	2020
40	6	2
80	10	11
120	2	5

    There is a personal deduction per exemption of $500.
    There are no other expense deductions. In addition, there is an exclusion of $3,000 for incomes less than $50,000 and $2,000 for incomes from $50,000 to $99,999.99. From $100,000 upward there is no exclusion.

The average net taxable income for the samples in thousands for 2019 is MOST NEARLY
  A. $67   B. $85   C. $10   D. $128

18. In the preceding question, the increase in average net taxable income for the sample (in thousands) between 2019 and 2020 is
  A. 16   B. 20   C. 24   D. 34

19. Assume that supervisor S has four subordinates—A, B, C, and D. The MAXIMUM number of relationships, assuming that all combinations are included, that can exist between S and his subordinates is
  A. 28   B. 15   C. 7   D. 4

20. If the workmen's compensation insurance rate for clerical workers is 93 cents per $100 of wages, the total premium paid by a city whose clerical staff earns $8,765,000 is MOST NEARLY
  A. $8,150   B. $81,515   C. $87,650   D. $93,765

21. Assume that a budget of $3,240,000,000 for the fiscal year beginning July 1, 2020 has been approved. A city sales tax is expected to provide $1,100,000,000; licenses, fees and sundry revenues ae expected to yield $121,600,000; the balance is to be raised from property taxes. A tax equalization board has appraised all property in the city at a fair value of $42,500,000,000. The council wishes to assess property at 60% of its fair value.
The tax rate would need to be MOST NEARLY _____ per $100 of assessed value.
  A. $12.70   B. $10.65   C. $7.90   D. $4.00

22. Men's white linen handkerchiefs cost $12.90 for 3.
The cost per dozen handkerchiefs is
  A. $77.40   B. $38.70   C. $144.80   D. $51.60

23. Assume that it is necessary to partition a room measuring 40 feet by 20 feet into eight smaller rooms of equal size.
Allowing no room for aisles, the MINIMUM amount of partitioning that would be needed is _____ feet.
  A. 90   B. 100   C. 110   D. 140

24. Assume that two types of files have been ordered: 200 of type A and 100 of type B. When the files are delivered, the buyer discovers that 25% of each type is damaged. Of the remaining files, 20% of type A and 40% of type B are the wrong color.
The total number of files that are the WRONG COLOR is
  A. 30   B. 40   C. 50   D. 60

25. In a unit of five inspectors, one inspector makes an average of 12 inspections a day, two inspectors make an average of 10 inspections a day, and two inspectors make an average of 9 inspections a day.
If in a certain week one of the inspectors who makes an average of nine inspections a day is out of work on Monday and Tuesday because of illness and all the inspectors do no inspections for half a day on Wednesday because of a special meeting, the number of inspections this unit can be expected to make in that week is MOST NEARLY

   A. 215   B. 225   C. 230   D. 250

25.____

KEY (CORRECT ANSWERS)

1. B
2. C
3. D
4. D
5. D

6. C
7. B
8. B
9. A
10. D

11. A
12. C
13. C
14. C
15. B

16. B
17. A
18. A
19. B
20. B

21. C
22. D
23. B
24. D
25. A

SOLUTIONS TO PROBLEMS

1. Since the number of weekly inspections ranged from 20 to 40, this implies that the average weekly number of inspections never fell below 20.

2. 591 ÷ 194 ≈ 3046, closest to 3,000 students

3. (591-268) ÷ 268 = 120%

4. Total processing cost = (268)(28) + (1,688)($21) = $42,952, closest to $40,000. [Note: Since 268 represents 13.7%, total freshman population = 268 ÷ .137 ≈ 1,956. Then, 1,956 − 268 = 1,688]

5. Let x = staff size in 2018-2019. Then, .80x = staff size in 2019-2020. Since the 2019-2020 staff produced 20% more work, this is represented by 1.20. However, to measure the productivity per staff member, the factor 1/.80 = 1.25 must also be used to equate the 2 staffs. Then, (1.20)(1.25) = 1.50. Thus, the 2019-2020 staff produced 50% more than the 2018-2019 staff.

6. The respective percent increases are ≈ 20%, 17%, 39%, 29%. The largest would be, over the previous fiscal year, for the current fiscal year 2018-2019

7. $\frac{P}{c}$ = number of buses needed per hour. If t = time (in hrs.), then $U_t = tP.c$

8. a = (2)(9) = 18 for 1 stop. Then, 288 ÷ 18 = 15 stops.

9. 560 ÷ .35 = 1600 grand larcenies.

10. 456 ÷ .226 = 2018; 560 ÷ .35 = 1600. Then, (1,600-2,018) ÷ 2,018 = -20% or a 20% decrease.

11. $(\frac{1}{6})(560) = 93\frac{1}{3}$. Then, $93\frac{1}{3}$ ÷ 1,600 = 5.8%

12. There are 5,000 brake jobs and 3,000 front-end jobs in one year.
5,000 ÷ 4 = 1,250 days, and 1,250 ÷ 240 ≈ 5.2. Also, 3,000 ÷ 3 = 1,000 days, and 1,000 ÷ 240 ≈ 4.2. Total number of workers needed ≈ 5.2 + 4.2 ≈ 10.

13. (.94)(1.05)(1.10) = 1.0857, which represents an overall increase by about 8.6%.

14. Average annual % change = $(1+TC)^{1/3} - 1 = (1.0857)^{1/3} - 1 ≈ 2.8\%$.

15. 357 ÷ .06 = 5,950

16. In 2020, $(h)(1-\frac{k}{100})$ pieces cost $(x)(1 + \frac{g}{100})$ dollars. To calculate the cost for 1 piece (average cost), find the value of $[(x)(1 + \frac{G}{100})] \div [(n)(1 - \frac{K}{100})] = [(x)(100+g)/100]$. $[100/\{n(100-k)\}] = [x(100+g)]/[n(100-k)]$

17.

	#	Deductions Up to 50,000		
40,000	6	2000	3000	40,000−3,000−2,000 = 35,000 × 6
80,000	10	2000	2000	80,000−2,000−2,000 = 76,000 × 10
20,000	2	2000		= 118000 × 2

35,000 × 6 = 210,000 = 210
76,000 × 10 = 760,000 = 760
118,800 × 2 = 236,000 = <u>236</u>
                                 1206

1206 ÷ 18 = 67

18. 2020   Deductions

40,000	2	2000	3000	35,000 × 2 =	70,000
80,000	11	2000	2000	76,000 × 11 =	836,000
120,000	5	2000		118,000 × 5 =	<u>590,000</u>
					1,496,000

1,496,000/18 = 83,111
83,111 − 67,000 = 16,111 = most nearly 16 (in thousands)

19. We are actually looking for the number of different groups of different sizes involving S. This reduces to $_4C_1 + {_4C_2} + {_4C_2} + {_4C_4} = 4 + 6 + 4 + 1 = 15$. The notation $_nC_r$ means combinations of n things taken R at a time = $[(n)(n-1)(n-2)(\ldots)(n-R+1)]/[(R)(R-1)(\ldots)(1)]$. The 15 groups are: SA, SB, SC, SD, SAB, SAC, SAD, SBC, SBD, SCD, SABC, SABD, SACD, SBCD, SABCD.

20. Let x = total premiums. Then, $\frac{.93}{100} = \frac{X}{8,765,000}$ Solving, x = $81,515

21. The balance, raised from property taxes, = $3,240,000,000 − $1,100,000,000 − $121,600,000 = $2,018,400,000. Now, (.60)($42,500,000,000) = $25,500,000. The tax rate per $100 of assessed value = ($2,018,400,000)($100)(/$25,500,000,00 = $7.90.

22. A dozen costs ($12.90)$(\frac{12}{3})$ = $51.60.

23. (40(20) ÷ 8 = 100 ft.

24. Total number of wrong-color files = (200)(.75)(.20)+(100)(.75)(.40) = 60

25. Weekly number of inspections = (12×5) + (10×5) + (10×5) + (9×5) + 9×5) = 250
Subtract: 9 Monday, 9 Tuesday, 25 Wednesday
Total: 250 − 9 − 9 − 25 = 207
Closest entry is choice A.

www.ingramcontent.com/pod-product-compliance
Lightning Source LLC
Chambersburg PA
CBHW081808300426
44116CB00014B/2283